DATE DUE			
Apr 28 '75			
May 19 '75			
Dec 8 '75			
Oct 25 78			
Nov 14 79			

Experiences in Music

Experiences in Music

R. PHYLLIS GELINEAU

Department of Music
Southern Connecticut State College

McGraw–Hill Book Company
New York   St. Louis   San Francisco
Düsseldorf   London   Mexico   Panama
Sydney   Toronto

This book was set in Bembo by Spottiswoode, Ballantyne and Co. Ltd., and printed on permanent paper and bound by George Banta Company, Inc. The designer was Joan O'Connor; the drawings were done by BMA Associates, Inc. The editors were James Mirrielees and Helen Greenberg. Robert R. Laffler supervised the production.

Experiences in Music

To Ray and Robin

"A man should hear a little music, read a little poetry, and see a fine picture every day of his life, in order that worldly cares may not obliterate the sense of the beautiful which God has implanted in the human soul."

Goethe

PREFACE

Dear Classroom Teacher (in training, in service and in spirit!)

Under this same cover a little further on, you'll find a small quote that reads "Please stop worrying about whether you sing or play well. You don't have to do either to be successful in teaching music in your classroom." This is the premise upon which this book is based. Be assured that having no voice is *not* akin to having two heads.

   Some of you may be resisting teaching music (you'd rather die!) because you fear your own inadequacies. Perhaps many of you lost your way as well as your courage at the hand of some stony-hearted music teacher who commanded that you "move your mouth but don't sing," or branded you a "crow" (front seat, please), or suggested (?!) that you be a "listener" (shameful-type activity). Take heart in the knowledge that in my many years of classroom music supervision experience, I have found that some of the best music comes from rooms where teachers can't sing. Their secret (a delightful one to share) is that they have a sincere desire in their hearts to bring joy into the lives of their children, and to share with them the deeply satisfying experience of making a real contribution where heretofore there has been none. This desire, strengthened by determination to "find a way" despite alleged vocal difficulties, reaps its reward not only in fine musical results but, even more important, in positive attitudes on the part of the children toward all phases of music. So you see, it's not so much what's in your head as what's in your heart.

Did you know that there are so many varied activities under the heading of "music" that every child in your room, regardless of his mental ability, will have an opportunity to achieve success in at least one musical experience? In this book, I have attempted to suggest many different musical activities suitable for kindergarten through grade six as well as procedures for their presentation to children. The suggestions are made in what I hope is an uncluttered manner, eliminating the usual textbook superfluity. It's quite specific because many of you have said you like it that way. We have even included fourteen transparency masters in the back of this book to get you started immediately. A further attempt has been made to keep everything flexible, so as to provide for teachers with no ability, for those with limited ability, and also for those of you who are downright talented!

All that's really required for teaching music in the elementary classroom is a few musical teaching aids and love in your heart.

And the greatest of these is love.

R. Phyllis Gelineau

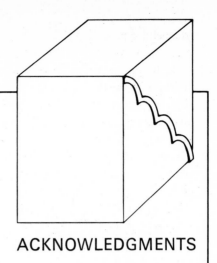

ACKNOWLEDGMENTS

The author is deeply indebted to all who so kindly gave permission to reprint copyrighted and other material. In a few instances, even careful research failed to uncover the source of some of the songs. The efforts in this direction were most extended and sincere, and should there be a lack of acknowledgment in the proper place, it is only because the source is unknown. The author would very much appreciate being informed about such materials so that proper acknowledgment may be made in future editions and so that the appropriate arrangements may be secured.

The author is also very grateful to the following persons and firms for special acts of kindness:

Dr. Hilton C. Buley—President, Southern Connecticut State College—for faith

American Society of Composers, Authors and Publishers (ASCAP)
Broadcast Music, Inc. (BMI)
Gracia Caines
James Hennessey, of United Features Syndicate
Jill Jackson, of Jan-Lee Music
Burton Litwin, of Mills Music, Inc.
Cooper McCarthy, of McGraw-Hill Book Company
Helen Paul, of Follett Publishing Company
Lynn Rohrbough, of Cooperative Recreation Service
Jerry Vogel, of Jerry Vogel Music Company
and

Dr. Robert Dowd—Southern Connecticut State College

R. Phyllis Gelineau

CONTENTS

xiii

Experiences in Music

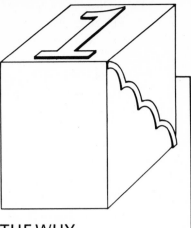

THE WHY,
THE WHAT,
AND THE HOW

*"When you work you are a flute
through whose heart the whispering of
the hours turns to music. . . ."*
From The Prophet, *by Khalil Gibran.
Published by Alfred A. Knopf, Inc.,
New York.*

The Why

Most of us occasionally experience the feeling of being totally surrounded by music in our daily living—music to eat by, drive by, dream by, shop by, work by, and feel totally exhausted by. This is not all. For some time now, experiments have been in progress to test the uses to which music might be put for human benefit.

Some scientists, for example, feel that music may possess heretofore undeveloped powers. Possibilities for the use of music therapy with mental patients are being continuously explored, and researchers are undertaking studies relating to the significance of the effect of music on the emotions.

More recently, music has been found to be a satisfactory anesthetic in the dentist's chair as well as on the surgeon's table. Its power to relieve tension and anxiety is being tested on preoperative patients as well as on those receiving specialized treatment that must be administered in isolation.

Some isolated studies reveal that music is even being used to grow better plants, improve a golf swing, increase efficiency, decrease resistance, and keep mosquitoes away!

Perhaps we who daily touch the lives of children might conceivably consider the provision of classroom musical experiences as one more contribution in terms of human benefit.

The very word "music" represents so many varied activities that every child can succeed in at least one, and often more than one, musical experience, regardless of his mental ability. Unlike achievement in many other subjects in the school curriculum, achievement in music is not contingent upon intellectual capacity. This is evidenced particularly in special classes, where despite apparent handicaps, children can participate totally and often make significant musical contributions.

Achievement in some area is necessary for maintaining self-respect as well as mental health. In short, a measure of success is good for all of us, but especially for the child as he grows. Certainly no one would deny that any healthy activity in life that contributes in a positive way to an individual's well-being is worthwhile. Music, happily, has something for everyone. If a child cannot sing well, he may explore his musical capabilities on many different instruments, such as song bells, rhythm instruments, Autoharps, harmonicas, ukuleles, recorders, and even simple water glasses or bottles. Other children may enjoy their musical achievements through listening experiences, music reading, body movement, or creating something uniquely their own.

The value of music is frequently felt in other areas of the curriculum as well, for it is a natural vitalizer of other subject matter. Singing the songs and doing the dances of the peoples of other cultures cannot help but give us a truer feeling for, and deeper understanding of, ways of life other than our own. Race and creed barriers cease to exist in the presence of music. Furthermore, the very nature and scope of music makes it possible for a child to participate as a cooperating group member as well as to enjoy numerous opportunities for individual expression.

It is an accepted fact that music releases tension. Participation in some musical activity during the school day offers refreshment, as well as a needed respite from the constant irritation of life's daily abrasions.

The skeptics who question the value of music as a discipline should be reminded that throughout the history of civilization, music has always been recognized as a discipline that is in many ways as exacting as mathematics or science.

The presence of music in a classroom also provides the teacher with the means toward fulfilling one of his many commitments to his children—that of helping to educate them for the advent of an ever-increasing amount of leisure time. Participation in the arts—of which music is one—has always been accepted as an excellent leisure-time activity. Can we predict which of our children will become consumers or producers of music, or even a little of each? Probably not. Of one thing we can be sure, however—music of many sorts will continue to rain upon them from all sides at most times, just as it does today. Should we not feel some responsibility for helping our young people to develop criteria for musical judgment so that in the future they may become more highly discriminating listeners? Are we not also committed to the possible discovery of any unusual ability or talent among our children that might, were it not for the medium of music and a teacher who cared, lie dormant too long or go unnoticed completely?

Finally, through music we are able to provide our children with abundant opportunities for self-realization and creative expression so that, hopefully, they may learn to live at a deeper level. Wars are fought so that men may remain free to express themselves through their creations. Music is one of these creations. We need it in the school curriculum.

The What

Where a well-planned, continuing music program exists in all grades throughout a given school system, each child can be assured of increased musical growth and involvement as he matures. This, in turn, should help to establish a foundation for even deeper satisfactions and pleasures to be derived from music in the future, as a consumer or producer, and to contribute toward a richer and fuller life for him. This richer and fuller life is our most highly desired outcome—one that we should try to keep uppermost in our hearts, especially when beset by the rigours of daily planning.

Since music does offer all children the unique opportunity to attain success in at least one area, hopefully many children will find their days a little brighter and themselves a little happier because of their musical experiences in the classroom. If we, as teachers, expect to accomplish this end, we must commit ourselves to the provision of a wide variety of musical activities to ensure each child's finding at least one in which he can achieve satisfactorily.

At each level of development, every child should be afforded the opportunity to explore the world of music through its sound, its literature, and its language—to move *to* it, to be moved *by* it, and finally to translate what he has experienced into musical creations of his own.

These endeavors constitute the "what." Their implementation varies with the grade level, of course. Basically, however, they are the same for all levels and for all children (who seem to be pretty much the same everywhere!).

The How

PORTRAIT OF A MUSIC PERIOD

Music time should be a happy time. Smile! Look alive, even if you don't feel that way. Remember the old saw, "Attitudes are caught—not taught." The children's attitude towards music will reflect yours. If you love it (you'll *grow* to), they will too, and it's important that they do. With children, enthusiasm can be more contagious than mumps.

Stop worrying about whether you play or sing well. You don't have to do either to be successful in teaching music in your classroom.

Now that we've cleared up those two vital points, let's go on with some general suggestions for planning procedures—success (practically) guaranteed.

In the beginning:

1. Have the children clear their desks of everything except their music books. This not only minimizes the distractions of rolling pencils, snapping rulers, and hidden comics books but also serves to reduce dangers from unidentified flying objects when your back is turned. (The life you save may be you know whose!)
2. Good posture is vital to good singing. A simple suggestion—"Feet flat on the floor"—is all that's necessary to secure proper placement of the affected parts. Please postpone the lecture on the basics of posture. Less talk means more music. After a few days of this reminder, all you'll have to do is *mention* that it's time for music and straighten your own tired old shoulders, and the children should respond likewise.
3. Begin the music period by having the class sing a song they know and like. Be sure to give them the correct starting pitch (more on this later). Frequent reminders to the class to use their *best* (not loudest) singing voices should aid in improving tone quality. (See "Securing Good Tone," p. 13.)
4. The choice of activities to be undertaken between the beginning song (above) and the concluding song (below) is unlimited. (Incidentally, they are the subject of this entire literary effort!) The point to be made here is that activities within a music period should be varied—the whole period should not be spent learning just one song or working entirely on music-reading skills, for example. Variety helps to maintain interest as well as enthusiasm.
5. End the music period the way you began it—by having the class sing a song they know and like. (The more songs you teach, the more they'll know.)

Translating the foregoing generalities into specifics, a given music period might be set up somewhat as follows:

A. Familiar song.

B. Tone-matching games at appropriate grade levels (p. 10).

C. Ear training (p. 108).

D. Music reading (p. 115)—to consist of any *one* or combinations of the following, depending on grade level:

    1. Introducing the class to basic skills for music reading (p. 120).

    2. Having the class sing simple melodies at sight with syllables from the chalkboard or a chart or book (pp. 128–135).

    3. Introducing the class to new melodic and rhythmic problems where appropriate, e.g., finding *do* with sharps and flats or introducing eighth notes, chromatics, or part singing.

E. New song with words—learned either by rote (p. 16) or through music reading.

F. Additional activities as desired,—e.g., playing classroom instruments, body movement, musical games. Of course there are endless possibilities here. Many of these activities alone or in combination, as well as others, can be blended with the aforementioned areas to heighten interest and deepen understandings.

G. Familiar song.

(It goes without saying that in all areas, opportunities to create would also be provided.)

The foregoing is a very bare framework, obviously. It is included here simply to point up the fact that singing a few songs does not constitute a music lesson—even at the kindergarten level. The activities were itemized merely as a reminder to ensure their inclusion in the planning, and not to convey the idea that a child's music experiences in the classroom should be fragmented.

Three of the five weekly periods could be structured as suggested above. While it is possible that some *listening* experiences might occasionally be included within this framework, any in-depth listening lesson would require an entire music period and should be scheduled at least once a week (see p. 244). The planning in this area would be totally different from that suggested above. Only where such activities as singing, using instruments, and body movement could be considered either logical outgrowths or integral parts of the listening experience should they be included.

Other related experiences such as watching a sound film, a filmstrip, or a television broadcast (or seeing other visual material dealing with musical subject matter); having local performers pay a visit to the classroom; attending concerts; or combining music with an art lesson, for example, would certainly require an entire music period, if not more. Furthermore, if a teacher should choose to expand the children's experience in some of the areas mentioned in item *F* above, he would need an entire music period in which to do so. The learning of a new classroom instrument, for example, especially when it is first being introduced, certainly requires more time than a small portion of a twenty- to thirty-minute period.

In summary, then, three of the five music periods each week could consist primarily of the types of lesson suggested on p. 4, one period could be set aside for a listening experience, and the remaining one might be used

5

for other related activities. This should provide the children with a well-rounded, ongoing music program.

At first glance it might appear that frameworks such as these tend to limit the scope of a more imaginative teacher. Closer inspection and use, however, will reveal that some structure will actually *increase* the opportunity for further activities by making it possible to use the time set aside more efficiently. With careful planning and budgeting of time, a teacher should be able to get in all the activities he plans for, and often more. There simply must be some structure and planning if any goals are to be achieved and growth is to occur. Too often there is a danger of being so whimsical and "way out" with what many choose to term "creative activities" that, in reality, children learn little and grow less because no real working challenges are being offered. Furthermore, when one attempts to examine the specific accomplishments of such a program, they often prove to be rather intangible.

Musical growth also requires some degree of continuity in the entire K-6 program. This means that every teacher who fulfills his responsibilities to the children by completing the desired program for his particular grade becomes a strong link in the curriculum. Sixth grade children, for example, will never accomplish all they can if the previously specified accomplishments have not taken place from kindergarten through grade five.

HOW MUCH TIME FOR MUSIC?

The amount of time allotted daily for music usually varies with the grade level; however, the important consideration is not always how *much* time is allotted but how it is used. Regularly scheduled *daily* periods produce much more desirable results, even if they are of shorter duration, than longer periods scheduled less often. The following have been proved successful time allotments for each grade:

Kindergarten	10 to 15 minutes daily
Grades one and two	15 to 20 minutes daily
Grade three	20 minutes daily
Grade four	20 to 25 minutes daily
Grade five	25 minutes daily
Grade six	25 to 30 minutes daily

It may be feasible, of course, to vary the time somewhat, depending on the class response and the chosen activity for any given day. Many teachers find that music often proves valuable when included during the school day at times other than the regularly scheduled music period for such purposes as providing relaxation or relief from tension or vitalizing other subject matter. Although this practice may tend to be more common in the primary grades, where schedules are inclined to be more flexible, music can and should be provided at unscheduled times during the day in the upper grades as well, when appropriate. In any event, it is wise to *schedule* a daily music period so that music won't be eliminated on a busy day.

Professional Reading

Bergethon, Bjornar, and Eunice Boardman: *Musical Growth in the Elementary School.* Holt, Rinehart and Winston, Inc., New York, 1963.

Cheyette, Irving, and Herbert Cheyette: *Teaching Music Creatively in the Elementary School.* McGraw-Hill Book Company, New York, 1969.

Hurd, Lyman III, and Edith J. Savage: *First Experiences in Music.* Wadsworth Publishing Co., Belmont, Calif., 1966.

Kaplan, Max: *Foundations and Frontiers of Music Education.* Holt, Rinehart and Winston, Inc., New York, 1966.

McMillan, Eileen: *Guiding Children's Growth through Music.* Ginn and Company, Boston, 1959.

Music Educator's National Conference: *The Study of Music in the Elementary School: A Conceptual Approach.* NEA Center, Washington, D.C., 1967.

Nye, Robert E., and Bernice T. Nye: *Music in the Elementary School*, rev. ed. Prentice-Hall, Inc., Englewood Cliffs, N.J., 1964.

Raebeck, Lois, and Lawrence Wheeler: *New Approaches to Music in the Elementary School.* Wm. C. Brown Co., Dubuque, Iowa, 1964.

Richards, Mary: *Threshold to Music.* Harper & Row, Publishers, Incorporated, New York, 1964. (This book is an adaptation of the Kodaly method.)

Runkle, Aleta, and Mary L. Erikson: *Music for Today's Boys and Girls.* Allyn and Bacon, Inc., Boston, 1966.

Schubert, Inez, and Lucille Wood: *The Craft of Music Teaching.* Silver Burdett Company, Morristown, N.J., 1964.

Sheehy, Emma: *There's Music in Children.* Holt, Rinehart and Winston, Inc., New York, 1952.

Slind, Lloyd H., and D. Evan Davis: *Bringing Music to Children.* Harper & Row, Publishers, Incorporated, New York, 1964.

Swanson, Bessie: *Music in the Education of Children*, 3rd ed. Wadsworth Publishing Co., Belmont, Calif., 1969.

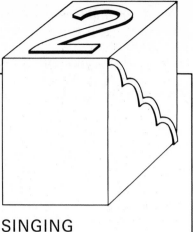

SINGING EXPERIENCES

*"Music
Is something inside of you
That sings."*
       Timothy Hawkins, age seven
From Let Them Write Poetry, *by*
Nina Willis Walter. Copyright
© *1962 by Holt, Rinehart and Winston,*
Inc. Reprinted by permission of Holt,
Rinehart and Winston, Inc.

Singing in Tune

Music educators have put forth many reasons why children sing out of tune. Lack of musical environment in the home is often suggested as a contributing factor. Incredible as it may seem, there are many children whose home environment has been so musically deprived that they aren't even aware that they have a singing voice, much less of how to use it. Emotional blocks and immaturity are also frequently mentioned as possible reasons why children sing out of tune (or don't sing at all).

While it is conceivable that these and various other factors may be operating in many cases to prevent children from singing in tune, it has been the author's observation that the most common cause of out-of-tune singing is *lack of concentration*. (Obviously, we are discounting the rare cases where some physical disability is involved.)

A child must *hear* a tone mentally as well as physically before he can be expected to reproduce it. If he isn't listening intently, he won't hear it in the first place. Any distractions—even minor ones—tend to interfere with the special kind of listening that this activity requires; thus a teacher should make every effort to provide an optimum listening environment for his class.

Children know when they sound different from someone else, and in most cases they'd like to do something about it. As teachers, we have an obligation to each child to help him discover his singing voice and to produce the best tone possible from it. This means that we are committed to providing the experiences that will enable children to accomplish these tasks. For some, it is no task; they just naturally sing in tune. For the out-of-tune or "uncertain" singers (as they are sometimes called), special procedures are required.

The following are some suggested devices for aiding out-of-tune singers wherever causes are such that improvement is possible.

HELPING OUT-OF-TUNE SINGERS

1. Encourage *every* child to sing. Never tell a child to be a listener while the rest of the class sings forth with joy. Welcome all contributions, no matter how froglike. Feeling that they are a part of the group is most vital to these children. If they hesitate to sing at first, try offering them a triangle or a drum or other rhythm instrument and suggest that they might like to accompany the singing. It is extremely important that they know that the teacher *cares* whether they participate or not.

2. Insist that every child give his complete attention when the music is being played or sung. Singing on pitch and getting the correct beginning pitch require concentration on the part of even the most experienced singers. In this connection, make certain that all songs are pitched in the right key and started on the right note.

3. Whenever possible, it is helpful to seat these children near a good singer so that they may have a desirable sound to try to imitate. Obviously, such seating should not be made an issue. Any humiliating identification such as labeling these children "blackbirds" or "crows" and telling them to sit in the front row with the rest of the out-of-tune singers should be avoided.

4. Stress light singing, never heavy or harsh. Call attention to proper posture, diction, and breathing. Such clues from the teacher as "Think high—way up here" (point to forehead) and "Feel as though you've grown an inch" often prove helpful in securing better tone placement. (See "Securing Good Tone," p. 13.)

5. Be generous with praise and encouragement, especially at the slightest sign of improvement.

9

6. Individual work in this area is a must. Since class time may be limited, it falls to the teacher to work with the more difficult cases alone whenever time permits. Time thus spent is so worthwhile. The teacher who one day suddenly hears a longtime out-of-tuner singing along on pitch with the rest of the class and sees the joy on his face is blessed with his own reward.

7. In lower grades, use tone-matching games and other similar devices, such as those given below. Further suggestions may be found in the teacher's editions of the children's music texts, or the teacher may wish to create some of his own to fit a season or situation. Whatever devices are chosen for tone matching, they should be used *every day*, for bringing a child up to pitch requires daily practice. Tone-matching games, as such, may be omitted in upper grades, although many teachers continue to use modified versions of them throughout all grades. (See "Helping Older Children," p. 12.)

TONE-MATCHING GAMES

(NOTE: Don't panic if you can't sing. See "Tone-matching Using Instruments," p. 12.)

T—Teacher   C—Child

5. Try a familiar tune with tone-matching words, e.g., "Are You Sleeping, Brother John?" (pitch G):

    T: Where is Betsy?
    C: Here is Betsy.
    T: Where is Mike?

C: Here is Mike.
T: Where is pretty Anna?
C: Here is pretty Anna.
T: Glad you're here.
Class: Glad you're here.

6. Tone matching may be related to rhythm instruments. The tune used below is a familiar children's chant. It may be varied as desired.

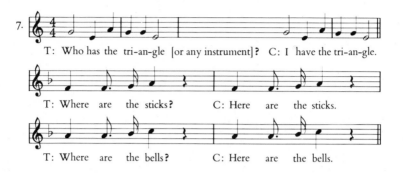

7.

T: Who has the tri-an-gle [or any instrument]?   C: I have the tri-an-gle.

T: Where are the sticks?   C: Here are the sticks.

T: Where are the bells?   C: Here are the bells.

8. You might also pass out such objects as colored paper, numbers, or geometric shapes to individual children. The child who has the appropriate article mentioned in the sung question must sing the answer on the same tune.

 T: Who has the circle? C: I have the circle.
 T: Where is the red? C: Here is the red.
 T: Where is forty-six? C: Here is forty-six.

9. A child might be asked to sing his initials:
 T: Where is [child's initials here]? C: Here is ———.

10. Classroom helpers could be identified:
 T: Where is the duster? C: Here is the duster.
 (Other possibilities—board cleaner, paper collector, line leader, etc.)

11. Tone-matching games may also be in the form of questions to which the child must originate an answer:

T: Do you like to read?	C: Yes, I like to read [or "No"].
T: What kind of animal are you?	C: I am a ——— [animal of choice].
T: What do you like to do?	C: I like to———[activity].
T: What color is your dress?	C: My dress is———[color].
T: How do you get to school?	C: I ——— to school.

In all the above, the teacher may ask the questions using any tune desired, as long as it is not too difficult for the child to reproduce. With very young children a simple tune such as the previously suggested children's chant is preferable to more complicated ones. Questions within a given lesson may vary in content, but it is less confusing to the children if the tune remains the same when this is done.

 Choosing children at random occasionally, rather than restricting the games to the out-of-tune singers, will lessen the possibility of embarrassing **11** the out-of-tune singers as well as help maintain attention and improve the listening habits of the whole class.

Despite the game aspect, the classroom situation at this time should be well controlled in order to secure optimum results. The teacher's manner and attitude should be such that the child feels that the teacher *really* cares whether he manages to sing a little more tunefully that day. Furthermore, caring can be contagious. If the teacher shows that he cares, the class will too, and soon the out-of-tune child feels that all this caring is surely worth some extra effort on his part. Result? He extends himself a little more, concentrates, and, in most cases, eventually "tunes up."

TONE MATCHING USING INSTRUMENTS

Whereas the previous suggestions for tone-matching games all indicate the use of the teacher's voice, it is possible to execute many of them through the use of melody instruments if the teacher doesn't sing. For example, a teacher may say to a child, "I am going to call your name [or "ask you a question" or whatever particular device he selects to use] with this instrument. It will sound like this." Then he plays the appropriate tune for the chosen tone-matching game on the piano, song bells, or any melody instrument and asks, "Can you sing back your answer using the same tune that I played?" If the answering tune is to be different from the tune used for the question, the teacher plays the answering tune on the instrument so that the child can hear it before he tries to answer. (The teacher would probably not want to vary the answering tune too often.)

After a few class sessions with the instrument, the teacher will find that the children have become familiar enough with the procedure to sing the appropriate responses to selected questions immediately, thus eliminating the need for any further explanations.

HELPING OLDER CHILDREN

In the upper grades, games may have to be replaced by more frequent attention to good posture, proper breathing, and clear diction and by more than an occasional reminder to "Use your best singing voices," "Think *up*," "Think high," "Get on *top* of the tone," etc. (See "Securing Good Tone," p. 13.)

While it is often more difficult to cure an out-of-tune singer in the upper grades, it is certainly not impossible, and hope should never be abandoned at any level. It requires merely more of the same patience and perseverance that are necessary in the primary grades, in addition to an intensive team effort on the part of the teacher and the child. Individual work outside class is even more vital when attempting to help older children.

Good tone results from a number of things, not the least of which is attention to posture, breathing, and diction. Helping a child to sit, breathe, and speak properly is one way of securing better tone quality in the classroom.

Good posture consists in having both feet flat on the floor, the back up (reasonably straight), and eyes front. It is neither a soldierlike rigidity nor a rag-doll fold-up, but rather something acceptably comfortable in between. If you care to put your postural instructions to music, try these words to the tune of "Are You Sleeping, Brother John?" (Key of G. Start G—second line.)

> Sit up straighter, sit up straighter
> Never slump, never slump
> Or you'll be a camel, yes, you'll be a camel
> With a hump, with a hump.
> (Origin unknown)

Proper breathing involves the use of the diaphragm. Try the following breathing exercise with your class:

Have the children put their hands on their hips (thumbs in back). Move their hands up their sides until the middle fingers of both hands are outlining the lowest rib. As they breathe, they should be concentrating on those fingers—*exhaling* means that the tips of the right- and left-hand middle fingers will *touch; inhaling* means that they will *separate.* The breathing should be done with this in mind—*making* the touching (or nontouching) of the fingers happen by moving the diaphragm during the exhaling and inhaling. Nothing happens to the fingers when only the chest moves. This shallow chest breathing is just what we are trying to avoid.

Try having the children exhale and inhale several times, allowing the diaphragm to push the tips of the fingers apart and together. Have them inhale deeply and then try to take a comfortable pitch and exhale on that pitch—little by little—so that the note is sustained as long as possible. (Try giving several different pitches in the upper grades and sustaining *chords* for nice sounds.)

The ability to sustain a tone, gained through practice in controlling the breath, will contribute to better phrasing in singing as well as to better tone quality. Lack of control often causes children to "explode" all their breath at once on the first few notes of a song, only to discover suddenly that they have run out of the necessary breath to complete the phrase. The result in any given song is a series of little "explosions," which produce a chopped-up sound and prevent a desirable smooth flow in the music. (Let's see now whether we can make it through the first line of "America"!)

Clear diction requires careful enunciation of the words of a song. Suggest to the children that they try to form their words in the front of their mouths, using much the same technique of exaggerated lip position that they use when trying to communicate inaudibly to a friend across the room when the teacher isn't looking.

Children need to be reminded often to use their best singing voices to avoid producing a heavy or harsh quality. If a class has a tendency to sing in a rather timid manner, a comment from the teacher in the nature of "I don't hear everyone singing" is preferable to suggesting that they sing louder. Almost invariably, the term "louder" seems to evoke a less desirable response as far as tone production is concerned. All this is not to say that children should never be allowed to sing heartily, with spirit and gusto, when the nature of the song warrants it, but even a lusty sea chantey can be properly interpreted without sacrificing tone quality.

A state of tension may often affect a person's tone production. Try the following relaxing exercises with the class before the singing starts. They're designed to "untie the knots."

1. "Be wooden soldiers!" (Stiffen whole body.) "Rag dolls!" (Immediately go limp.) Repeat. This exercise may be varied by using two different chords on the piano (or two different rhythm instruments) as cues to change positions—a high one for soldiers and a low one for dolls, etc.
2. Standing with arms stretched high over the head, *drop* each suggested part of the body on the designated count, as follows:

One:	right wrist
Two:	left wrist
Three:	right forearm
Four:	left forearm
Five:	right upper arm
Six:	left upper arm
Seven:	head (let fall on chest)
Eight:	trunk (end in bent-over position with head down and arms hanging down loosely in front)

This exercise may also be cued musically by singing or playing a *descending* scale. (Any key will do.)

Attention to light singing and open mouths can also help children to produce some of the higher tones with greater ease. If they encounter difficulty in this area, suggest that an attack on a high note should be from *above*—down on it, as it were—rather than from beneath, trying to push up to it. Mental set is a most important factor here. A child·must hear the tone in his mind before he can produce it. His subsequent physical production of it depends to a large degree on how he perceives it mentally. Raising the chin and eyes skyward simply will not suffice!

Using the Pitch Pipe

Your children will probably call it your "spit pipe," "peace pipe" (even "pig pipe"!), or some other travesty on its real name; however, by any name it does serve to provide the needed starting pitches for songs, and that makes it a rather important little music tool.

In Fig. 2-1 you'll notice that the pitch pipe has two sides. One side is black, imprinted with arrows, letters, sharps, and flats. The reverse silver side has all these, plus five concentric circles with notes located on various lines and spaces. These five circles represent the staff "in the round," as it were. The notes located on the round staff correspond to the letters shown directly below them.

The sharp at the right and the flat at the left of each of the arrows indicate that the sound produced by blowing over the opening above the arrow may be called by two different letter names (E♭ or D♯, for example), but they refer to only *one* sound. The opening, in effect, corresponds to the black key located between two white keys on the piano keyboard. Only *one* sound is produced by striking the black key, but when written on the staff it may be notated as either E♭ or D♯, for example, depending on the key of the song. Some songs are written in sharp keys, and others in flat keys. The pitch pipe is made to accommodate either.

Pitch pipes are usually available in two different ranges:

1. The C to C octave:

from

middle C   to   C third space

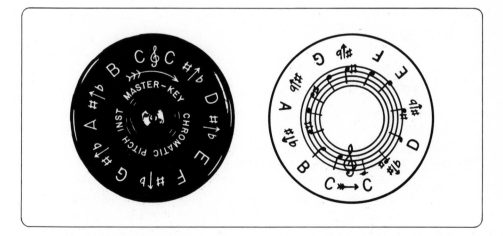

FIGURE 2–1 *Pitch pipe (2 views).*

2. The F to F octave:

from

F first space   to   F fifth line

Either is satisfactory for classroom use, depending on which range is best for your purpose. Sometimes it's hard to tell until you've worked with them awhile.

The pitch pipe shown in Fig. 2-1 is a C to C octave. You notice that there are two C's written right next to each other. The black side of the pitch pipe gives no clue as to which C is the middle C and which is the third-space C, as far as locating them on the staff is concerned; however, careful examination will reveal a curved arrow pointing to the right and indicating that the range of tones *ascends* in this direction up to the higher C on the third space. Haste and inexperience can often cause a teacher to blow the high note when he meant to blow the low note and throw the song all out of range. When everyone in the class is squeaking in too high a register, it's pretty hard to keep them from breaking up in laughter. Be safe. Check the silver side too.

Fundamentally, the pitch pipe is meant for the teacher's use alone. It is designed merely to allow him to sound the *do* or keynote of any given song so that he may reproduce it for the children with his voice. Some teachers, however, experience vocal difficulty and find it necessary to ask the children to take their pitch *directly* from the sound of the pitch pipe, rather than from the teacher's voice. Although sounding a pitch with the voice is preferable, either method is perfectly acceptable, and we love you just the same.

More specific instructions can be found under "Giving the Starting Pitch," p. 20.

Rote Songs

INTRODUCTION

Learning a song by rote is much like learning anything else by rote—it is, in effect, learning "by ear." If a teacher sings or plays a song on an instrument or from a record and the children sing back the words and tune they have heard, they are learning the song by rote. All songs taught in this manner are referred to as "rote songs."

Rote songs may be taught through the use of the voice, melody instrument, or record—whichever is most comfortable for the teacher. Suggested procedures for all three are given below. (With so many teaching aids available, there are simply no excuses left!)

SELECTING THE SONG

When selecting a song to be taught by rote to your class, the first consideration is that it be a song of good quality. It is important that you like it and that you feel the children will, too. (We *all* make mistakes!) Do not choose a song merely because it is seasonal or happens to fit a particular unit of work at the time. These considerations are important, to be sure, but more important is the quality of the music chosen and the sincerity with which you can teach it.

The range of the song should be on the staff, as far as possible, especially in the primary grades. In the upper grades this may vary.

PREPARATION

Familiarize yourself with the song so that you can devote your entire attention to teaching and not risk losing the children's attention by having to refer to a book. A well-known conductor once commented that when you have the music in your head, you won't have your head in the music. It's helpful, of course, if you *know* that the music you have in your head is the right music for the song you're going to teach. (One student teacher was observed earnestly teaching "Home on the Range" to the tune of "The Man on the Flying Trapeze." Somehow or other, he made it fit.)

TEACHING A SONG BY VOICE

When teaching any song to children, it is well to remember that they always deserve the best example possible; thus it behooves the teacher to give careful attention to his own phrasing, tone quality, diction, etc., for the children will imitate what they hear. Our most common deficiency in this area seems to be a failure to pronounce the words of a song distinctly enough for children to understand them. This results in what the child *thinks* is imitation, but really turns out to be *improvisation*, in many instances. When they can't understand what you say, they sing what they thought you said—with some rather startling results:

("Silent Night")
    Holy infant so tender and wild
       and
    Round your furniture mother and child
       and
    Round your furnace mother and child

("God Bless America")
    . . . through the night with a light from a bulb

("America, the Beautiful")
    O beautiful, for spaceships flies

17

("The Farmer in the Dell")
Heigh, ho, the Cheerios

Surely you've heard this classic before:

("Battle Hymn of the Republic")
He is tramping out the village where the great giraffes are stored

So, let's watch our language!

Try to teach any given song in the key in which it is written if you possibly can. (If you use a very light tone, you'll find that your range is wider than you suspected.) If you feel that the song is pitched too high for you to sing comfortably without squeaks, try teaching it in a key more comfortable for you. When the class has learned it well enough to carry on alone, give them the *correct* starting pitch and then let them sing it in the right key.

PROCEDURE FOR PHRASE METHOD

1. Arouse the children's interest (especially in the primary grades) through some motivational device such as a picture, story, puppet, etc.
2. Sing the entire song through, giving careful attention to the spirit of the song, expression, phrasing, diction, and tone quality.
3. Ask a few appropriate questions and discuss poetic content, if desired. This is a good means of securing a reasonably proper interpretation of the song when learned.
4. Sing the first phrase and have the class repeat it.
5. Sing the second phrase and have the class repeat it.
6. Sing the third phrase and have the class repeat it.
7. Sing the fourth phrase and have the class repeat it.
8. Sing the first and second phrases and have the class repeat them.
9. Sing the third and fourth phrases and have the class repeat them.
10. Sing the entire song through with the class.

The above procedure is intended primarily for the lower grades; it may be modified in the upper grades. For example, older children can follow the words on the chalkboard or in their books while the song is being taught. They can probably hear and repeat two phrases at a time instead of just one. If the song is familiar in part, they may be able to sing along with the teacher the *first* time the song is sung. After the first trial, any rough spots can be isolated and then practiced as needed.

PROCEDURE FOR WHOLE METHOD

Some primary songs are so easily grasped after one or two hearings that it is more satisfactory to teach them by what is known as the "whole method." This consists of merely singing the *whole* song through *each* time the children hear it, rather than breaking it up into short phrases for teaching purposes. This method is often appropriate for teaching upper-grade songs also, as when a song is partially familiar or is easily remembered for any other reason. Obviously, if certain passages in the song present difficulty, they may be isolated for practice, as previously suggested.

TEACHING BY MELODY INSTRUMENT

It is possible to teach a rote song through the use of any instrument on which one note can be played at a time—piano, song bells, recorder, etc. The teaching procedure is much the same as with the voice except that the words (if they are not in the children's music books) can be put on the chalkboard or on a chart. In using the *phrase* method, the whole song is played through once while the children follow the words, and then each phrase is played separately and repeated, with the children *singing* the appropriate words for that phrase. At the end of the last phrase, the whole song is played through, with the children singing.

In using the *whole* method, the entire song is played through the first time while the children listen to the tune and follow the words. On successive playings, while the children sing the words, the song is played through in its entirety, not broken up into phrases (except when a trouble spot occurs, of course).

When teaching a song by use of the melody instrument, the starting pitch should be given from the *instrument*, not the pitch pipe.

TEACHING BY RECORD

Many of the recent recordings that accompany children's music textbooks are so well done that it's a real joy to use them often, even if the teacher *is* able to sing. The children enjoy the instrumental accompaniment—much of which is strongly rhythmical—and the feeling of fullness of the support as they sing along. Records other than those which accompany the songbook series may also be used. (See suggestions at the end of this chapter.)

The procedure for teaching any new song by record is very simple. If the children have the textbooks that go along with the records, they merely open their books to the proper page and look and listen while the song is played through once. Following the first playing, there should be some discussion about the location of like phrases (if any), form, mood, dynamics, or any other appropriate points that will help to enhance the children's feeling for the song. The second time the song is played, the class joins in where they feel they can. The third time they join in singing the entire song. Three playings are sufficient for one day. There's always tomorrow. By the end of the week, the class should be able to start with the record and then continue without it. If the class does not have the textbooks to go with the records, the teacher may wish to put the words on the board or simply have the class listen and try to 19 remember as much as possible. Obviously, when teaching a song by record, it will be impossible to use the phrase method; only the whole method is feasible here.

In kindergarten or first grade before the children have learned to read, it will be necessary to discuss the words *heard* on the record (during the first playing) to make sure that every child knows what they are before attempting to have them sing the song through the first time. When using records to teach rote songs, always pitch the song from the record. Do not attempt to use any other pitch-producing instrument at the same time.

GIVING THE STARTING PITCH

Obviously, the easiest way for children to get started on the right pitch is to hear the teacher singing it. The most acceptable method for giving the starting pitch to a class is for the teacher first to sound the keynote (*do*) of the song, sing the tonic chord (*do-mi-so*) in that key to establish a feeling for the tonality, and then *sing* the correct starting pitch for the class. Once the class has the pitch, the command "Sing!" is given so that everyone will start together. It has been found, however, that not all people are able to match the pitches they hear. A teacher who has this problem certainly deserves to be provided with a way of giving his class the correct starting pitch by means other than his voice. He should also relax in the assurance that the children will continue to love him whether he can match pitches or not. Try the following method if you find it difficult to match a pitch that you hear from the pitch pipe or other instrument:

1. Say to the class, "Take your note," and then sound the starting pitch of the song either from the pitch pipe or from some melody instrument.
2. *Sustain* the tone long enough for the class to repeat it. (They simply *cannot* retain very short sounds blown in haste.) When you feel that the children have it, give the firm command "Sing!" The chances are good that they will start together on the right pitch. If you fail to say "Sing!" but instead simply nod your head or timidly whisper "Sing?" or delay with a long introduction such as "All ready to begin now, 1, 2, 3" (by this time they have forgotten what the starting tone sounded like), you may find the class having difficulty getting started at all.
3. When teaching a song by record, let the children get their starting pitch from the record.
4. If you are using an instrument to accompany the song, give the starting pitch from that instrument.

Please pitch all songs in their given key. This also applies to "America" and "The Star-spangled Banner," both of which frequently suffer countless indignities in opening exercises.

ACCOMPANYING A ROTE SONG

After the children have learned a song, they will enjoy hearing it accompanied by piano, Autoharp, song bells, or some other classroom instrument. Individual children may play portions of songs or simple ostinati (fragment of a tune repeated over and over) on selected instruments. Using rhythm instruments such as tambourines, maracas, drums, finger cymbals, woodblocks, etc., for special effects where appropriate will also heighten interest. When available, native instruments may be used with folk songs of various origins for added flavor as well as authenticity. It is not necessary to use *all* the instruments all the time. For variety, try *whistling* a verse or two of a song occasionally. (Even if you can't, the children will be able to!)

IN GENERAL

If the song is included in the children's music textbooks, each child should have his music book open to the song and follow along as the teacher sings it through. This is appropriate at any grade level where children have music books.

Observing songs in the books while they are being taught by rote often provides opportunities for other musical learnings such as the meaning of certain symbols (holds, repeat signs, etc.), as well as discovery of like and unlike phrases by sight as well as by sound, terms to indicate variations in dynamics, etc.

Establish the habit early of having the class listen when you sing and of listening when the class sings. This will help to improve concentration on the part of the children and will cut down considerably on the time that it takes to teach a song by rote.

Once they have learned a song, the children need only to be given the starting pitch and command to sing, and they should be able to continue by themselves.

A large repertoire of songs is not only a source of pride for teacher and children alike, but also it serves as a basis for a broader range of activities in other areas of music. In ear training, for example, trying to identify a familiar song from hearing snatches of it played or sung or hearing the rhythm pattern clapped becomes much more challenging when there are more songs from which to choose. More songs generate more opportunities for experimentation in accompaniment styles, composing descants, exploring related instrumental experiences, and other creative pursuits. Furthermore, a teacher whose class can boast of knowing many fine songs well is at least partially prepared when suddenly called upon to present a program, whether for an assembly or other occasion.

Many schools schedule assembly "sings" regularly, in which all grades participate. The program consists of one or two selected songs (or other musical contributions) prepared by each grade, plus other songs that are sung by the whole school together. This necessitates the learning of some "common" songs in all rooms so that everyone can participate. If the "sing" takes place at a holiday time, the program is usually in keeping with the holiday theme. Occasionally, the singing might be interspersed with a psalm, choral speaking, a prayer, or a reading, depending on what is appropriate for the occasion. In addition to their musical benefits, these "sings" are an excellent means of developing and maintaining group spirit within a school.

Meanwhile, back in the room, keep a list handy of songs the children know. (Be sure to include the *starting pitches* for quick and easy reference.) If there's an attractive way to display at least a partial list somewhere in the room, so much the better. The children will take pride in watching it grow. (And it's bound to impress someone!)

Repertoire

HERITAGE SONGS

Many songs have come to be considered part of a child's musical heritage, and it is generally felt that the learning of them should take place throughout his musical education. The teaching of a few such songs each year at the appropriate grade level, in addition to the reviewing of others previously learned, should ensure a child's becoming familiar with at least a portion of these "heritage" songs.

The list below, while not complete by any means, is suggestive of this type of song. Many of these may be found in most of the basic music texts published for classroom use or in various other collections. (See the list at the end of this chapter.)

Words and music for the songs marked with an asterisk (★) are included elsewhere in this text. (See Song Index, p. 369.)

The categorical grouping is for convenience only.

NURSERY RHYMES, SINGING GAMES

Little Bo-Peep
Lazy Mary
One, Two, Buckle My Shoe
This Old Man
Hickory Dickory Dock
Hot Cross Buns
Little Jack Horner
Eensy Weensy Spider
Old King Cole
London Bridge
Muffin Man
Looby Loo
A-hunting We Will Go
Soldier Boy
'Round and 'round the Village

Jack and Jill
Oh Where, Oh Where Has My
Little Dog Gone?
Pussy Cat, Pussy Cat
Three Little Kittens
Humpty Dumpty
Ride a Cock-horse
Little Miss Muffet
I'm a Little Teapot
See-Saw, Margery Daw
Hey Diddle, Diddle
I Know a Little Pussy
Baa, Baa, Black Sheep
Little Boy Blue
Mary, Mary, Quite Contrary

Shoo Fly
Here We Go round the Mountain
Lavender's Blue
Sing a Song of Sixpence
Ten Little Indians
Bluebird, Bluebird
Here We Go 'round the Mulberry
    Bush

Twinkle, Twinkle, Little Star★
Mary Had a Little Lamb
Oats, Peas, Beans and Barley Grow
The Farmer in the Dell
Did You Ever See a Lassie ?
Skip to My Lou★

ROUNDS

Row, Row, Row Your Boat★
Three Blind Mice
White Coral Bells★
Are You Sleeping, Brother John ?★
Oh How Lovely Is the Evening
Kookaburra
For Health and Strength (Round
    of Thanks)

Scotland's Burning
Make New Friends★
Down by the Station
Sweetly Sings the Donkey
Hey, Ho! Nobody Home★
Dona Nobis Pacem★

FOLK SONGS

Cindy
Riddle Song
Rig a Jig Jig
Sourwood Mountain
Red River Valley★
Down in the Valley★
Pop Goes the Weasel
Shenandoah
Billy Boy
Polly Wolly Doodle
Blue Tail Fly
Animal Fair
Reuben and Rachael
Comin' 'round the Mountain

Ridin' That New River Train
Go Tell Aunt Rhody
Get Along Little Dogies
Old Chisholm Trail
Erie Canal
On Top of Old Smoky★
Fiddle Dee Dee (Fly and the
    Bumblebee)
Turkey in the Straw
Sweet Betsy from Pike
Ole Dan Tucker
Wait for the Wagon
I Had a Rooster

PATRIOTIC SONGS

America
America, the Beautiful
Battle Hymn of the Republic
Columbia, the Gem of the Ocean
Dixie

The Star-spangled Banner
Yankee Doodle
When Johnny Comes Marching
    Home

SERVICE SONGS

Marine's Hymn
Anchors Aweigh
Coast Guard Song

Air Corps Song
Caisson Song

23

SONGS OF GEORGE M. COHAN

Yankee Doodle Boy★

You're a Grand Old Flag★

Over There

SONGS OF DEVOTION

A Mighty Fortress Is Our God
We Gather Together
Faith of Our Fathers
For the Beauty of the Earth
The Lord Is My Shepherd
Crusader's Hymn

Now Thank We All Our God
Come Ye Thankful People
O God, Beneath Thy Guiding
Hand
O God Our Help in Ages Past
Jesu, Joy of Man's Desiring

SPIRITUALS

Jacob's Ladder★
Swing Low, Sweet Chariot
When the Saints Go Marching In
Kum Ba Yah★
I Ain't Gonna Grieve My Lord
No More

Steal Away
Deep River
Ain't Goin' to Study War No
More
There's a Little Wheel A-turning
in My Heart

OLD FAVORITES

Sidewalks of New York
Bicycle Built for Two
Take Me out to the Ball Game
For He's a Jolly Good Fellow
The Bear Went over the Mountain
Keep the Home Fires Burning
Camptown Races
Oh, Susanna
Vive L'amour
Auld Lang Syne
Tell Me Why★
I Had a Dream, Dear
In the Good Old Summertime
Old Grey Bonnet
Down by the Old Mill Stream
Old Folks at Home (Swanee River)
My Bonnie
Man on the Flying Trapeze
Alouette
In the Evening by the Moonlight
Moonlight Bay

School Days
Wait till the Sun Shines, Nellie
I Want a Girl
When You Wore a Tulip
Captain Jinks
Home on the Range
Blow the Man Down
When You and I Were Young
Maggie★
It's a Long Way to Tipperary
Finiculi, Finicula
Clementine
Good Night Ladies
Buffalo Girl
Old Grey Mare
Old MacDonald Had a Farm
And the Band Played On
Long, Long Trail A-winding
Spanish Cavalier
Solomon Levi
Smiles

HOLIDAY SONGS (See·"Songs of Devotion")

Over the River and through the
  Wood*
Up on the Housetop

Jolly Old St. Nicholas
Jingle Bells

OTHERS

Santa Lucia
Blue Bells of Scotland
Oh Dear, What Can the Matter
  Be?
Londonderry Air
Annie Laurie
Comin' through the Rye
Flow Gently, Sweet Afton
Drink to Me Only with Thine
  Eyes
Loch Lomond
Frog Went a Courtin'
All through the Night

Heigh, Ho, Come to the Fair
Juanita
Beautiful Dreamer
Little Brown Church in the Vale
My Old Kentucky Home
Love's Old Sweet Song
Sweet and Low
Sailing, Sailing
Home Sweet Home
Long, Long Ago
Grandfather's Clock
Bendemeer Stream

SELECTED FAVORITES

Although many of the following may not be considered heritage songs as such, they are songs that have been found to be well liked by children, and that in itself is enough to justify their inclusion here. Some of these songs are merely *listed*, with the publisher or source given where known. (Publishers' addresses may be found in the Appendix.) A few appear with only the words given because their tunes are usually so familiar. Still others are complete with words and music in this text so that you'll be sure to try them with your children. Some of these extra-special favorites are also scattered throughout the section "Singing in Harmony," p. 64, and Chapter 8, Experiences in Movement.

FINGER-PLAY, COUNTING, AND ACTION SONGS

Finger-play and counting songs are often in demand by teachers in early childhood education. Action songs are requested by teachers at all levels. Those listed below are from some of the basic music texts.

From *Sharing Music* (American Book)
  Where Is Thumbkin?
  Here Is the Church
  Knock at the Door
  Mother's Knives and Forks
  The Family
  Five Little Alligators
  Eency Weency Spider
  Finger, Nose and Toes

When We March
Wiggle Song
Roll That Red Ball
From *Music for Early Childhood* (Silver Burdett)
Open Them, Shut Them
Dance Thumbkin Dance
Two Blackbirds
From *Music through the Day* (Silver Burdett)
Three Blue Pigeons
Stamping Land
From *Growing with Music*, Book 1 (Prentice-Hall)
Ten Little Indians
This Old Man
From *Growing with Music*, Book 2 (Prentice-Hall)
Smoke Went up the Chimney
From *Magic of Music*, Book 1 (Ginn)
One Potato
Clap Your Hands
From *Meeting Music* (American Book)
Ten Little Pennies
Jimmy Cracked Corn
From *Experiences in Music for First Grade Children* (Silver Burdett)
Busy
From *Exploring Music*, Book 1 (Holt)
Johnny Works with One Hammer
Little Cabin in the Wood
From *Singing and Rhyming* (Ginn)
The Bus
From *Singing Fun* (Bowmar Records)
I Wiggle
Two Little Hands
From *More Singing Fun* (Bowmar Records)
Touch Your Head
From *Discovering Music Together*, Book 2 (Follett)
Playing in the Band

ACTION SONGS TO FAMILIAR TUNES★

TUNE: "Here We Go 'round the Mulberry Bush" (Key of G. Start G *do*)
Words 1. Head, shoulders, knees, and toes (Sing three times)
        Clap, clap, bow.
Words 2. This is the way the [animal] goes (Sing three times)
        All around the zoo. [May substitute "farm" for "zoo"]
Words 3. This is the way the children [skip, run, walk, etc.]
        All around the room. [or "on their way to school," etc.]

★ Words and music to more action songs are included elsewhere in this text. (See Song
Index, p. 369.)

TUNE: "Battle Hymn of the Republic" (Key of B♭. Start F—first space *sol*)

Words 1. "The Emperor Napoleon" had twenty-thousand men (Sing three
   times)
    And they all went marching on.

Actions

  Omit one word at the end of the first line and substitute a nod of the
  head, then omit two words and substitute two nods, etc., until the
  whole first line is simply a series of seven nods (done three times). At
  the end of all the nods each time the song is sung, everyone joins in
  on "And they all went marching on."

Words 2. "John Brown's Flivver" had a puncture in the tire (Sing three times)
    And he fixed it with a piece of gum.

Actions

  Substitute cranking motion for "flivver."
  Make *ssst* noise for "puncture."
  Draw circle with hand for "tire."
  Imitate pulling gum back and forth from mouth on "piece of gum".

Words 3. "Little Peter Rabbit" had a flea upon his ear (Sing three times)
    And he brushed it and it flew away.

Actions

  Make ears on top of head for "Peter Rabbit."
  Put thumb and forefinger close together to indicate small flea on "flea."
  Point to ear on "ear."
  Brush ear on "brushed it."
  Make flying motion with hand on "flew away."
  Repeat the whole song, omitting a word and substituting an action each
   time until all four actions have been completed.

Words 4. "John Brown's Baby" had a cold upon his chest (Sing three times)
    And he rubbed it with camphorated oil.

Actions

  Substitute short cough for "cold".
  Hit chest for "chest."
  Hold nose for "camphorated oil."

TUNE: "Yankee Doodle" (Key G. Start G *do*)

Words 1. Chester, have you heard about Harry
    Just got back from the Army
    I hear he knows how to wear a rose
    Hip, Hip, hooray for the Army.

Actions

  On "Chester" put hands on chest.
  On "heard" cup hand over ear as though listening.
  On "Harry" pull hair.
  On "back" point to back.
  On "Army" cross arms over chest and slap hands on arms twice.
  On "hear" point to ear.
  On "knows" point to nose.
  On "wear a rose" pat lapel three times.
  On "hip hip" slap hip twice.

27

On "hooray" circle hand in air as though waving and cheering.
On "Army" cross arms over chest and slap hands on arms twice, as
before.

SONGS FROM MUSICALS, MOTION PICTURES, AND OPERETTAS

From *Oklahoma*
  Oklahoma
  Oh, What a Beautiful Morning
  Surrey with the Fringe on Top
From *The Sound of Music*
  Do Re Mi
  My Favorite Things
  Climb Every Mountain
From *The King and I*
  Getting to Know You
  I Whistle a Happy Tune
From *Miss Liberty*
  Give Me Your Tired, Your Poor
From *Carousel*:
  You'll Never Walk Alone
From *The Wizard of Oz*
  Over the Rainbow

From *South Pacific*
  Dites Moi
From *Pinocchio*
  When You Wish upon a Star
From *Song of the South*
  Zip-adee-doo-dah
From selected *Gilbert and Sullivan*
  operettas
  When I Was a Lad
  I Am the Monarch of the Sea
  Major General's Song

OLD STANDARDS	PUBLISHER OR SOURCE
Side by Side	Shapiro-Bernstein
McNamara's Band	Jerry Vogel
Heart of My Heart	Big Three Music Corporation
Rudolph, the Red-nosed Reindeer	St. Nicholas Music Co.
Peter Cottontail	*Growing with Music*, Book 2 (Prentice-Hall)
Easter Parade	Irving Berlin Music Co.
White Christmas	Irving Berlin Music Co.
Silver Bells	*Fred Waring Song Book*
April Showers	Warner Bros.–Seven Arts

Despite the diversified content of the following songs, children usually
like them all:

Happy Wanderer	*This is Music*, Book 2 (Allyn and Bacon)
Bless This House	Boosey & Hawkes
This Land Is Your Land	*Exploring Music*, Book 5 (Holt)
America, I Love You	Mills Music, Inc.
Marching along Together	Big Three Music Corporation
Good News	*Growing with Music*, Book 6 (Prentice-Hall)
Trampin'	*Studying Music* (American Book)

I Like to Catch Brass Rings
    on the Merry Go Round   Unknown
L O double L Y POP spells
    Lollypop   Unknown
I Want Two Wings   *Making Music* (American Book)

FOREIGN-LANGUAGE SONGS

Children frequently enjoy singing songs in foreign languages. Many, such as *Frère Jacques* (see Song Index), are commonly found in children's music books.

The following songs in Spanish are included here because the tunes are probably familiar to most teachers and children:

"Felices Navidades"
TUNE: "We Wish You a Merry Christmas"
    Felices Navidades, Felices Navidades, Felices Navidades
    Y un prospero año nuevo.
Translation: We wish you a merry Christmas, we wish you a merry Christmas,
        We wish you a merry Christmas and a happy New Year.

"Buenos Dias"
TUNE: "Are You Sleeping, Brother John?"
    Buenos dias, buenos dias, como estan, como estan?
    Estamos muy bienes, estamos muy bienes,
    Muchas gracias, muchas gracias.
Translation: Good day, how are you?
        I am fine, thank you.

"Mi Escuelita"
TUNE: "La Cucaracha"
    Mi escuelita, mi escuelita, yo la quero con pasion
    Porque en ella, porque en ella, es que aprende la leccion.
Translation: My little school, I like it very much
        Because in it lessons are learned.

"Noche de Paz"
TUNE: "Silent Night"
    Noche de paz, noche de amor, todo duerme en derredor,
    Entre los astros que esparcen su lus, bella annunciando
        al niño Jesús,
    Brilla la estrella de paz, brilla la estrella de paz.
Translation: "Silent Night" (English words).

"Cascabel"
TUNE: "Jingle Bells" (chorus only)
    Cascabel, cascabel, música de amor,

Dulces horas, gratas horas, juventud en flor,
Cascabel, cascabel, tan sentimental,
No dejes casbelito de repiquetear.

Translation: "Jingle Bells" (chorus only, English words).

Let There Be Peace on Earth

(Let It Begin with Me)

Sy Miller & Jill Jackson

30

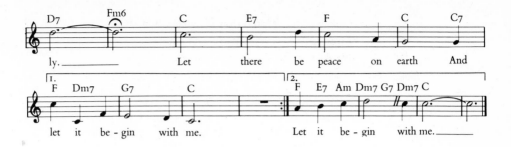

ly._____ Let there be peace on earth And
let it be-gin with me. Let it be-gin with me._____

CREDIT: By Sy Miller and Jill Jackson. Used by permission Jan-Lee Music. Beverly Hills, California
© 1955.

You're a Grand Old Flag

Majestically

George M. Cohan

You're a grand old flag, you're a high-fly - ing flag;

And for - ev - er, in peace may you wave;_____

You're the em - blem of the land I love,

The home of the free and the brave._____

Ev - 'ry heart beats true, un - der Red, White, and Blue;

Where there's nev - er a boast or brag;_____

But, should auld ac - quaint - ance be for - got,

Keep your eye on the grand old flag._____

3 I

Morning Song

With easy movement   *Gracia Caines*

1. I a-wake to the day on a moun-tain high, Where the sun is
2. I a-wake to the day when the shad-ows of night Have dis-ap-

bright in a per-fect sky; The pines, like ar-rows, are
peared in the morn-ing light; The trees' green branch-es look

point-ing a-bove, My world is peace-ful be-cause of God's love.
down from a-bove, My world is peace-ful be-cause of God's love.

This day is my own; I must use it with care,

So when night comes, and I say my prayers, I'll thank you, God,

For a beau-ti-ful day. This is my morn-ing song.

CREDIT: *Words and music by Gracia Caines, from* Voices of America, © *Follett Publishing Company, 1957, 1960, 1963.*

This is one of the loveliest and most appealing songs ever written for children. All children who have ever sung it feel the same way. Be sure to try it with the chords suggested for accompaniment. It transposes easily to the key of F and may then be accompanied on the Autoharp, substituting chords in the key of F for those given above as follows:

For:	*Substitute:*	*For:*	*Substitute:*
E♭	F	F7	G7
Gm	Am	A♭	B♭
Cm	Dm	Fm	Gm
B♭7	C7		

Yankee Doodle Boy

George M. Cohan

I'm a Yan-kee Doo-dle Dan-dy, A Yan-kee Doo-dle, do or die;— A real live neph-ew of my Un-cle Sam, Born on the Fourth of Ju-ly.— I've got a Yan-kee Doo-dle sweet-heart, She's my Yan-kee Doo-dle joy.— Yan-kee Doo-dle came to Lon-don, just to ride the po - nies, I am a Yan-kee Doo-dle boy.—

Kum Ba Yah

Spiritual

Kum ba yah, my Lord, Kum ba yah! Kum ba yah, my Lord, Kum ba yah! Kum ba yah, my Lord, Kum ba yah! O Lord, Kum ba yah.—

2. Someone's crying, Lord, Kum ba yah!
3. Someone's singing, Lord, Kum ba yah!
4. Someone's praying, Lord, Kum ba yah!

CREDIT: *From* Look Away. *Used by permission of Cooperative Recreation Service, Delaware, Ohio.*

Cert'nly Lord

1. Have you got re - li - gion? Cert'n-ly, Lord. Have you got re - li - gion?
2. Have you been bap - tized? Cert'n-ly, Lord. Have you been bap - tized?

Cert'n-ly, Lord. Have you got re - li - gion? Cert'n-ly, Lord.
Cert'n-ly, Lord. Have you been bap - tized? Cert'n-ly, Lord.

O cert'n-ly Lord._____

Cert'n-ly, cert'n-ly, cert'n-ly, Lord. O

_____ O cert'n-ly Lord._____

cert'n-ly Lord. O cert'n-ly, Lord.

Cert'n - ly, cert'n - ly, cert'n - ly, cert'n - ly, Lord.

CREDIT: *From* Chansons de Notre Chalet, © *1962. Used by permission of Cooperative Recrea-tion Service, Delaware, Ohio.*

All Night, All Day

Spiritual

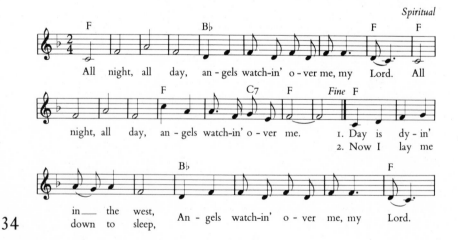

All night, all day, an - gels watch-in' o - ver me, my Lord. All

night, all day, an - gels watch-in' o - ver me.
1. Day is dy - in'
2. Now I lay me

in _____ the west, An - gels watch-in' o - ver me, my Lord.
down to sleep,

34

Sleep, my child, and take your rest,
Pray the Lord my soul to keep,
An - gels watch-in' o - ver me.

CREDIT: *From* Chansons de Notre Chalet, © *1962. Used by permission of Cooperative Service,*
Delaware, Ohio.

The Angel Band

Choose a different instrument for each of the angels. Play a different instrument each time you sing a number.

South Carolina Folk Song

There was one, there were two, there were three lit - tle an - gels,

There were four, there were five, there were six lit - tle an - gels,

There were sev'n, there were eight, there were nine lit - tle an-gels,

Ten lit - tle an - gels in the band.

Refrain

Was-n't that a band, Sun - day morn - ing, Sun - day

morn - ing, Sun - day morn - ing? Was-n't that a band,

Sun - day morn - ing, Sun - day morn - ing soon?

CREDIT: *By permission from G. Schirmer, from* 36 South Carolina Spirituals, *by Carl Diton,*
1930, 1957.

35

Hush, Little Baby

American Folk Song

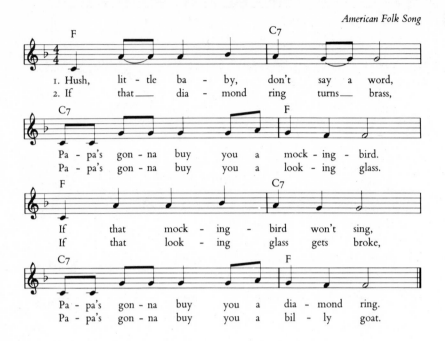

1. Hush, lit - tle ba - by, don't say a word,
2. If that dia - mond ring turns brass,

Pa - pa's gon - na buy you a mock - ing - bird.
Pa - pa's gon - na buy you a look - ing glass.

If that mock - ing - bird won't sing,
If that look - ing glass gets broke,

Pa - pa's gon - na buy you a dia - mond ring.
Pa - pa's gon - na buy you a bil - ly goat.

Little Red Caboose

Lit - tle red ca - boose, lit - tle red ca - boose,

Lit - tle red ca - boose be - hind the train.

Smoke-stack on its back, rum-blin' down the track,

F C7 F

Lit-tle red ca - boose be - hind the train.___

CREDIT: By special permission of the publishers, Holt, Rinehart and Winston. From Book 1, Exploring Music series, © 1966.

Little Boy Song

Chorus

C G7 G7 C

I am a lit-tle boy from Tri-ni - dad, some-times I am good, some-times I am bad.

Claves

Barrel Drum

C G7 G7 C

Ma-ma she talk, talk all the day How I should grow up and how I should play.

Second Verse

Go to the school get smart you'll see,
Go to the school get smart you'll see,
I don't believe her,
Try to deceive her,
I play hookey, but they soon catch me.

CREDIT: *From* Little Calypsos, *by Lillian Krugman and Alice Ludwig,* © *1955, Carl Van Roy Publishing Co., Far Rockaway, N.Y. Subsidiary of Peripole. Used with permission.*

Little Girl Song

(To the Tune of the Little Boy Song)

Chorus:

I am a little girl from Trinidad,
Sometimes I am good, sometimes I am bad.
Mama she talk, talk all day
How I should grow up and how I should play.

Verse:

Walk straight as Tree, Mama she said,
Walk straight as Tree, Mamma she said.
  If I will heed her
  Then I won't need her
To help me carry baskets on my head.

Second Verse:

Learn how to cook and you will see,
Learn how to cook and you will see,
  If I will heed her,
  Then I won't need her
To catch a fellow who will marry me!

CREDIT: From Little Calypsos, *by Lillian Krugman and Alice Ludwig,* © *1955, Carl Van Roy Publishing Co., Far Rockaway, N.Y. Subsidiary of Peripole. Used with permission.*

Honey, You Can't Love One

Traditional American Song

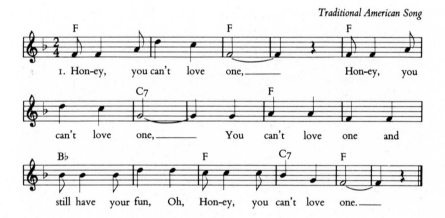

2. Honey, you can't love two, (*2 times*)
   You can't love two and always be true,
   Oh, Honey, you can't love two.
3. Honey, you can't love three, (*2 times*)
   You can't love three and still go with me,
   Oh, Honey, you can't love three.

Can you add some new verses to this song?

   Honey, you can't love four, (*2 times*)
   You can't love four and. . . . .
   Oh, Honey, you can't love four.

CREDIT: *By special permission of the publishers, Holt, Rinehart and Winston. From Book 2,* Exploring Music *series,* © *1966.*

Five Hundred Miles

Folk Song

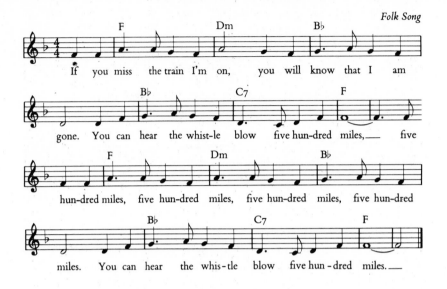

If you miss the train I'm on, you will know that I am gone. You can hear the whist-le blow five hun-dred miles,—— five hun-dred miles, five hun-dred miles, five hun-dred miles, five hun-dred miles. You can hear the whis-tle blow five hun-dred miles.——

2. Lord, I'm one, Lord, I'm two, Lord, I'm three, Lord, I'm four, Lord I'm five hundred miles from my home.
   Away from home, away from home, away from home, away from home, Lord, I'm five hundred miles away from home.
3. Not a shirt on my back, not a penny to my name, No, I can't go home this-a way, this-a way, this-a way, this-a way, this-a way, No, I can't go home this-a way.
4. Repeat first verse.

There Was an Old Woman

American Folk Song

Easily

1. There was an old wom-an who swal-lowed a fly, And I don't know why she swal-lowed a fly, Per-haps she'll die.

2. There was an old wom-an who swal-lowed a spi-der That
3. There was an old wom-an who swal-lowed a bird,——

wig - gled and jig - gled and tick - led in - side her,
How___ ab - surd___ to swal - low a bird,___

Verses accumulate

2. She swal-lowed the spi - der to swal - low a fly,
3. { She swal-lowed a bird___ } And
   { to swal - low a spi - der to swal - low a fly, }

I don't know why she swal-lowed the fly, Per - haps she'll die.

4. There was an old woman who swallowed a cat;
   Imagine that—to swallow a cat.
   She swallowed a cat—to swallow a bird—to swallow a spider—
   to swallow a fly, And I don't know why she swallowed a fly,
   Perhaps she'll die.

5. There was an old woman who swallowed a dog;
   What a hog to swallow a dog.
   She swallowed a dog—to swallow a cat—to swallow a bird—
   to swallow a spider—to swallow a fly,
   And I don't know why she swallowed a fly,
   Perhaps she'll die.

6. There was an old woman who swallowed a goat;
   Just opened her throat and swallowed a goat.
   She swallowed a goat —to swallow a dog—to swallow a cat—
   to swallow a bird—to swallow a spider—to swallow a fly,
   And I don't know why she swallowed a fly,
   Perhaps she'll die.

7. There was an old woman who swallowed a cow;
   I don't know how she swallowed a cow.
   She swallowed a cow—to swallow a goat—to swallow a dog—
   to swallow a cat—to swallow a bird—to swallow a spider—
   to swallow a fly, And I don't know why she swallowed a fly,
   Perhaps she'll die.

8. There was an old wom-an who swal-lowed a horse; She's dead of course.

CREDIT: *From* Growing with Music, *Book 4, by R. H. Wilson et al.,* © *1966 by Prentice-Hall, Inc., Englewood Cliffs, N.J. Reprinted with permission.*

Michael Finnigin

Traditional

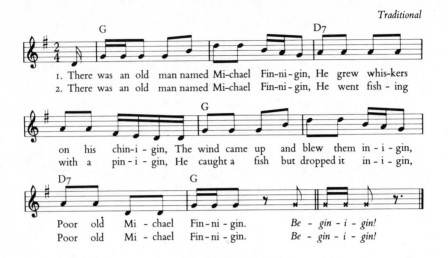

1. There was an old man named Mi-chael Fin-ni-gin, He grew whis-kers
2. There was an old man named Mi-chael Fin-ni-gin, He went fish - ing

on his chin-i-gin, The wind came up and blew them in-i-gin,
with a pin - i - gin, He caught a fish but dropped it in - i - gin,

Poor old Mi - chael Fin - ni - gin. *Be - gin - i - gin!*
Poor old Mi - chael Fin - ni - gin. *Be - gin - i - gin!*

3. There was an old man named Michael Finnigin,
   Climbed a tree and barked his shinigin,
   He took off many years of skiningin,
   Poor old Michael Finnigin! Beginigin!
4. There was an old man named Michael Finnigin,
   He grew fat and then grew thinigin,
   He died and then he had to beginigin,
   Poor old Michael Finnigin. It's the endigin!

For variation, sing it a little softer on each repetition until the song is barely audible. (Note that the word "beginigin!" is to be spoken, not sung.)

CREDIT: By special permission of the publishers, Holt, Rinehart and Winston. From Book 1, Exploring Music series, © 1966.

Six Little Ducks

Six lit - tle ducks that I once knew, Fat ones, skin-ny ones,

fair ones too, But the one lit - tle duck with a feath-er on his back,

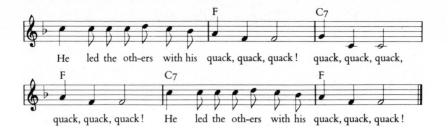

He led the oth-ers with his quack, quack, quack! quack, quack, quack,

quack, quack, quack! He led the oth-ers with his quack, quack, quack!

2. Down to the river they would go,
   Wibble, Wabble, Wibble, Wabble to and fro.
3. Home from the river they would come,
   Wibble, Wabble, Wibble, Wabble, Ho-hum-hum!

CREDIT: *From* Sing a Tune, © 1966. *Used by permission of Cooperative Service, Delaware, Ohio.*

Tongo

Polynesia

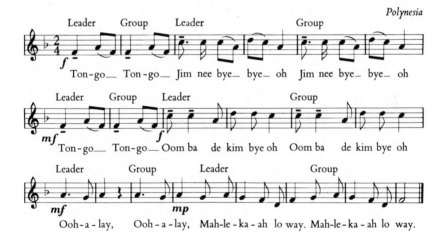

Ton-go— Ton-go— Jim nee bye— bye— oh Jim nee bye— bye— oh

Ton-go— Ton-go— Oom ba de kim bye oh Oom ba de kim bye oh

Ooh-a-lay, Ooh-a-lay, Mah-le-ka-ah lo way. Mah-le-ka-ah lo way.

CREDIT: *From* Good Fellowship Songs, © 1963. *Used by permission of Cooperative Recreation Service, Delaware, Ohio.*

Paddlers echo the chant from one canoe to another. The effect of echoing voices is enhanced if both the leader and the group hold the last note of each phrase while the other sings.

43

I Had a Little Dog

Source Unknown

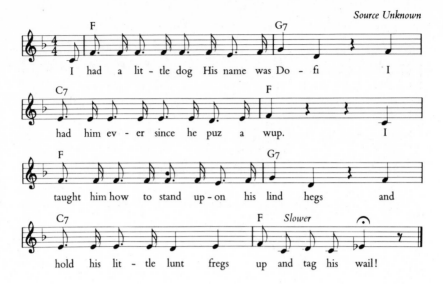

I had a lit - tle dog His name was Do - fi I

had him ev - er since he puz a wup. I

taught him how to stand up - on his lind hegs and

hold his lit - tle lunt fregs up and tag his wail!

I've Got That Happy Feeling

Origin Unknown

I've got that hap - py feel - ing here in my heart, Here in my heart,

Here in my heart. I've got that hap - py feel - ing

here in my heart, Here in my heart to stay.

2. I've got that happy feeling down in my feet, etc. [march in place].
3. I've got that happy feeling here in my hands [clap hands].
4. I've got that happy feeling all over me, etc.

Have children add other verses.

Wake Me

Lively

Adapted from a Folk Song

1. Wake me! Shake me! Don't let me sleep too late; ___ Got to get up bright and ear-ly in the morn-ing, Going to swing on the gold-en gate.

2. Wake me! Shake me!
   Don't let me sleep too late;
   Got to comb my hair this morning,
   Going to swing on the golden gate.
3. Got to brush my teeth this morning
4. Got to dress myself this morning.

   Can the children think of other activities?

CREDIT: By permission from American Book Company. From Sharing Music, *Music for Young Americans* series, © 1966.

Noble Duke of York

English Folk Song.
Added verses by Mary Dutre

Briskly
mf

1. Oh, the no - ble Duke of York, He
2. Oh, when they were up they were up, When

had ten thou - sand men, He marched them up to the
they were down they were down, But when they were on - ly

top of the hill, And he marched them down a - gain.
half - way up, They were nei - ther up nor down.

3. Oh, the noble Duke of York
   Saluted all his men,
   Saluted with his left and right,
   And saluted them again.
4. Oh, the noble Duke of York
   Rode a noble mount, of course,
   But he fell on his head and thought he was dead
   Till he got back on his horse.

ACTIONS:

"*Up*"—*stand up every time the word is sung.*
"*Down*"—*sit down every time the word is sung.*
"*Halfway*"—*assume position halfway between up and down.*
"*Fell on his head*"—*drop forehead to desk.*
"*Got back on his horse*"—*resume sitting position.*

Crocodile Song

Happily
Traditional

She sailed a-way on a bright and sun-ny day, On the
back of a croc-o dile. "You see," said she, "He's as
tame as he can be As I float him down the Nile." The
Croc winked his eye as she waved a mer-ry bye,
Wear-ing a hap-py smile. At the end of the ride, the
la-dy was in-side, And the smile was on the croc-o-dile. (*Clap Clap*)

ACTIONS:

Measures

1– 4 *Hands pointed away from the body; move them rhythmically, in a waving motion.*

5– 8 *Stroke the left arm with right hand, or vice versa.*

9–12 *Give a big wink; wave goodbye; smile very broadly, using index fingers to pull lips up at corners.*

13–16 *Palms together, open and shut hands like crocodile's mouth. Give two sharp claps at the end.*

CREDIT: *From* Growing with Music, *Book 3, by H. R. Wilson et al.,* © *1966 by Prentice-Hall, Inc., Englewood Cliffs, N.J. Reprinted with permission.*

I Am a Musician

Origin Unknown

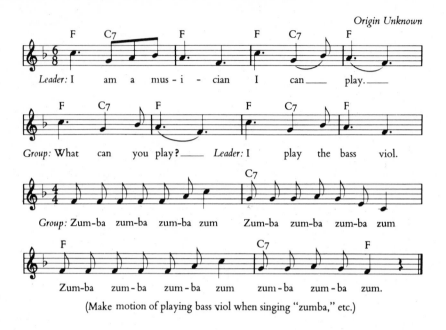

Leader: I am a mus-i-cian I can___ play.___

Group: What can you play?___ Leader: I play the bass viol.

Group: Zum-ba zum-ba zum-ba zum Zum-ba zum-ba zum-ba zum

Zum-ba zum-ba zum-ba zum zum-ba zum-ba zum.

(Make motion of playing bass viol when singing "zumba," etc.)

2. Leader: I am a musician, I can play. I play the piccolo.   Group: What can you play?
Group: (Whistle above tune starting with "zumba," etc.)

3. violin   vee-o- vee-o vee-o la   (make motion of playing violin)
4. bass drum boomba boomba, etc.   (make motion of playing bass drum)
5. cymbals   zimba zimba, etc.   (make motion of playing cymbals)
6. trumpet   ta ta ta, etc.   (make motion of holding and playing trumpet)
7. "I am the leader"   (silence while conducting in time)

Add other instruments as desired.

"I Am a Musician" is a cumulative song. This means that each previous instrument must be returned to as each new one is added. For example, after whistling the chorus tune for the piccolo, go immediately to repetition of "zumba zumba," etc., for the bass viol. When the violin chorus of "vee-o vee-o," etc., is completed, repeat the whistle of the piccolo and the "zumba zumba" of the bass viol. The last verse then will include the beating silence plus the addition of *all* the previously mentioned instruments, ending with "zumba zumba," etc.

The Wise Man Built His House upon the Rock

Origin Unknown

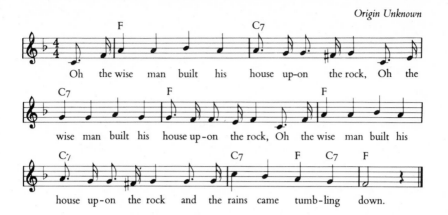

Oh the wise man built his house up-on the rock, Oh the wise man built his house up-on the rock, Oh the wise man built his house up-on the rock and the rains came tumb-ling down.

2. Oh the rains came down and the floods came up,
   Oh the rains came down and the floods came up,
   Oh the rains came down and the floods came up,
   But the house on the rock stood firm.
3. Oh the silly man built his house upon the sand,
   Oh the silly man built his house upon the sand,
   Oh the silly man built his house upon the sand,
   And the rains came tumbling down.
4. Oh the rains came down, etc.
   And the house on the sand went swisssssssssssh.

ACTIONS:

"Wise"—point to head.

"Built"—one fist on top of the other.

"House"—tips of fingers to make pointed roof.

"Rock"—hands clasped.

"Silly"—circling motion with finger at side of head.

"Sand"—sweeping motion with forearms in opposite direction.

"Swish"—large sweeping motion to indicate washing away.

Pow Wow

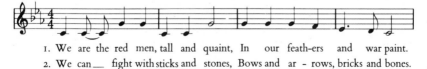

1. We are the red men, tall and quaint, In our feath-ers and war paint.
2. We can fight with sticks and stones, Bows and ar - rows, bricks and bones.

49

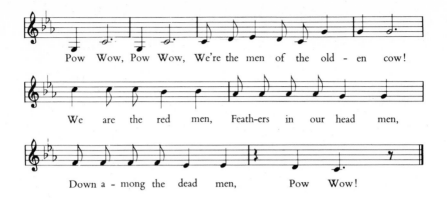

Pow Wow, Pow Wow, We're the men of the old - en cow!

We are the red men, Feath-ers in our head men,

Down a - mong the dead men, Pow Wow!

3. We return from hunting far,
   Greeted by our long-nosed squaw.
   Pow Wow, Pow Wow,—(chorus)

ACTIONS:

"Red men"—cross arms in front in "chief" position.

"Feathers"—make feathers in back of head with three fingers.

"War paint"—stroke both cheeks.

"Pow wow"—cross arms in front as for "red men,"—but this time slap upper arms with hands, one at a time, in time with the music on words "pow wow."

"Olden cow"—extend right arm forward; clasp upper arm with left hand.

"Red men"—repeat as above.

"Feathers"—repeat as above.

"Down"—make "scooping" motion leaning over.

"Pow wow"—repeat as above.

Vary actions as desired for this verse and others.

CREDIT: From Happy Days. Used by permission of Cooperative Recreation Service, Delaware, Ohio.

My Beloved Laddie, Nicky

Mine hand on mine-self, Vas iss das here? Das iss mine schwet box-er,

My Mam - ma dear. Schwet box - er, schwet box - er,

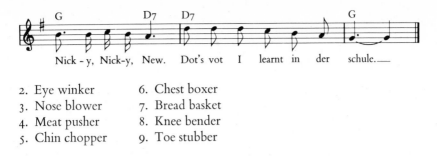

Nick - y, Nick-y, New. Dot's vot I learnt in der schule.——

2. Eye winker
3. Nose blower
4. Meat pusher
5. Chin chopper

6. Chest boxer
7. Bread basket
8. Knee bender
9. Toe stubber

CREDIT: *From* Happy Days. *Used by permission of Cooperative Recreation Service, Delaware, Ohio.*

If You're Happy

If you're hap - py and you know it wear a smile If you're
hap-py and you know it wear a smile If you're hap-py and you know it then your
life will sure-ly show it, if you're hap-py and you know it wear a smile.

2. If you're happy, etc., clap your hands. (Clap two times.)
3. If you're happy, etc., tap your feet. (Tap feet two times.)
4. If you're happy, etc., say "amen." (Say "amen".)
5. If you're happy, etc., sing a song tra-la-la.

At the end of each verse, add the last action of the preceding verse to make a cumulative song. Words should be sung with the action, of course. The last verse then would be: "Sing a song tra-la-la, say amen, tap your feet, clap your hands, wear a smile."

6. Have the children create verses of their own.

A Pat on the Back

Lively but not too fast

Oh, give your friend a pat on the back, a pat on the back, a
pat on the back, and say to your-self it's jol - ly good health we've
had a good day_ to - day. Yes - ter - day was full of trou - ble and sor - row,
No - bod - y knows what's goin' to hap - pen to - mor - row, So,

CREDIT: *From* Songs of Many Nations, © 1966. *Used by permission of Cooperative Recreation Service, Delaware, Ohio.*

Downright, Upright

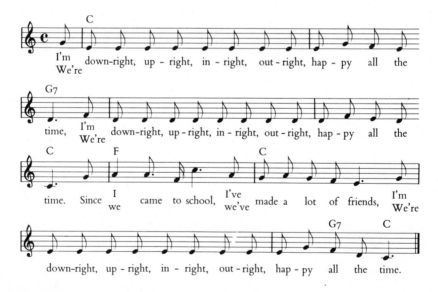

I'm / We're down-right, up - right, in - right, out - right, hap - py all the
time, I'm / We're down-right, up - right, in - right, out - right, hap - py all the
time. Since I / we came to school, I've / we've made a lot of friends, I'm / We're
down-right, up - right, in - right, out - right, hap - py all the time.

CREDIT: *From* Second Fun and Folk Song Proof Book. *Used by permission of Cooperative Recreation Service, Delaware, Ohio.*

52

My Hat

(Mein Hut)

German Folk Song

Eng: My hat it had three cor - ners, _____ Three cor - ners
Ger: Mein Hut er hat drei Eck - en, _____ Drei Eck - en

had my hat; _____ And had it not three
hat mein Hut; _____ Und hat er nicht drei

cor - ners _____ It would not be my hat. _____
Eck - en _____ Dann ist er nicht mein Hut. _____

ACTIONS:

"My"—point to self.

"Hat"—touch head.

"Three"—hold up three fingers.

"Corners"—bend left arm to make elbow, then touch elbow with right hand.

Repeat the song five times, leaving out one of the action words each time and substituting the action in time to the music.

CREDIT: By special permission of the publishers, Holt, Rinehart and Winston. From Book 1, Exploring Music series, © 1966.

Over the River and through the Wood

Happily

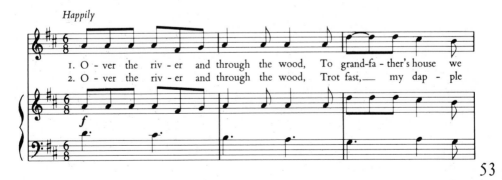

1. O - ver the riv - er and through the wood, To grand-fa - ther's house we
2. O - ver the riv - er and through the wood, Trot fast, _____ my dap - ple

Winter Wonderland

(Children's Words) (*Key of C. Start G sol*)

Sleigh bells ring, are you list'nin'?
In the lane, snow is glist'nin'
A beautiful sight, we're happy tonight
Walkin' in a winter wonderland.
Gone away is the bluebird
Here to stay is a new bird
He's singing a song as we go along
Walkin' in a winter wonderland.
In the meadow we can build a snowman
And pretend that he's a circus clown
We'll have lots of fun with Mister Snowman
Until the other kiddies knock 'im down.
When it snows, ain't it thrillin'
Tho' your nose gets a chillin'
We'll frolic and play the Eskimo way
Walkin' in a winter wonderland.

CREDIT: Words by Dick Smith. Music by Felix Bernard. Used by permission of the copyright owners: Bregman, Vocco and Conn, Inc., New York.

Children Go

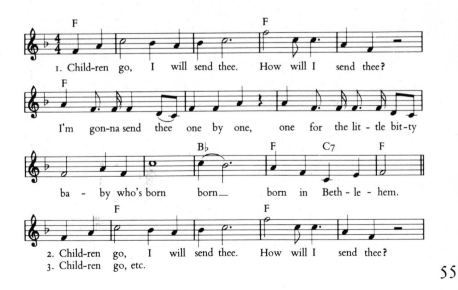

1. Child-ren go, I will send thee. How will I send thee? I'm gon-na send thee one by one, one for the lit-tle bit-ty ba - by who's born born— born in Beth - le - hem.

2. Child-ren go, I will send thee. How will I send thee?
3. Child-ren go, etc.

55

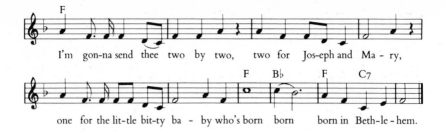

I'm gon-na send thee two by two, two for Jos-eph and Ma - ry,

one for the lit-tle bit-ty ba - by who's born born born in Beth-le - hem.

Three for the three old wise men.
Two for Joseph and Mary.
One for the little bitty baby who's born, born, born in Bethlehem.

Mary Had a Baby

Spiritual

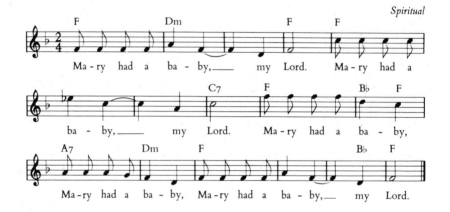

Ma - ry had a ba - by,____ my Lord. Ma - ry had a

ba - by,____ my Lord. Ma - ry had a ba - by,

Ma - ry had a ba - by, Ma - ry had a ba - by,____ my Lord.

2. What did she name him, my Lord?
3. Named him King Jesus, my Lord.
4. Where was he born, my Lord?
5. Born in a manger, my Lord.

Amen

Arranged by Marion Downs

Chorus

A - - men, A - - men, A - - men, A -

Solo   Obbligato

1. See   the   ba - by,
2. See Him in the   tem - ple,
3. See Him at the   sea - side,
4. See Him in the   gar - den,
5. Yes, He   is my   Sav - ior,

1 Chorus   2

men, A - men.   men, A - men.   A - -

Ly - ing in   a   man-ger   One   Christ - mas   morn - ing.
Talk - ing to the El - ders, How   they marvelled at   His wis-dom.
Preach - ing   and heal-ing,   To   the   blind   and the fee-ble.
Pray - ing to His Fa - ther,   In   deep - est   sor - row.
Je - sus died to   save us,   And   He   rose   on Eas - ter.

men,   A - - men,   A - -

6. Hal - le - lu - jah   In   the King -

men, A - men, A - men.   A - - men,

dom   with my Sav - ior.   A - men, A - men,

A - - men,   A - - men, A - men, A - men.

Amen—pronounce A as in bay.

CREDIT: From Look Away. Used by permission of Cooperative Recreation Service, Delaware, Ohio.

Christmas Is Coming

Traditional English Round

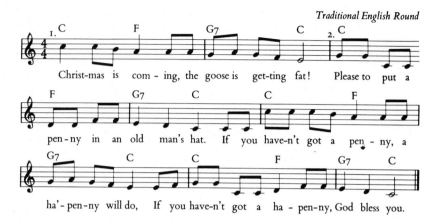

Christ-mas is com-ing, the goose is get-ting fat! Please to put a
pen-ny in an old man's hat. If you have-n't got a pen-ny, a
ha'-pen-ny will do, If you have-n't got a ha-pen-ny, God bless you.

CREDIT: *By special permission of the publishers, Holt, Rinehart and Winston. From Book 6,* Exploring Music *series,* © *1966.*

Child of God

Not too fast

Southern Folk Song

Key: F

A-3-Mi

1. If an-y-bod-y asks you who I am,____ Who I
2. The lit-tle cra-dle rocks to-night in glo-ry, Night in
3. ____ Peace on earth,__ Ma-ry, rock the cra-dle, Rock the

am,____ Who I am,__ If an-y-bod-y asks you
glo-ry, Night in glo-ry, The lit-tle cra-dle rocks to-
cra-dle, Rock the cra-dle, ____ Peace on earth,__ Ma-ry,

who I am,____ Tell him I'm a child of God.____
night in glo-ry, Rocks to-night in glo-ry.____
rock the cra-dle, Ma-ry, rock the cra-dle.____

CREDIT: *By permission from American Book Company. From* Exploring Music, Music for Young Americans *series,* © *1966.*

Bed Is Too Small

Anonymous

Bed is too small for my ti - red - ness. Give me a hill topp'd with trees; _____ Tuck a cloud up un - der my chin, _____ Lord; _____ blow the moon out, _____ please.

Rock me to sleep in a cra - dle of dreams, Sing me a lul - la - by of leaves. _____ Tuck a cloud up un - der my chin, Lord; blow the moon out, _____ please.

CREDIT: From Happy Days. *Used by permission of Cooperative Recreation Service, Delaware, Ohio.*

Singing Materials

BASIC CLASSROOM MUSIC TEXTS

Birchard Music Series, Summy-Birchard Company, Evanston, Ill., 1962.

Discovering Music Together (grades K–8), Follett Publishing Company, Chicago, 1967.

Exploring Music (grades K–8), Holt, Rinehart and Winston, Inc., New York, 1966.

Growing with Music (grades 1–6), Prentice-Hall, Inc., Englewood Cliffs, N.J., 1963.

The Magic of Music (grades K–8), Ginn and Company, Boston, 1950.

Making Music Your Own (grades 1–6), Silver Burdett Company, Morristown, N.J., 1965.

Music for Living (grades K–6), Silver Burdett Company, Morristown, N.J., 1956.

Music for Young Americans (grades K–9), American Book Company, New York, 1966.

Our Singing World (grades K–8), Ginn and Company, Boston, 1950.

This Is Music (grades K–8), Allyn and Bacon, Inc., Boston, 1962.

Together We Sing, rev. ed. (grades K–8), Follett Publishing Company, Chicago, 1959.

When ordering books for the children, be sure to specify the *teacher's edition* for yourself.

All series have related record albums. Many of these albums contain not only the songs from the books but some listening selections as well. Themes for these listening selections are usually included in the children's books.

SONG COLLECTIONS

American Folk Songs for Children (Ruth Seeger: Doubleday & Company, Inc., Garden City, N.Y.)*

American Folk Songs for Christmas (Ruth Seeger: Doubleday & Company, Inc., Garden City, N.Y.)*

American Song Bag (Carl Sandburg: Harcourt, Brace & World, Inc., New York.)

Animal Folk Songs for Children (Ruth Seeger: Doubleday & Company, Inc., Garden City, N.Y.)*

Around the World in Song (Silver Burdett Company, Morristown, N.J.)*

Best Loved American Folk Songs (John Lomax and Alan Lomax: Grosset & Dunlap, Inc., New York.)

The Ditty Bag (compiled by Janet E. Tobitt, Box 97, Pleasantville, N.Y.)

Fireside Book of Folk Songs (Simon and Schuster, Inc., New York.)

Folk Song Collections (songs available from most countries; specify country when ordering. Edward B. Marks Music Corporation, New York.)

Folk Songs for Children (Ruth Seeger: Doubleday & Company, Inc., Garden City, N.Y.)*

Folk Songster (Leon Dallin and Lynn Dallin: Wm. C. Brown Co., Dubuque, Iowa.)

Fred Waring Song Book (Shawnee Press, Delaware Water Gap, Pa.)

Get on Board (Beatrice Landeck: Edward B. Marks Music Corporation, New York.)*

* Record available.

Golden Book of Favorite Songs (Schmitt, Hall & McCreary, Minneapolis, Minn.)

Heritage Songster (Leon Dallin and Lynn Dallin: Wm. C. Brown Co., Dubuque, Iowa.)

Little Calypsos (Krugman and Ludwig: Carl Van Roy Co., Far Rockaway, N.Y.)

More Partner Songs (Frederick Beckman: Ginn and Company, Boston.)

More Singing Fun (Lucille Wood: Bowmar Records, North Hollywood, Calif.)★

More Songs to Grow On (Beatrice Landeck: Edward B. Marks Music Corporation, New York.)★

Partner Songs (Frederick Beckman: Ginn and Company, Boston.)

Pooh Song Book (Fraser-Simpson: E. P. Dutton & Co., Inc., New York.)

Sing a Song (McLaughlin and Wood: Prentice-Hall, Inc., Englewood Cliffs, N.J.)★

Sing Together (Girl Scout Handbook, Girl Scouts of the USA, New York.)

Singing Fun (Lucille Wood: Bowmar Records, North Hollywood, Calif.)★

Songs for all Seasons and Rhymes without Reasons (Marquis. Orff principles included. Edward B. Marks Music Corporation, New York.)

Songs to Grow On (Beatrice Landeck: Edward B. Marks Music Corporation, New York.)★

357 Songs We Love to Sing (Schmitt, Hall & McCreary, Minneapolis, Minn.)

The Cooperative Recreation Service of Delaware, Ohio, has an abundant library of song collections of all types published in inexpensive pamphlet form, the catalog of which is available upon request. Many of these are standard favorites with children. A few of the pamphlets are:

Chansons de Notre Chalet
Good Fellowship Songs
Life on the H₂O
101 Rounds for Singing
Songs of Many Nations

SONG RECORDS

FOLKWAYS

Birds, Beasts, Bugs and Little Fishes   Pete Seeger
Birds, Beasts, Bugs and Bigger Fishes   Pete Seeger
Camp Songs (Six- to eleven-year-old children)   Seeger, Darling, and the Song Swappers
You Sing a Song and I'll Sing a Song   Ella Jenkins

★ Record available.

Follow the Sunset (beginning geography with nine songs from around the world)
Christmas Songs
   Christmas Songs from Many Lands (sung in English)
   Christmas Songs of Portugal
   Christmas Songs of Spain
   German Christmas Songs

BOWMAR RECORDS

Children's Songs of Mexico
Favorite Songs of Japanese Children
Folk Songs of Africa
Folk Songs of Many People
Latin American Folk Songs
Little Favorites
North American Indian Songs
Nursery and Mother Goose Songs
Sing'n Do Songs (six albums)
Songs from "Singing Fun" and "More Singing Fun"

CHILDREN'S RECORD GUILD AND YOUNG PEOPLE'S RECORDS

Little Red Wagon
Sing Along
Where Do Songs Begin?
"Yankee Doodle" and Other Folk Songs

RCA VICTOR

"Deep River" and Other Spirituals   Robert Shaw Chorale
Holiday Songs
   Christmas Hymn and Carols   Robert Shaw Chorale
   Thanksgiving Hymns   Robert Shaw Chorale
Stephen Foster Favorites   Robert Shaw Chorale
This Is My Country (or *America, the Beautiful*)   Robert Shaw Chorale

COLUMBIA RECORDS

Songs of the Sea   Norman Luboff Choir
Songs of the West   Norman Luboff Choir
Songs of the World   Norman Luboff Choir

CAPITOL RECORDS

Folk Songs of the New World   Roger Wagner Chorale
Folk Songs of the Old World, vols. 1 and 2   Roger Wagner Chorale

SONG FILMSTRIPS

SOCIETY FOR VISUAL EDUCATION
1345 Diversey Parkway,
Chicago, Ill., 60614

Our American Heritage of Folk Music
Group 1: Six filmstrips with records
Group 2: Six filmstrips with records

Our American Heritage of Patriotic Songs (two filmstrips with records)
America, the Beautiful (captioned filmstrip only; no record)
Christmas Celebrated in Song (two filmstrips with record)
The Story of Good King Wenceslas (filmstrip with record)
The Twelve Days of Christmas (filmstrip with record)

WASP FILMSTRIPS
Palmer Lane West,
Pleasantville, N.Y.

Folk Songs in American History (six filmstrips and six records)
Civil War
Early Colony Days
In Search of Gold
Revolutionary War
The South
Workers of America

HARMONIZING EXPERIENCES

"Each singing what belongs to him or her and to none else. . . ."
Whitman, "I hear America Singing"

Singing in Harmony

Children love the sound of harmony. Through the use of appropriate song material, they can be provided with the experience of singing in harmony as early as the second grade (sometimes even in *first* grade).

There are developmental stages of singing in harmony as well as in other areas of musical learning. Partner songs, rounds, and simple descants (in that order) are very satisfactory means of introducing children to harmony, following which they may enjoy more complex harmonic experiences in two and three parts.

PARTNER SONGS

The term "partner songs" is used to designate two different songs that may be sung together with a pleasing, harmonious result. Half of the class sings one song, while the other half sings the other song. The important thing, of course, is to make sure that they are pitched in the same key and that the groups get started together. Even more important, the class should be thoroughly familiar with both songs individually before trying to sing them together. The class should also be encouraged to use their very best singing voices when singing in harmony. There seems to be a tendency, especially in the lower grades, for children to try to "outshout" one another when singing rounds and partner songs.

The following songs may be sung as partner songs when this activity is first begun. They are short, simple, and somewhat familiar to the children:

Key of F Skip to My Lou (start A) and Ten Little Indians (start F)
(All)   Little Red Wagon (start F) and Skip to My Lou (start A)
     Are You Sleeping, Brother John? (start F) and Three Blind
      Mice (start A)
     Row, Row, Row Your Boat (start F) and The Farmer in the
      Dell (start *middle* C)

It is possible to sing "Are You Sleeping, Brother John?" "Three Blind Mice," "Row, Row, Row Your Boat," and "The Farmer in the Dell" all at the same time, if you care to try. Furthermore, you've probably figured out by now that any combination of these four songs will work as partner songs. Just be sure to pitch them in the same key and give the proper starting pitch for each song in the beginning.

Upper-grade children will enjoy singing combinations of the above songs also, as well as longer and more difficult ones such as:

White Coral Bells and Vesper Hymn (Jubilate section only)
Man on the Flying Trapeze and My Bonnie (chorus only)
Swing Low, Sweet Chariot and She'll Be Comin' 'round the Mountain
Home on the Range (omit chorus) and My Home's in Montana
In the Good Old Summertime and Bicycle Built for Two
Wait till the Sun Shines, Nellie and When You Wore a Tulip
When the Saints Go Marching In and Good Night, Ladies
Spanish Cavalier and Solomon Levi

For additional suggestions, see *Partner Songs*, © 1958, and *More Partner Songs*, © 1962, by Frederick Beckman, published by Ginn and Company.

Songs may be sung as partner songs when they have the same chord accompaniment or background in the same accented places in the song. They must be parallel in this respect, or they cannot be sung together with a desirable effect.

65

Some songs are almost partner songs within themselves. In the little Czechoslovakian dance song "Tancuj," the chorus may be sung as a partner with the verse, if desired. Note the repeat on the chorus.

Tancuj

(Dance)

CREDIT: *From Girl Scout Pocket Songbook, © 1956. Used by permission of Girl Scouts of the USA.*

The two songs that follow ("No Need to Hurry" and "There's Work to Be Done") were apparently written with the intent that they be sung as partner songs as well as individually. Children in the fifth and sixth grades find their word content and calypso beat most appealing, especially when used with appropriate instrumental accompaniment such as claves, maracas, bongo drums, etc. These songs—sung individually and then together as partner songs—have been used very successfully as a program number.

There's Work to Be Done

Play this on the claves for measures 1–7.

Play this on the bongo drums and maracas for measures 1–7.

Play this for the last measure.

CREDIT: By permission from American Book Company. From Studying Music, *Music for Young Americans* series. Copyright 1966.

No Need to Hurry

In Calypso Rhythm   *Richard C. Berg*

1. All right, I come now; all right, I come; No need to hur - ry,
2. Don't be so nois - y, my lit - tle one, You'll wake the town be -

no need to run. It is too ear - ly, where is the sun?
fore you are done. If I should work hard out in the sun,

I am so tired that I can - not run.
I'll be so tired that I'll have no fun.

CREDIT: By permission from American Book Company. From Studying Music, *Music for Young Americans series. Copyright 1966.*

ROUNDS

The same melody sung by several different groups starting at different times, resulting in a pleasing harmony, is referred to as a "round." No song should be sung in round form unless it is specifically designated as a round. The little numbers printed over the rounds in textbooks indicate where each group is to enter (always singing the song from the *beginning* upon entrance) as well as how many groups may be used. Rounds may be in two, three, or four parts, or even more, depending on the song and the level of difficulty.

Simple rounds in two parts may be sung at the second grade level (and occasionally late in the year in the first grade); however, it has been the author's experience that partner songs are easier to carry against each other at these low levels than sections of rounds. In this text, the introduction of rounds *follows* the successful singing of several groups of partner songs, but this is not meant to be arbitrary by any means.

Perhaps the simplest round of all is the familiar "Row, Row, Row Your Boat." There are many others that children enjoy singing, such as those listed below. Words and music for those marked with an asterisk are included in this text. (See Song Index, p. 369.)

Row, Row, Row Your Boat★
Are You Sleeping, Brother John?★
Sweetly Sings the Donkey
Scotland's Burning
Three Blind Mice
Oh, How Lovely Is the Evening
White Coral Bells★

There are many other appealing rounds that are heard less often, perhaps. The music for some of them is included here so that the children may be given the opportunity to broaden their singing experiences as well as their round repertoire.

Little Bitty Man

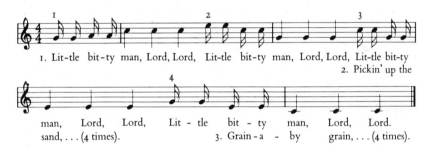

1. Lit-tle bit-ty man, Lord, Lord, Lit-tle bit-ty man, Lord, Lord, Lit-tle bit-ty
2. Pickin' up the
man, Lord, Lord, Lit - tle bit - ty man, Lord, Lord.
sand, . . . (4 times).   3. Grain-a - by   grain, . . . (4 times).

CREDIT: *From* 101 Rounds. *Used by permission of Cooperative Recreation Service, Delaware, Ohio.*

Make New Friends

Moderately slow

Make new friends but keep the_ old;__ One is   sil-ver and the oth-er gold.

CREDIT: *From* Chansons de Notre Chalet, © *1962. Used by permission of Cooperative Recreation Service, Delaware, Ohio.*

The Swan Sings

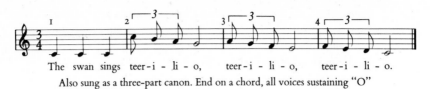

The swan sings teer - i - li - o, teer - i - li - o, teer - i - li - o.

Also sung as a three-part canon. End on a chord, all voices sustaining "O"

CREDIT: From Chansons de Notre Chalet, © 1962. Used by permission of Cooperative Recreation Service, Delaware, Ohio.

Hey, Ho! Nobody Home

Briskly   Traditional English Round

Hey, ho! No - bod-y home, Meat nor drink nor mon-ey have I none,

Yet I will be hap - - py,— Hey, ho! No-bod-y home.

CREDIT: From Growing with Music, Book 6, by H. R. Wilson et al., © 1966 by Prentice-Hall, Inc., Englewood Cliffs, N.J. Reprinted with permission.

Music Shall Live

Three-part Round

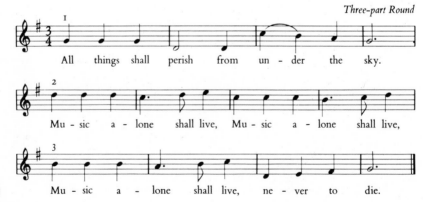

All things shall perish from un - der the sky.

Mu - sic a - lone shall live, Mu - sic a - lone shall live,

Mu - sic a - lone shall live, ne - ver to die.

DANISH	FRENCH	GERMAN
Himmel og Jord	*Tout doit sur terre*	*Himmel und Erde*
Engång förgår,	*Mourir un jour,*	*Müssen vergehn,*
Men Musikanterne	*Mais la musique*	*Aber die Musica*
Men Musikanterne	*Mais la musique*	*Aber die Musica*
Men Musikanterne	*Mais la musique*	*Aber die Musica*
Evig består.	*Vive toujours.*	*Bleibet bestehn.*

CREDIT: *From* Girl Scout Pocket Songbook, © *1956. Used by permission of Girl Scouts of the USA.*

Alleluia

Allegro — Mozart, Adapted by H.R.W.

Al – le-lu – ia, al-le-le-lu – ia,___ al – le – lu – ia, al-le-lu –
ia, Al – le-lu – ia, al-le-lu – ia,___ al – le – lu – ia, al-
le – lu – ia, Al – le-lu – ia, al – le – lu – ia.

CREDIT: *From* Rounds and Canons. *Used by permission of the publishers, Schmitt, Hall &*
McCreary Co., Minneapolis, Minn.

Let Us Sing Together

Adapted from Czech Folk Tune

Let us sing to-geth – er, Let us sing to-geth – er, One and all a
joy – ous song. Let us sing to-geth – er, One and all a joy – ous song.

71

Let us sing a-gain and a-gain, Let us sing a-gain and a-gain,

Let us sing a-gain and a-gain. One and all a joy - ous song.

CREDIT: *From* Sing a Tune, © 1966. *Used by permission of Cooperative Recreation Service, Delaware, Ohio.*

Dona Nobis Pacem

Slowly   *Three-part Round*

Do - na no - bis pa - cem, pa-cem, do - na no - bis pa - - cem.

Do - na no - bis pa-cem, do-na no-bis pa - - cem.

Do - na no - bis pa-cem; do-na no-bis pa - - cem.

For variation in singing rounds, as each group completes its singing of the round for the last time, let it hold the final note until all the remaining groups have arrived on that note.

The round below may be taught using the syllables for words. If your class is able to sing with syllables, have them try to sing it alone with the given syllables; if not, try teaching it by rote. The original words were "Ave Maria" repeated all the way through; however, the children may wish to put their own words to the tune when they have learned it.

Ave Maria Round

Do Re Mi Fa Mi Re Do Mi Fa Sol La Sol Fa Mi Do Do Do Do Ti Do
A - ve Ma-ri - - a A - ve Ma-ri - - a A - ve Ma-ri - a

CANONS

"Canons," another form of imitative singing, are similar to rounds in that the singers enter at spaced intervals. In many instances, it is difficult to distinguish a round from a canon except by title, as in the "Thanksgiving Canon" below. The minor mode of this piece makes it especially appealing:

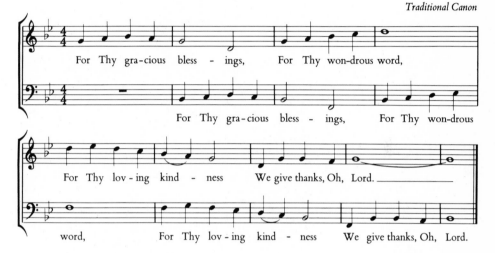

Thanksgiving Canon

Traditional Canon

For Thy gra-cious bless - ings, For Thy won-drous word,

For Thy gra-cious bless - ings, For Thy won-drous

For Thy lov - ing kind - ness We give thanks, Oh, Lord.

word, For Thy lov - ing kind - ness We give thanks, Oh, Lord.

CREDIT: *By special permission of the publishers, Holt, Rinehart and Winston. From Book 5,* Exploring Music *series,* © *1966.*

Canons may be simple or elaborate, and they are often very beautiful. Many familiar and less familiar canons are found in the basic music texts.

DESCANTS

A "descant" is simply a melody that may be sung, whistled, played, or hummed against another melody to produce a harmonizing effect.

Teachers can compose their own descants for use in lower grades, while in upper grades the children can do the composing themselves. (See "Making up Descants," p. 103.)

Descants vary in degree of difficulty. Those which drone away on one pitch are actually more like chants than descants, e.g., the "boom-da" that is 73 sung with the spinning song "Sarasponda" to represent the sound of the spinning wheel:

Sarasponda

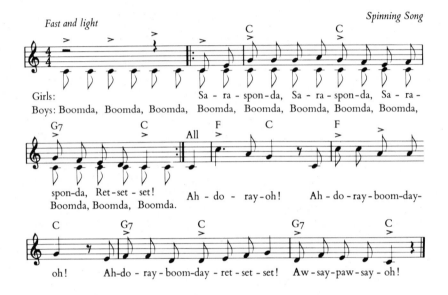

Fast and light

Spinning Song

Girls: Sa - ra - spon - da, Sa - ra - spon - da, Sa - ra -
Boys: Boomda, Boomda, Boomda, Boomda, Boomda, Boomda, Boomda, Boomda,

spon-da, Ret-set-set!   Ah - do - ray-oh!   Ah - do - ray-boom-day-
Boomda, Boomda, Boomda.

oh!   Ah-do - ray - boom-day - ret-set-set!   Aw-say-paw-say-oh!

A little less chantlike are the "ostinati" (repeated melodic fragments), which are easily composed and frequently used as preliminary devices for introducing children to singing in harmony. Because of their simplicity, they may be used as early as the first or second grade with familiar songs. Rounds such as "Are You Sleeping, Brother John?" and "Row, Row, Row Your Boat," for example, may be accompanied either vocally or instrumentally with short fragments such as the following:

"Are You Sleeping, Brother John?"   "Row, Row, Row Your Boat"

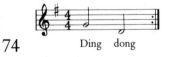

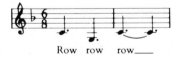

Ding   dong

Row row row___

Are You Sleeping, Brother John?

Are you sleep-ing, are you sleep-ing, Broth-er John, Broth-er John?

Morn-ing bells are ring-ing, morn-ing bells are ring-ing, Ding ding dong, ding ding dong.

Frère Jacques, Frère Jacques,
Dormez-vous, dormez-vous?
Sonnez les matines, sonnez les matines,
Din din don, din din don.

Row, Row, Row Your Boat

Four-part Round

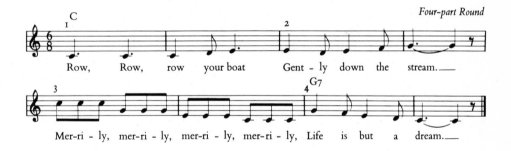

Row, Row, row your boat Gent - ly down the stream.___

Mer-ri - ly, mer-ri - ly, mer-ri - ly, mer-ri - ly, Life is but a dream.___

In "I Love the Mountains," which follows, sing the four measures of the "boom-dee-ah-da" portion of the song by itself first, as an introduction, and then continue repeating the same *two* measures as an ostinato against the melody throughout the song. This song may also be sung as a round.

75

I Love the Mountains

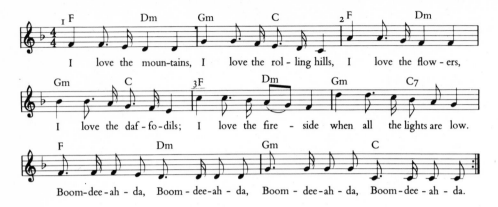

I love the moun-tains, I love the rol-ling hills, I love the flow-ers,

I love the daf-fo-dils; I love the fire - side when all the lights are low.

Boom-dee-ah - da, Boom - dee-ah - da, Boom - dee-ah - da, Boom - dee-ah - da.

CREDIT: *From* Sing a Tune, © *1966. Used by permission of Cooperative Recreation Service, Delaware, Ohio.*

"Zum Gali Gali" is a longtime favorite of children. In the same manner that "boom-dee-ah-da" was used in the song "I Love the Mountains," use "Zum gali gali gali, zum gali gali" as an introduction and then continue singing it throughout the song.

Zum Gali Gali

Palestinian Song

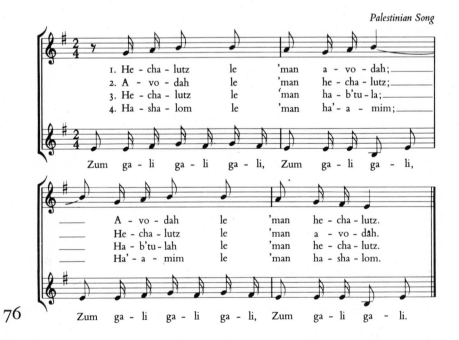

1. He - cha - lutz   le   'man   a - vo - dah;_____
2. A - vo - dah   le   'man   he - cha - lutz;_____
3. He - cha - lutz   le   'man   ha - b'tu - la;_____
4. Ha - sha - lom   le   'man   ha' - a - mim;_____

Zum   ga - li   ga - li   ga - li,   Zum   ga - li   ga - li,

_____ A - vo - dah   le   'man   he - cha - lutz.
_____ He - cha - lutz   le   'man   a - vo - dah.
_____ Ha - b'tu - lah   le   'man   he - cha - lutz.
_____ Ha' - a - mim   le   'man   ha - sha - lom.

Zum   ga - li   ga - li   ga - li,   Zum   ga - li   ga - li.

An approximate translation of the Hebrew words is:

1 and 2. The pioneer's purpose is for labor.

3. The pioneer is for his girl; his girl is for the pioneer.

4. Peace for all the nations.

Pronunciation: *a* as in "father"; *he* as in "hay"; *le* with short *e* as in "end"; *i* as in "machine"; *o* as in "come"; *u* as in "rule"; *ch* as in the German *ach*.

CREDIT: *From* Joyful Singing, *n.d., Cooperative Recreation Service, Delaware, Ohio. Used by permission.*

The descant for "Streets of Laredo" is melodically simple but very effective when sung or played along with the song. Children may sing the descant on "oo" or hum (try using "hn" with mouths slightly open instead of the closed "hm" sound) if desired.

Streets of Laredo

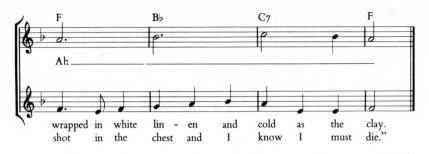

wrapped in white lin - en and cold as the clay.
shot in the chest and I know I must die."

CREDIT: *By permission from American Book Company. From* Studying Music, Music for Young Americans *series. Copyright 1966.*

The descant below is a simple scalewise progression that may be sung with "White Coral Bells." It is also effective when played on the song bells.

Descant for "White Coral Bells":

Ding dong ding dong hear the bells ding dong

White Coral Bells

Traditional

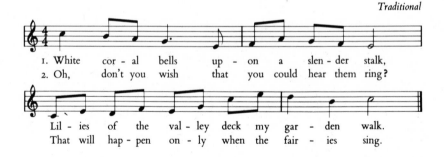

1. White cor - al bells up - on a slen - der stalk,
2. Oh, don't you wish that you could hear them ring?

Lil - ies of the val - ley deck my gar - den walk.
That will hap - pen on - ly when the fair - ies sing.

Some descants are melodically interesting enough to be a complete tune by themselves. The syncopation in "When You and I Were Young Maggie Blues" makes it a great favorite with the children in fifth and sixth grades. This is also an excellent program number.

When You and I Were Young Maggie Blues

ROOT-CHORDING SONGS

"Root-chording songs" are a very simple form of harmonic experience, in which the "harmonizing" part is limited to the use of three tones—*do, fa,* or *sol*, depending on the chord indicated for each measure of the song.

Half of the class sings the *root note* of the chord designated for the measure (or *portion* of the measure—some measures require more than one chord), while the other half of the class sings the words and melody of the given song. *Do, fa,* and *sol* are the syllable root names of the three principal triads, I, IV, and V7(V), respectively, and thus would be the most frequently used root-chording tones. In the beginning, perhaps it might be wise to select songs for root chording that contain only the three principal triads (I, IV, and V7) and then go on to others later, if desired.

Some children's music books contain chording songs with the root syllables already written out directly beneath the words with which they are to be sung, as in the song below:

On Top of Old Smoky

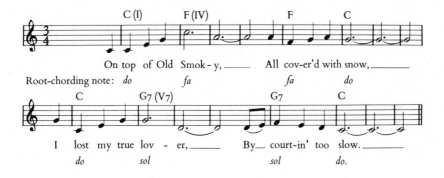

This simplifies things considerably for the children as well as for the teacher; however, in the event that the root syllables are not written out, the teacher can construct his own chording song simply by selecting the proper root syllable for the indicated chord. (Most songs now have the proper chords designated by either number or letter in order that they may be accompanied.) The procedure for doing this is a simple one, and can even be carried out by the children in upper grades. (See "Constructing a Root-chording Song," p. 101.)

TWO-PART SINGING

While it is possible for some children at the third grade level to sing more elaborate descants, as well as songs written in two parts, it is usually toward the end of the fourth grade that two-part music, as such, is introduced, continuing into fifth grade with songs of gradually increasing difficulty. By the end of the school year, an average fifth grader who has been provided with a sufficient background in two-part singing experiences is often able to add a third part to selected songs in the form of an easy descant or ostinato or the appropriate root-chord syllable.

Sixth grade children are capable of singing three-part music with ease, provided that they have been blessed at previous grade levels with an adequate foundation in two-part singing.

As a prelude to actual two-part singing, the use of some transitional songs such as those given below is often helpful in bridging the gap between the previously discussed *introductory* experiences (partner songs, rounds, descants, etc.) and those which will require a greater degree of skill to execute. In "Goin' to Leave Ol' Texas," for example, the second voice merely *echoes* what the first voice has already sung (very much like a round), while the first voice is sustaining a note of the phrase.

Goin' to Leave Ol' Texas

CREDIT: From Growing with Music, Book 4, by H. R. Wilson et al., © 1966 by Prentice-Hall, Inc., Englewood Cliffs, N.J. Reprinted with permission.

In "Tina Singu," the melody indicated for Part II is simply *mi fa mi re do* repeated.

Tina Singu

CREDIT: From Chansons de Notre Chalet, © 1962. Used by permission of Cooperative Recreation Service, Delaware, Ohio.

Adding a bit of harmony to a *small fragment* of some familiar songs is also a means of developing a feeling for harmony. The three songs from which the fragments below have been taken may be found elsewhere in this text. (See Song Index, p. 369.)

All Night, All Day

Down in the Valley

On Top of Old Smoky

Most of the short harmonizing parts shown above move in "thirds"; that is, the upper note is an interval of a third (three notes) away from the lower note. This is a frequently used way to harmonize in two parts. The chorus of "Marching to Pretoria" is also harmonized in thirds; however, here the melody is on the top, with the harmonizing note a third *below* the melody:

84

Marching to Pretoria

Lively   By Josef Marais

1. I'm with you and you're with me and so, we are all to-geth-er,
2. I love food and you love food and so, we shall eat to-geth-er,

So, we are all to-geth-er, So, we are all to-geth-er,
So, we shall eat to-geth-er, So, we shall eat to-geth-er.

Sing with me, I'll sing with you and so, we will sing to-geth-er,

Refrain

As we march a-long.___ We are march-ing to Pre-to-ri-a,___

Pre-to-ri-a,___ Pre-to-ri-a,___ We are march-ing

to Pre-to-ri-a,___ Pre-to-ri-a, Hur-rah!___

CREDIT: By permission from G. Schirmer from Songs from the Veld, by Josef Marais, © 1942.

In the well-loved "Peace of the River," the melody is also on top, with the harmonizing part below, moving for the most part in thirds but with an occasional deviation to another interval:

Peace of the River

Glendora Gosling
& Viola Wood

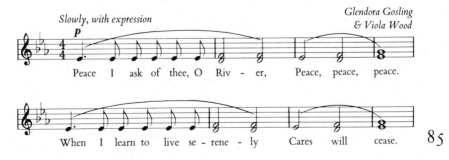

Slowly, with expression
p

Peace I ask of thee, O Riv-er, Peace, peace, peace.

When I learn to live se-rene-ly Cares will cease.

85

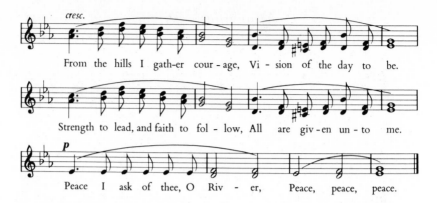

From the hills I gath-er cour-age, Vi - sion of the day to be.

Strength to lead, and faith to fol - low, All are giv-en un - to me.

Peace I ask of thee, O Riv - er, Peace, peace, peace.

CREDIT: *Reprinted by permission of Janet E. Tobitt, Box 97, Pleasantville, N.Y. From* The Ditty Bag, *1946. Revised 1960.*

Another commonly used harmonizing interval is that of the sixth—six notes *below* the melody. In "Standin' in the Need of Prayer," note that the harmonizing part moves in the same direction as the melody, but is six notes lower:

Standin' in the Need of Prayer

Spiritual

Not my broth - er, not my sis - ter, but it's me, O Lord, stand-in' in the need of

prayer. Not my broth-er, not my sis - ter, but it's me, O Lord, stand-in' in the need of

prayer. It's a - me, it's me, it's me, O Lord, stand-in' in the need of

prayer. It's a - me, it's me, it's me, O Lord, stand-in' in the need of prayer.

2. Not my father, not my mother, but it's me, O Lord. . . .

3. Not the preacher, not the deacon, but it's me, O Lord . . . .

Of course there are other possible ways of harmonizing besides in thirds and sixths. In "Tell Me Why," portions of the harmony part move in a direction completely counter to that of the melody line:

Tell Me Why

In the second and tenth measures of the song "Little Ships," note that one part descends while the other continues to repeat the same note:

Little Ships

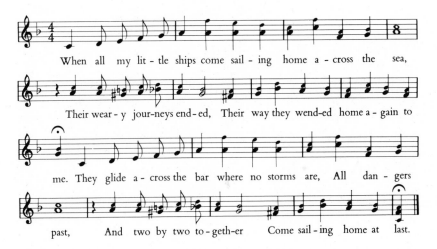

CREDIT: *From* Life on the H₂O, ©1964. *Used by permission of Cooperative Recreation Service, Delaware, Ohio.*

The song "Witchcraft" harmonizes beautifully in two parts in a rather unusual manner. Sing the tune indicated for the part beginning "But in this real world" in harmony with the tune at the beginning of the song—"If there were witchcraft. . . ."

Witchcraft

Margarett Snyder

If there were witch-craft   I'd   make two wish-es,   A   wind-ing road   that
And then I'd   wish   for   a   blaz-ing camp-fire,   To   wel-come me   when

beck-ons me to   roam,   But in   this   real   world there is   no
I'm re-turn-ing   home.   Our fond-est   day-dreams must be   the

witch-craft,   and gold-en wish-es   do not grow on   trees.
mag-ic   to   bring us back these hap-py mem-o   -   ries. Mem-'ries that

lin-ger,   con-stant and true,   Mem-'ries we cher-ish,   -   -   -   of you.

CREDIT: *From* Good Fellowship Songs, © *1963. Used by permission of Cooperative Recreation Service, Delaware, Ohio.*

In any part-singing activity, every child should, at one time or another during the year, have the opportunity to sing different parts; thus children should not be permanently assigned to either soprano or alto for the entire year, nor should boys *always* be asked to sing the lower part.

TWO-PART MUSIC-READING EXPERIENCES

It is assumed that all the part-singing experiences suggested so far will be learned by rote; however, once children are able to carry one part against another with ease, they should begin to expand their music-reading experiences into those which involve simple part singing. The following melodic fragments might be used for introductory practice in this area:

1. Divide the class into two groups (not girls and boys, please). Call them Group I and Group II.
2. In the short exercises below, briefly review each group's part separately and have the two groups sing both parts together. One or two of these exercises per day is sufficient when first introducing this.

		GROUP I	GROUP II
1.	Pitch G	do re do	mi fa mi
2.	Pitch G	do re mi	mi fa sol
3.	Pitch A	do ti do	mi re mi
4.	Pitch F (first space)	do re mi re do	mi fa sol fa mi
5.	Pitch E♭ (low)	do ti la ti do	mi re do re mi
6.	Pitch G	do re do ti do	mi fa mi re mi
7.	Pitch D (low)	do sol do	mi fa mi

As the class masters the above, try longer and slightly more difficult exercises such as:

		GROUP I	GROUP II
1.	Pitch G	do ti re fa mi	mi re fa sol sol
2.	Pitch E♭ (low)	mi sol mi fa re do	sol mi sol la fa mi

and so on. When the class can carry the two parts in the preceding exercises easily, they should then be given more of the same to read *at sight*, without first hearing each part sung separately. The teacher blows *do* in the key specified. Each group should then sound its own starting note and hold it until the command "Sing!" is given. The syllables in the above exercises may then be transferred onto the staff, to be sung at sight from notation (omit stems on the notes for the present). Following this, the class should be ready for easy beginning music-reading experiences in *two parts* from the board in simple melodies (using regular notation, *with* stems this time) and then from the music books. This means *independent* music reading (*not rote*) preceded by the usual preparatory devices (see p. 133), which will include practice on the skips and rhythms of both parts.

The songs selected for music reading in parts from the music books should, of necessity, be rhythmically simple, containing only those rhythms which the class has previously mastered. As new rhythms come under study, they may be practiced in part songs as well as in unison songs.

THREE-PART SINGING

By the sixth grade level, the average class should be able to sing in three parts, assuming that the preceding foundation in unison and two-part singing has been well established.

Adding a root-chording note or a descant to a two-part song offers a good beginning because it serves as a transitional device between two- and three-part singing, providing the class with a feeling of three-part harmony with a minimum of effort.

The important factor in part singing is to help the child become secure enough in holding his own part against others, so that he is free to enjoy the total sound of all parts singing together. This becomes difficult for him to do if he is asked to concern himself with trying to *read* the music and at the same time carry his part against others; therefore, it is suggested that the *initial* experiences in *three*-part harmony be *rote* experiences (as they were in unison and two-part singing). Some songs fit this purpose beautifully. In the following arrangement of "Chopsticks," for example, two of the three parts are already somewhat familiar to the children. They pick up the tune of the third part very quickly from simply hearing it played or sung by the teacher. The simplicity of this particular arrangement should enable a child to achieve exactly what we hope for, namely, the ability to enjoy the total sound of all the parts while contributing one of his own.

Chopsticks

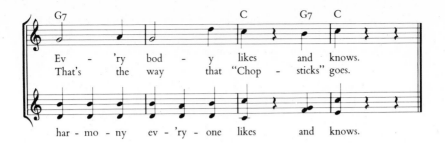

VOCAL CHORDING IN THREE PARTS

"Vocal chording" means simply executing chords vocally rather than instrumentally and is a good means of providing practice in learning to sing in three parts, as well as pleasure in hearing three-part harmony immediately.

It consists merely of the I, IV, and V7 chords arranged for voices in such a way as to provide the smoothest voice progression from one chord to another. (Reading "Chord Structure," p. 96, which contains further information on these chords, would be an aid to further use and understanding of vocal chording.)

PROCEDURE

Write the following on the board, using a different colored chalk for the notes that each group is to sing. (Use of colored chalk is optional, of course.) The notes may also be written in their melodic direction, as shown below, or in a straight line, if preferred.

By reading *up* from the Roman numerals below, we find the appropriate notes for the indicated chord. Thus the I chord is found to contain *do-mi-sol*; the IV chord, *fa-la-do* (arranged in inverted order, *do-fa-la*, for better voice progression); and the V7 chord, *sol-ti-(re)-fa* (also arranged in inverted order, *ti-fa-sol*). In the V7 chord, the fifth of the chord (*re*) has been omitted to maintain the three-voice limit. This does not disturb the feeling of the chord and is frequently done. (It is interesting to note that the chord progressions shown here are in exactly the same positions as for the left-hand piano chording. See "Piano Chording," p. 214.)

Group III sings → sol ↗ *la* ↘ sol → sol

Group II sings → mi ↗ fa → fa ↘ mi

Group I sings → do → do ↘ ti ↗ do

Chord: I   IV V7   I

1. Divide the class into three groups. Point to Roman numeral I to indicate the I chord. Sound the pitch of *do* (try G just for a beginning). Have Group I sound their note *do*. Let Groups II and III try to sound their notes (*mi* and *sol*) from the *do* sounded by Group I.

2. Point to Roman numeral IV. Group I should sing *do* again while Group II moves up to *fa* and Group III moves up to *la* to sound the IV chord. Point to Roman numeral I again. Group I should sing *do* while Group II moves back to *mi* and Group III moves back to *sol*.

3. You may point to the Roman numerals in any order desired, simply for practice, for example, I, IV, I, V7, I, IV, V7, I. Each group should move horizontally to their appropriate note as you point to the chords below.

4. Try the following progression as a vocal accompaniment for "Twinkle, Twinkle, Little Star." Pitch the *do* on the indicated key of the song. (Music for "Twinkle, Twinkle, Little Star" may be found on p. 145.) Let groups II and III take their starting notes *mi* and *sol* from the *do* given.

Twinkle, Twinkle, Little Star

Twinkle, Twinkle, little star, How I wonder what you are!

Chords	I	I	IV	I	IV	I	V7	I

Only a portion of the song is given here; however, the remainder of the song as well as the chords may be found on p. 145.

"Down in the Valley" (words and music on p. 199) has similar chords but a different rhythm:

Down in the Valley

Down in the valley, the valley so low
I   I   I   V7

Hang your head over, hear the wind blow.
V7   V7   V7   I

Have several children sing the melody and words of the songs while others sing the vocal accompaniment as indicated by the teacher pointing to the appropriate Roman numerals where they occur in the song. Try other songs from the books, following the chords indicated in the given songs.

Once the procedure has become familiar, individual children may wish to do the pointing. Many sixth grade children become intrigued with the idea of providing their own vocal accompaniment and work on it to the point where they can sing directly from the chords indicated in the book without anyone having to point from the board. Most books give the chord *letter* rather than the numeral. Once the teacher indicates the formula for translating letters into numbers according to the key signature of the song, the number of songs for which a class may provide vocal accompaniment becomes greatly increased. (See "Chord Structure," p. 96.) This type of vocal accompaniment may also be used along with the melody of a song being played on a melody instrument such as the song bells, piano, or recorder.

The arrangement of the song "Red River Valley" (below) shows how these vocal accompaniments look when written out on the staff in notation. Group I would sing the lowest note of each chord; Group II, the middle note of each chord; and Group III, the highest note of each chord. Try it with syllables first (each group singing the syllables appropriate for their part) and then on "oo" or humming.

Red River Valley

CREDIT: *From* Musicianship for the Elementary Teacher, *by Anne Pierce and Neal Glenn.* McGraw-Hill, © 1967.

Tune Uke: G C E A (Tuning for Key of F)

F chord   B♭ chord   C₇ chord

THREE-PART MUSIC-READING EXPERIENCES

As an introduction to music-reading experiences in three parts, have the class try a few melodic fragments similar to those suggested for practice in two-part music reading, for example,

	GROUP I	GROUP II	GROUP III
1. Pitch G	do re do	mi fa mi	sol la sol
2. Pitch F (first space)	do ti do	mi re mi	sol sol sol
3. Pitch E♭ (first line)	do re mi do	mi fa sol mi	sol la ti do

Blow the specified *do* and have Group I sound *do*. Groups II and III should try to sound their starting notes from the given *do*. Sustain until all starting tones are sounded and then give the command "Sing!"

Transfer the above short exercises (and other longer ones) onto the staff and sing at sight from notation, following which the class should be ready for easy beginning music-reading experiences in three parts from notation on the board and from their textbooks. Prepare these songs in the same manner as any new song is prepared for music reading (see p. 133), using appropriate preparatory experiences for each which will include the skips and rhythms of all three parts of the song. The rhythms contained in the songs for music reading should be only those which the class has previously mastered. As new rhythms, and also new melodic problems, come under study, they may be applied in the three-part songs as well as in the unison and two-part songs.

The three-part arrangement of "Jacob's Ladder" (pp. 94–95) is especially beautiful and is representative of the type of easy material that should be chosen for beginning music-reading experiences in three parts in the sixth grade:

Jacob's Ladder

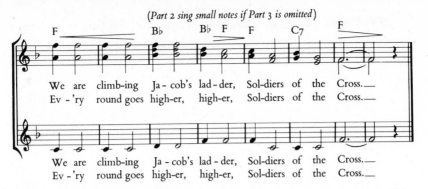

CREDIT: *By permission from American Book Company. From* Studying Music, *Music for Young Americans series. Copyright 1966.*

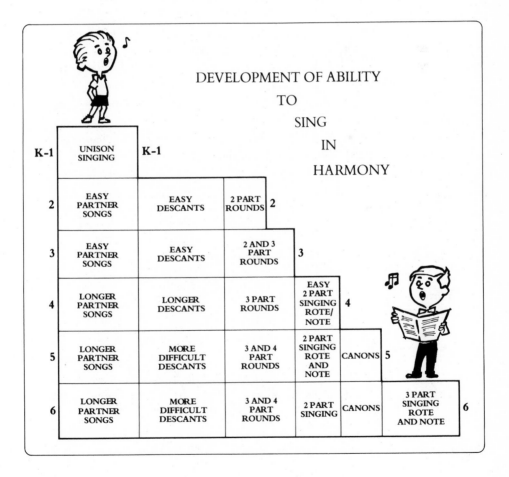

FIGURE 3–1 *Chart showing the development of the ability to sing in harmony. (Southern Connecticut State Multi Media Studio Production)*

A feeling for harmony may also be developed through the use of certain harmony instruments such as the Autoharp or the ukulele or through chording on the piano. Strum or play a chord and have the class hum whatever note of the chord they hear. Change the chord and ask them to hum another note that they hear in the new chord. Different children should hear different notes, so there should be several notes being hummed at once. Chord progressions of I, V7, I or I, IV, I or I, IV, V7, I are a good beginning. Other chords and progressions may be added as the class becomes more familiar with the procedure.

As a result of a broad range of experiences in part singing, some children are able to harmonize "by ear," as it were, after hearing the melody of a song a few times. Songs such as "Good Night, Ladies," "I've Been Working on the Railroad," and "Moonlight Bay" lend themselves well to the barbershop type of harmonization. Development of the ability to harmonize by ear is highly desirable, for it holds promise of playing a vital part in the child's future participation in musical activities and, hopefully, in his enjoyment of music.

Chord Structure

Whether harmony is provided vocally or instrumentally, the basic principles of harmonic structure remain the same.

A chord is simply a selected group of tones sounded simultaneously. A chord containing only three tones is known as a "triad." Triads may be built on any tone of the scale:

Scale in C major

Beginning with any one of the basic tones of the scale (*do, re, mi, fa, sol, la, ti*), simply add a third and fifth (interval distance from the scale tone) above it:

Triads built on each tone of the scale in C major

96

The note upon which each triad is built is known as the "root" of the triad. When triads are sung or played in the position shown below (with the root occurring as the *lowest* tone of the triad, that is, in the lowest position), we say that they are being sung or played in "root position." The root of each chord shown below is indicated in *black* for easier identification:

Triads in root position, key of C major

Each tone of the scale is numbered according to the position it occupies in the scale; e.g., *do* is the first tone of the scale and thus is numbered 1, *re* is numbered 2, *mi* is numbered 3, etc.

A triad built on *do* (the *first* tone of the scale) that contains the prescribed tones *do-mi-sol* (the first, third, and fifth tones of the given scale) is called a "I chord" (Roman numerals are used to designate chords).

A triad built on *fa* (the *fourth* tone of the scale) and containing the prescribed tones *fa-la-do* is called a "IV chord."

A triad built on *sol* and containing the prescribed tones *sol-ti-re* is called a "V chord" since it is built on the *fifth* tone of the scale.

Principal triads in key of C major (by number)

I   IV   V

Each tone of the scale has a name as well as a number. The first tone *do* is known as the "tonic." *Fa* is known as the "subdominant." *Sol* is known as the "dominant" note of the scale.

When a chord is built on one of these notes, it takes the name of the note, just as it takes the number of the scale note.

Principal triads in key of C major (by name)

I	IV	V
tonic	subdominant	dominant

Chords may consist of *four* tones also. When one more tone is added a third above the already-existing three-tone triad, the chord becomes known as a "seventh chord" because the added tone is *seven* notes away from the root. Any chord may be made into a seventh chord; however, for our purposes we shall limit our use of seventh chords to the dominant seventh (V7). Note that the chord is identified by its regular Roman numeral plus the figure "7" immediately following. The word "seventh" (or "seven") is added to its name when it is referred to; thus "dominant seventh" means simply the dominant chord with a fourth tone added a third above the three basic tones of the chord. In the music literature with which we shall be concerned, the V7 chord is encountered more frequently than the plain V (dominant) chord. (Obviously, the root remains the same whether it's the V or the V7 chord that is being used.) The added seventh not only provides greater harmonizing possibilities but also results in a more interesting sound.

Principal chords in key of C major (by name and number)

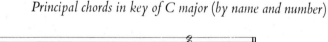

I	IV	V7
tonic	subdominant	dominant seventh

Although the foregoing examples have all been in the key of C major, the procedure for determining the tonic (I), sub-dominant (IV), and dominant seventh (V7), as well as the dominant (V), chords remains the same in *any* key.

The name of the key is always the *do*, or first tone of the scale. In the key of F, for example, *do* is on F; thus F is the first tone of the scale—the tonic note—and a triad built on F will be known as the "tonic chord" (I chord) in the key of F major:

Principal chords in key of F major (by name and number)

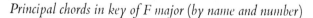

I	IV	V7
tonic	subdominant	dominant seventh

Counting up to *fa* from F as *do*, we arrive at the fourth tone of the scale of F major. It is upon this tone that the subdominant chord will be built. Counting up to *sol* from F as *do*, we arrive at the fifth tone of the scale of F. It is upon this tone that the dominant seventh (or dominant) chord will be built.

In the key of G, *do* is on G; thus G is the first tone of the scale, and a triad built on G will be known as the "tonic chord" (I chord) in the key of G major. The procedure for finding the root of the subdominant chord in the key of G major is the same as it is for the other keys—using G as I (since we are in the *key* of G), count up 4 (*fa*). To find the root of the dominant seventh (V7) or the dominant (V), count up 5 (*sol*).

Principal chords in key of G major (by name and number)

I   IV   V7
tonic   subdominant   dominant seventh

DETERMINING CHORD LETTER NAMES

Now that we have learned how to identify the tonic, subdominant, and dominant seventh chords in any given key and to assign the proper Roman numerals, we should be able to determine the proper *letter* names for the chords in the various keys.

The chord letter name is derived directly from the root of the chord. If we look again at the tonic, subdominant, and dominant seventh chords in the key of C major in their root positions, we note that the root of the I, or tonic, chord is on C; thus the chord letter name for the tonic chord in the key of C is the "C chord." The root of the IV, or subdominant, chord is on F; thus the IV chord in the key of C is appropriately called the "F chord." The root of the V7, or dominant seventh, chord is on G. Since it is a seventh chord, the chord letter name will be "G7." If it were a dominant chord *without* the added *seventh*, the chord letter name would be simply "G."

Principal chords in key of C major (by number and chord letter name)

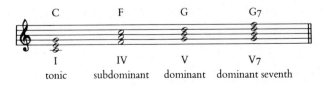

I   IV   V   V7
tonic   subdominant   dominant   dominant seventh

99

Chords are named in like manner in all keys. In the key of G major, for example, the root of the I, or tonic, chord is on G; thus the chord letter name for the tonic chord in the key of G is "G"; the subdominant (IV) chord in the key of G would be called a "C chord" because the root of the subdominant chord falls on C. The dominant seventh chord would be called a "D7 chord" because the root of the chord is on D. The dominant chord (without the added seventh tone) would be called simply a "D chord."

Principal chords in key of G major (by number and chord letter name)

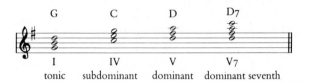

In the key of F, the root of the I, or tonic, chord is on F; thus the chord letter name for the *tonic* chord in the key of F is "F"; the subdominant (IV) chord in the key of F will be called a "B♭ chord" because the fourth tone up (the tone upon which the subdominant chord is built) from *do* in the scale of F is B♭. The dominant seventh chord would be called a "C7 chord" because the fifth tone up (the tone upon which the dominant chord is built) from *do* in the scale of F is C. The dominant chord (without the added seventh tone) would be called simply a "C chord."

Principal chords in key of F major (by number and chord letter name)

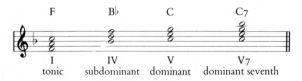

Chords may not always appear written in their root positions. For the sake of smoother voice leading, many chords may be placed in what is known as an "inversion" position, in which the third or the fifth of the chord, rather than the *root*, appears in the lowest position. This does not change the basic components of the chord; they remain the same. It is only their geographical position on the staff that changes. Therefore, the Roman numerals and chord letter names are designated by the same process as before. Whether a C chord is written:

root position   or   first inversion   or   second inversion

it is still a C major chord because it contains the notes C-E-G, which are the basic components of a C major chord. A C chord is a C chord whether it occurs in the key of C as the *tonic*, in the key of G as the *subdominant*, or in the key of F as the dominant chord. The same principle applies to all chords. An F major chord always contains the notes F-A-C. A chord containing the notes G-B-D is a G major chord regardless of the key of the song or the inversion in which the chord is written.

Constructing a Root-chording Song

1. Note the key of the song.
2. Note the chord letter names written above the music. (When trying this for the first time, avoid using any song that does not have these letter names.) The letter names are the clues to the chords (see "Chord Structure," p. 96), for they indicate the letter name of the *root* of any given chord, and it is the root with which we are concerned when constructing a root-chording song. Look at the song below:

Skip to My Lou

The children choose partners and skip in a circle.

1. The key is F; thus the F chord indicated above the first measure means that it is the *tonic* (I) chord of this key and is built on the scale tone *do*; thus the proper chording note for the F chord is *do*.

2. No chord over the second measure indicates that the same harmony is to be used for this measure also; thus the root-chording note for that measure would also be *do*.

3. The C7 over the third measure indicates a dominant seventh (V7) chord built on the fifth tone of the scale, which is *sol*; thus the proper root-chording note for this measure is *sol*.

4. The C7 is held through the fourth measure, which means that the root-chording note for the fourth measure would also be *sol*.

5. When the F reoccurs in the fifth measure, the tonic (I) chord is indicated (as it was at the beginning), and the root-chording note would be *do* again.

In summary, then, every time an F appears in the above song, the root-chording note to be sung would be *do*. Every time a C7 appears, the root-chording note to be sung would be *sol*. This particular song does not happen to have a subdominant (IV) harmony indicated; thus *fa* is not used here.

The procedure is the same for all keys—only the letter names will vary. Simply identify the key of the song so that the letter name of the *tonic* (I) chord may be evident immediately; then count from the tonic to the other given letter names (musical-alphabet-wise) to determine whether the subdominant (IV) or the dominant seventh (V7) chord is indicated. The name of the root-chording note is derived from these letter names, which are almost always written above the music. The root-chording note is to be sung each time the appropriate chord letter for that note occurs in the song.

Upper-grade children are capable of finding the proper root-chording notes for themselves. This type of activity provides a *reason* for learning the names of the lines and spaces, for there is an opportunity for immediate application of the knowledge, just as there is in playing various classroom instruments. (See Chapter 6, Instrumental Experiences.)

Making up Descants

A teacher can create simple descants of his own simply by using notes that are within the basic chord structure indicated for each measure on the accented beats.

In the song "Little Red Wagon," for example, the first two measures are tonic-chord (I) harmony; thus any of the three notes contained in the tonic chord (*do-mi-sol*) would be appropriate for descant notes for those measures. A measure may also contain a *combination* of the chord tones—e.g., *do-sol*, *do-mi*, or *mi-sol*—depending on how many notes were desired for the descant in each measure. It is also possible to vary the character of the descant through the use of different rhythm patterns:

Song (*first phrase only*)

Ri - ding up and down in my lit - tle red wa - gon

Descant for a smooth ride

Ri - - ding ri - - ding

Descant for a bouncy ride

Ri - ding ri - ding ri - ding ri - ding

The next two measures of the song are dominant seventh (V7) harmony; thus a simple descant should appropriately include any of the dominant seventh chord notes (*sol-ti-re-fa*) or combinations thereof:

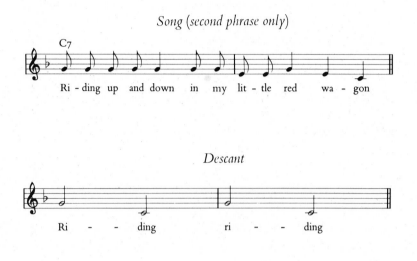

Song (second phrase only)

Ri - ding up and down in my lit - tle red wa - gon

Descant

Ri - - ding ri - - ding

The song is not complete, obviously, but the few measures shown should be sufficient to illustrate the point. Descants as simple as those suggested above may be sung in very early grades. Of course, more interesting ones are possible, if a little imagination is used. Older children may create their own descants.

Selecting Appropriate Chords for Accompaniment

Occasionally, the chord letter names and/or numbers (which usually appear above the music of the song) may be missing. In such a case, it is helpful if one has some basic idea of how to go about selecting the proper chords for accompanying or for creating some harmony device such as a descant or a root-chording note. With a minimum of knowledge of the three basic chords (I, IV, V7), it becomes a simple task to write one's own chords to any given melody in which these three chords would furnish appropriate harmony. The information given below might prove helpful toward this end:

The following are true no matter what the key in which a song is written:

1. The I chord always contains *do-mi-sol*.
2. The IV chord always contains *fa-la-do*.
3. The V7 chord always contains *sol-ti-re-fa*.

As any of these tones occur in a given song, appropriate chord accompaniment may be selected simply by referring to the above to discover in which chord the note is contained. Whichever chord the note is found in then becomes the appropriate chord for accompanying that particular note.

Let's take a simple seven-note tune for a working sample:

The first tone is *do*. Referring to items 1 to 3 above, we note that *do* is contained in the I chord *and* the IV chord. For our present purposes, we shall assume that most of our songs will begin and end on the I chord. Since this *do* occurs as the *first* chord, we shall use I instead of IV in this case; thus we place the Roman numeral I under the first *do*.

The second tone is *re*, which, as we have noted above, is contained *only* in the V7 chord; thus it is safe to assume that V7 harmony will be most suitable to accompany *re*, and we indicate this by placing V7 under *re*.

The third note *mi* is contained only in the I chord; thus we use the I chord again for accompanying *mi*, just as we used it the first time for *do*.

The fourth note *fa* requires that we choose between V7 and IV. Either one is acceptable in this particular place. (In this connection, it might be well to mention that this choice is often determined by what follows; e.g., the IV to V7 progression is preferable to the V7 to IV progression.) Since we are free to use either V7 or IV here, let's use IV since we'll soon be using V7 again on the next-to-the-last note.

The fifth note *mi* requires I.

The sixth note *re* requires V7.

The last note *do*, of course, requires I.

Having chosen the chords, they should look something like this when written under the notes:

Since most songs are chorded by letter name rather than by Roman numeral, we should, as a second step, translate the Roman numerals into the proper letter names. Note that up to this point there has been no need to be concerned with the name of the key—we had only to find *do* to determine the names of the syllables in the above tune.

In translating Roman numerals into letter names of the chords, the numeral I is always the name of the given key—in this case G major; thus I here refers to the G major chord. To determine the chord letter names for this particular tune in G, everything must now be figured mathematically and alphabetically from G as I.

Using G as I and counting up to IV, alphabetically we land on the letter "C"; thus the IV chord would be translated into the letter name "C chord."

Using G as I and counting up to V from G, alphabetically we land on the letter "D". (Since it is the V7 chord, the chord letter name is D7.)

Using Roman numerals and chord, letter names, our tune shapes up something like this:

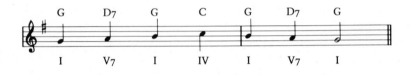

NOTE: Once the Roman numerals have been selected according to the system suggested above, care should be taken that the chord letter names correspond correctly to the numerals, according to the key in which the song is written.

With the letters of the chords now supplied, it becomes possible for a teacher or a child to chord this accompaniment on the Autoharp, the ukulele, the piano, or any other chording instrument with which he is familiar.

Just for a little extra practice, suppose we use the same working tune, but put it in another key:

The tune is still *do re mi fa mi re do*. Using the rule for choosing Roman numerals, we find that we come out with the same sequence of Roman numerals since we are dealing with the same sequence of syllable names that we were in our original key of G. It is only when we begin to translate the syllable names into the chord letter names that things change. As noted, the key for this tune is F major. This means that F is *do*, and therefore we must immediately begin thinking in terms of F as I, and all other chord letter names must be figured from F as I.

Counting alphabetically up to IV from F bring us to B♭ (B is always flatted in the key of F). Counting up to V brings us to C (C7 is written because the Roman numeral given is V7).

Thus we have the same tune as before—only now in the key of F major. When numbered and lettered, it looks like this:

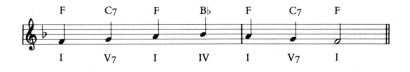

We have chorded *every* note in the working tune above simply for illustration and practice in chord selection. This is not what is usually found in most songs. Generally, just one or two chords are used for each *measure*—either because *all* the notes in the given measure are contained in a single chord as in "On Top of Old Smoky" (p. 81), which starts out *do do mi sol*—or because *most* of the notes in a given measure are contained in a single chord, with the remaining notes falling on *unaccented* beats. "Row, Row, Row Your Boat" is a good example of this (see p. 75). The first two measures of "Row, Row, Row Your Boat" are mainly tonic-chord (I) harmony. *Re* is contained in the second measure, to be sure, but it occurs in a rather unobtrusive place on the unaccented beat; consequently, the I chord may be considered appropriate harmony for the entire measure.

The ability to determine whether to use only one chord or more than one chord for a whole measure in any given song comes with practice in playing, singing, and listening. It is not a deciding factor in going to heaven.

Chord Summary

IN THE KEY OF	I OR (TONIC CHORD) LETTER NAME	IV OR (SUBDOMINANT CHORD) LETTER NAME	V7 OR (DOMINANT SEVENTH CHORD) LETTER NAME
C	C	F	G7
F	F	B♭	C7
G	G	C	D7

EAR TRAINING
EXPERIENCES

*"There's music in all things if men
had ears. . . ."*
Byron

Ear Training

It is hardly surprising in this century of many and constant sounds that adults as well as children appear to have lost the ability to listen. There is simply too much to hear. Children, it seems, must be *taught* to listen. (See Chapter 7, Listening Experiences.)

Perhaps the most valuable contribution a teacher can make toward promoting good listening habits in the classroom is to keep his own talking to a minimum. An overtalkative teacher may cause the children to feel that much of what he says is not worth listening to, and they simply "tune him out," much the same as they switch television channels at home.

The term "ear training," as used in this book, refers to any set of devices or techniques used in an attempt to improve musical acuity, for, in effect, this should be the main purpose of ear training. In addition, hopefully, the art of listening may also be improved.

Obviously, the better a child hears the music, the greater his chances of enjoying it will be. Many adults are found to be musically "color-blind," as it were. That is, they fail to hear differences in musical pitches. As a result, music sounds very much like noise to them.

In an effort to prevent children from missing the joy of hearing music as it should sound throughout their lives, the following suggestions are presented for classroom use. Care should be exercised not to spend too much time on ear training alone. *One or two minutes daily* is sufficient. *Individual answers* from the children are preferable to class answers, for it is only through their individual answers that the children who are most in need of help may be identified. Using the information presented here as a guide, classroom teachers may whistle, sing, or use any melody instrument such as song bells, the piano, plastic melody bells, a recorder, or a tonette to sound the tones for identification by the children. (See "Small Winds," p. 174.) Even the lowly pitch pipe is useful as a possible means of sounding individual tones.

The suggested procedures that follow are listed in order of difficulty as far as possible, in order to convey a general overview of the levels of development in this area. Regardless of grade level, when a given class has had no previous ear-training experience, the starting point is still with the simple beginning devices; the class then progresses through each succeeding level until they reach the appropriate one for the grade.

Before any pitch discrimination in ear training is attempted, hold a class discussion centering around sounds commonly heard by the children, with a suggestion that they "open their ears" to foster increased awareness of the many different sounds in the environment. The teacher might also tape-record some familiar classroom or other environmental sounds★ and then play them back to see whether the children can identify them. Another possibility is to play a few sounds on various classroom instruments such as the tambourine, triangle, and harmonica while the children have their eyes closed; then they try to identify the instruments in the order played.

At the early primary level, discriminatory powers are less acute than they will become as the child grows older; consequently, ear-training experiences should begin with the identification of very high as opposed to very low tones, loud and soft music, and fast and slow music. Many of these distinctions that children are called upon to discern are contingent upon their understanding of the words themselves ("high" and "low," "soft" and "loud," etc.). Furthermore, they are also expected to translate the words into musical meanings before they can make a proper response. Relating the terms by means of reference to familiar objects in the child's world, such as seesaws, slides, the school bus (getting on—"up"; getting off—"down"), plus having the children

★ Recorded sounds available from theatre-supply companies such as T. S. Denison & Co., Inc., 321 Fifth Ave., Minneapolis, Minn., 55415. Also Folkways.

execute appropriate physical responses according to the music heard, may prove helpful at the outset. Little song snatches such as the following might also be used:

T—Teacher   C—Class

T: Let's sing a high note. C: We sing a high note.

T: Let's sing a low note. C: We sing a low note.

PROCEDURES

I. Inform the class, "I am going to play (or sing) two tones. Listen and tell me whether they are the same or different."

II. Inform the class, "I am going to play (or sing) a little tune. Listen and tell me whether the music goes up or down." (The melody should be short and totally in one direction—either up or down.) As the children progress, try going up *and* down. Very young children may be asked to close their eyes (to prevent them from getting visual cues from others) and move their bodies according to the direction of the music heard.

GAMES AND DEVICES FOR EARLY EAR TRAINING

A. A modified version of Musical Chairs can be used. Play on the drum or tom-tom while the children march around chairs. When you sound a different instrument, the children try to find a chair.

B. Illustrate *high* and *low* tones visually by showing a man on the top rung of a ladder or on the lowest rung. Make the cutout of the man movable so that a child can place it in the correct position according to the music heard.

1. Ask the children to name some things that stand high (or low).

2. Ask the children to name some animals that stand high (or low).

3. Inform the children that sounds in music may also stand high or low. Illustrate high and low sounds with your voice

or an instrument. Place pictures of high- and low-standing things or animals in the front of the room where the children can see them. Play a high or a low tone. Ask individual children to indicate the picture to which the sound relates.

4. After reading "The Three Bears" to the children, ask which bear had the lowest-sounding voice. Ask other questions such as, "Was baby bear's voice higher or lower than mamma bear's voice?"

5. Have the children try to say their names using a high (or low) speaking voice; then have them transfer high and low sounds to *singing* voices.

C. Illustrate *up* and *down* with a visual showing Jack climbing up or sliding down the beanstalk, Jack and Jill climbing up or falling down the hill, or a fireman climbing up a ladder or sliding down a pole, for example. The children can place the cutout figures in the appropriate position on the picture, according to the music heard.

1. Ask the children, "Do you go *up* or *down* to reach a giraffe's neck?" "To reach a worm?" "To reach a turtle?" "To touch the floor?" "To touch the ceiling?"

2. Play a melody while showing a visual with steps leading up to an elephant at the top and another visual with steps leading down to a turtle at the bottom. Ask the children whether the melody they heard was going *up* to the elephant or *down* to the turtle.

III. Inform the class, "I am going to play (or sing) two tones. Listen and tell me whether the second tone is higher or lower than the first." The interval distance between the two tones should be wide at first and then gradually decreased in size until half-step intervals are being played or sung for recognition. *Avoid* saying, "Which tone is higher?" This deprives the child of a point of reference and requires an answer phrased in numerical terms (the first or second tone) rather than in musical terms.

IV. Children at all levels enjoy trying to guess familiar songs hummed, whistled, played, or sung on a neutral syllable by the teacher. You can make this more interesting by playing (or singing on a neutral syllable) only a short phrase from somewhere in the *middle* of the song.

V. When the class has learned a song with words, try singing half a line and letting the class complete the singing of that line. This may be done throughout the entire song. (The idea here is to come in on time. You too!)

VI. Play two short melodies (each three or four notes long) and then ask the children whether the melodies were the same or different.

VII. Inform the class, "I am going to play a short melody. Who can go to the board and draw a picture of it?" (The children may use

lines _ — ‾ or curves ⌒ .)

VIII. Reverse the above process by drawing lines or curves and asking who can sing a tune that fits the direction shown.

IX. Play three tones (two of which are the same, and one different). Then ask the children which two sounded alike.

X. As the children progress, after music reading has been introduced, they will be able to name the syllables to simple, short melodies that you sing or play. (Melodies should be stepwise and start on *do*. As skips are introduced in music reading, ear training should include skips for recognition in the melodies also.

XI. As chromatic tones are introduced in music reading, they too should be included in the ear-training tunes used for recognition of syllables (upper grades).

XII. In upper grades "melodic dictation" is possible with classes who have had adequate experience with basic skills. Indicate where *do* will be on the staff for the tune and then play a short tune beginning on *do*. The class writes the tune on the staff as played. If preferred, individual children may write the tune on the board while the rest of the class watches for errors.

XIII. Play one line of a familiar tune (*very* familiar) and then tell the class that you are going to change the music in one of three ways— the *key* will be different, the *melody* will change, or the rhythm (or meter) will be modified in some way. Play the melody again, changing it in one of the three ways, and ask the class to identify which change was made.

Other types of ear training which are not totally related to pitch but which provide further opportunities for learning to listen are discussed below.

LISTENING FOR RHYTHM PATTERNS

1. Recognizing familiar songs through hearing the rhythm of the song clapped. When doing this activity, it is important that every syllable of the words be clapped; otherwise the song may not be recognizable. The children will enjoy clapping various songs for others to guess.

2. Identifying same or different rhythm patterns tapped or clapped by you or by the children. A four-beat pattern is usually sufficient. The word "and" must be spoken by the person doing the clapping so that it is clear to the rest of the class where one rhythm pattern ends and the other begins, e.g.,

♩ ♩ ♫ ♩ *and* ♩ ♫ ♩ ♩

3. Clapping a rhythm pattern and having the class imitate it.

LISTENING FOR CONTRAST IN DYNAMICS (soft-loud)

1. Ask the children, "What are some things that make a *loud* sound?" "A soft sound?" "What do we sometimes do when a sound is *too* loud?" "What kind of a movement might a loud sound cause us to make?"

2. Clap or beat a drum—very softly at first. Ask the children to clap along, imitating the soft clapping or beating. Gradually let the drum or clapping get louder. The children should respond with louder clapping. Alternate loud and soft beating or clapping through gradual increase and decrease in the intensity of the beat. The children should listen carefully for these changes and respond accordingly.
3. Play a short musical selection—either loud (e.g., a march) or soft (e.g., a lullaby). Ask the children to identify whether it is loud or soft music. Have the children suggest some things they associate with loud (or soft) music and then have them suggest rhythm instruments that they feel would be most appropriate to play with the music heard.
4. Play a musical selection containing contrasting loud and soft sections. Have the children listen and identify each section as soft or loud. Divide the class into two groups—one for loud and one for soft. Have each group respond with body movements of their own creation when their music is heard. Add rhythm instruments previously selected by the children as appropriate for the loud and soft sections.

LISTENING FOR CONTRAST IN TEMPO (fast-slow)

Techniques similar to those suggested for listening for dynamics may also be applied to listening for contrast in tempo.

TESTING RESULTS

It might be of interest to some teachers to learn of a small pilot experiment with two groups of first grade children in which an attempt was made to test the value of some of the devices suggested in this chapter. Most teachers would surely be able to devise more interesting visuals than the ones used and undoubtedly would conduct the whole experiment on a much more scientific basis; however, in the interest of expediency at the time, the experiment proceeded as follows: Group I had a regular music lesson daily with no ear training as such, and Group II had a regular music lesson daily, plus one to two minutes of ear training related to distinguishing between melodies that go up and down, higher and lower tones, as well as same and different tones.

Before the experiment began, a pretest was given, and a final test was administered at the end of eight weeks. Results showed definite improvement in ability to distinguish differences (in the areas tested) by Group II, whose music periods had included the ear training.

An abbreviated sample of the test form is given below in the event that any teacher might like to try something similar in his own school. Instructions to the children as well as the musical portion of the test itself were on tape. Song bells were used to sound the tones.

A. (Same and Different)	B. (Up and Down)	C. (Higher and Lower)
S D	U D	⊙
1.	1.	1.
through	through	through
10.	10.	10.

In Part A, the children were asked to draw a line through either S or D to indicate whether the tones they heard were the *same* or *different*.

In Part B, the children were asked to draw a line through either U or D to indicate whether the succession of tones they heard was going *up* or *down*.

In Part C, the children were instructed to put the point of a pencil right on the dot in the center of the circle. If the second tone played sounded *higher* than the first, they drew a line from the dot *upward*. If the second tone played sounded *lower* than the first, they drew a line *downward*. There were ten separate items in each of the columns.

MUSIC READING EXPERIENCES

". . . from delight . . . to wisdom . . ."

How to teach children to read music has always been one of the most disputed areas in music education. This is understandable, of course, since psychologists have yet to come forth with a completely satisfactory explanation as to how children learn.

Perhaps the most familiar method of teaching music reading is the one in which the syllables *do, re, mi, fa, sol, la,* and *ti* are used; however, many music educators feel that since a child is already familiar with numbers, applying the number system to notes is more logical. Others insist that letter names of notes are the real musical language, equally at home with voice or instrument. Still another group advocates the teaching of music reading through the use of intervals.

Within the same framework lies the dispute over what grade level is the appropriate one to begin teaching children to read music. The question here, of course, concerns what is meant by "reading music." Should the child be able to sing a new tune at sight by himself with little or no help from the teacher, or should he be allowed to depend on the teacher's picking it all apart first, like chicken from a bone, and then singing it for him so that actually it becomes a *rote* experience? The term "reading music," as used in this book, refers to the singing of a *new* (not previously sung or heard) melody at sight, appropriate to the grade level, using the basic skills (melodic and rhythmic) that have been previously learned. The teacher neither plays nor sings the material before the class attempts it by themselves.

Children's abilities too often go unrecognized, untapped, and unchallenged in many areas of education, and music is no exception. There are, for example, school systems where, musically, children "get ready" for four years before they are expected to exert any real effort toward personal discovery. The result is that the child can talk in a few musical terms, but because the learnings have been rather at random, he is totally unable to perform. He simply does not have the security born of a background of well-planned and practiced skills to be able to produce independently when called upon to do so.

Surely, it is agreed that skills should be taught within the context of the musical experience and not in isolation; however, a too literal interpretation of this philosophy could conceivably manifest itself in the rather casual approach of leaving the learning of the skills to chance—the chance that the opportunity for their presentation *might* arise *sometime* during the course of the year.

The procedures suggested herein for teaching music reading were evolved in the process of trying many other ways while observing and working with classroom teachers in service, students in training, and children in abundance. They were selected for inclusion here because they proved to be the most musical and the easiest to administer, especially by an inexperienced teacher or one who feels vocally inadequate, for they put the burden of performance on the children—not on the teacher. Any system of teaching music reading that requires a great deal of vocal ability on the part of the teacher is almost certainly doomed to failure in classrooms where the teacher feels vocally insecure. Lack of success in this area could cause the teacher to feel frustrated in other musical areas as well, resulting, perhaps, in less positive attitudes on the part of the children and/or the elimination of music entirely in that classroom. (Good grief!)

In order to enable a teacher to better understand the significance of his contribution to a given grade, it is often helpful to provide him with an overview of the total curriculum. He may then be more aware of what tasks were previously required of his present class, as well as what will be expected of them in future. The following chart is intended to provide such an overview.

It shows the grade level at which each new skill is to be introduced, according

Chart of Basic Skills for Music Reading
(Arranged in Developmental Order)

GRADE LEVEL	MELODIC SKILLS	RHYTHMIC SKILLS
I second half of year	Singing scale down and up Singing simple tunes from ladder scale Recognizing staff, location of lines and spaces (first on bottom), G clef, bar line, double bar Finding *do* with X Reading easy stepwise melodies written on staff in note heads only—no stems Reading easy stepwise melodies written on one staff using rhythms of ——→	♪ 𝄾, ♩ ▬ in $\frac{2}{4},\frac{3}{4},\frac{4}{4}$ meters only
II	Reading stepwise melodies written on staff using ————————→ Reading songs containing *do-mi-sol* skips Reading songs from two or more staves Reading music from *books* (selected songs containing only afore-mentioned skills)	♩., o in $\frac{2}{4},\frac{3}{4},\frac{4}{4}$ meters only Interpreting the upper figure of a meter (time) signature
III	Reading music from *books*—songs containing ————————→ Reading songs containing skips other than *do-mi-sol* Reading songs starting on tones other than *do* Finding *do* with *sharps* Finding *do* with *flats*	♫ in $\frac{2}{4},\frac{3}{4},\frac{4}{4}$ meters only Interpreting the lower figure of a meter (time) signature
IV	Reading music from *books*—songs containing ————————→ Recognition of *minor* mode through sight and sound	♩. ♪
V	Reading music from *books*—songs containing ————————→ Reading music containing chromatic tones in simple melodic progressions	$\frac{6}{8},\frac{9}{8},\frac{12}{8},\frac{3}{2},\frac{2}{2}$ etc., meter signatures
VI	Reading music from *books*—songs containing ————————→ Reading music containing chromatic tones in more difficult melodic progressions	♬♬, ♬♪, ♪♪ triplet and syncopation ♪♪♪ ♪♪ ♪ ⌣3⌣ Translating meter signatures into conducting patterns.

117

to the suggested plan in this text for teaching music reading. The division into the areas of *melodic* and *rhythmic* skills has been made merely for the sake of clarity and serves to point up the fact that they should be taught one at a time.

At a glance, a teacher can easily determine the appropriate review material for earlier levels, as well as the new skills for his own grade. Not all areas of classroom musical experiences lend themselves to this kind of arrangement; however, since basic skills are fairly well defined, it was felt that they might be a suitable subject. (Specific procedures for teaching each of the skills listed will be found on pp. 120 to 172.)

Teaching Music Reading

IN GENERAL

The following step-by-step procedures for presenting basic music-reading skills to children are intended to further a child's knowledge so that he may become independent in his music-reading ability. The procedures, as suggested, also seek to provide for more actual practice in *performing* each new skill in place of merely talking about it. They are listed in order of difficulty, which is also the order in which they should be introduced to children, for ease of presentation as well as ease of learning. When "taken as directed," they have been known to produce very acceptable results. It is vital to the success of this program that the skills be presented in the indicated order and that the mastery of each skill be ensured before attempting the skill to follow. The order suggested here bases new musical learning on previous knowledge; i.e., each succeeding skill emerges as a logical outgrowth of the one immediately preceding it.

As shown on the Chart of Basic Skills (p. 117), children may be introduced to music reading as early as the latter half of the first grade. Some educators prefer to delay this area until a later grade. The point to be made here in connection with the following suggested procedures is that regardless of the grade level one chooses for the introduction of music reading, the *order* of presentation of the skills as well as the procedures for presentation (except for slight modifications where indicated) remains the same. This should enable any teacher whose class has never had any experience with music-reading skills to start them at the suggested beginning and to proceed through each succeeding skill to the desired level as quickly as the class can master each one. Obviously, a teacher in a higher grade may expect to cover some of the more basic material more rapidly than a teacher in a first or second grade.

The principle is the same when using review procedures. When a class begins to falter anywhere in the review, the teacher merely begins his "teaching" at this point, following the procedures suggested for teaching the given skill. As with any skill, only a prescribed amount of time should be allotted for practice each day, but the practice as well as the time should be efficiently planned so as to ensure some measurable achievement. The following con-

118

siderations should be taken into account in the planning of the *music-reading* portion of any given music period.

1. The attitude of the teacher is probably the most significant factor contributing to success or failure in this phase of music. Children enjoy meeting the challenge of music skills when properly taught. If these skills are presented with enthusiasm, sparked by the spirit of adventure into new learnings, the children cannot help but "catch" some of the fire.

2. Five to seven minutes in any given twenty-minute music period is sufficient amount of time to devote to the music-reading aspect. To avoid tiresome drill, the teacher should plan well and work quickly. Much can be accomplished in this amount of time.

3. The music-reading experience should be scheduled in the early part of any given music period. It should certainly not be scheduled first, but rather should come *between* other planned music activities. In addition, of course, practice in music reading may also be gained through participation in other related musical experiences such as playing classroom instruments, for example.

4. When introducing a new music-reading skill, the teacher should make certain that the skill is appropriate for his grade level.

5. Shorter practice periods scheduled every day will produce more measurable results than longer periods scheduled less frequently.

6. Magnetic music boards, flannel boards, and similar aids can be significant timesaving devices when teaching music reading to children. (Other devices and games for adding interest are suggested in the appropriate sections of this text.)

PREPARATORY EXPERIENCES

Before introducing a class to any basic music-reading skills, the teacher should make sure of the following:

1. That many rote songs have been learned well.
2. That out-of-tune singers have received proper attention.
3. That opportunities for participation by each child have been provided in all other areas of music, such as listening, moving, playing, and ear training.
4. That through a variety of such musical experiences the children have become somewhat familiar with the concepts of:
   high–low
   up–down
   same–different
   fast–slow
   soft–loud
   as they relate to music. (Suggested procedures for introducing children to these concepts in their relation to music may be found in Chapter 4, Ear Training Experiences.)

If the children have *not* had the foregoing range of musical experiences, introduction to music-reading skills should be delayed until they have been provided.

BASIC SKILLS (in order of presentation)

THE SCALE (by sound)

a. Introduce the scale by *sound* only, not on the staff. This may be done through the use of a melody instrument (the piano, a recorder, song bells, etc.) for your vocal support, if needed, or through the teaching of a rote song containing the scale, e.g.,

I like to   go out-side and play, es - peci-ally on a   sun-ny day!
(es - pesh -ly)

b. Teach the syllable names of the scale—descending first and then ascending. (This is an aid to better tone production and also provides for more practice where it's needed—on the descending scale.)

c. Have the class and individual children practice singing scales starting on different pitches: E, fourth space; E♭, fourth space; D, fourth line; D♭, fourth line; C, third space, etc., descending first and then ascending. Be sure to pronounce all syllable names correctly. Take care to sustain the foregoing starting pitches long enough so that the class can hear and reproduce each one as given.

Games and Devices for Practice

a. Have one child sing the scale descending and immediately afterward, another child sing the scale ascending.

b. Using plastic Melodé bells of various colors (see Fig. 6-5), line the children up in order of scale tones (low *do* on left). Ring and sing individually, or ring and have the class sing each syllable as it is rung. These bells are usually manufactured in the F to F octave.

c. Have individual children play scales descending and ascending on song bells, xylophones, or the piano. When available, hang song bells or xylophones on the wall with the small bars on top (ascending-scale order).

d. When you play the ascending scale, the children climb the fireman's ladder; when you play the descending scale, the children slide down the fireman's pole.

120

THE SCALE (by sight)

a. Write the syllable names of the scale on the board in ladder form:

do

ti

la

sol

fa

mi

re

do

Using the pointer, start on either low *do* or high *do*. Sound the correct pitch for the class and then point to various syllables on the ladder, asking the children to sing each syllable as you point to it. Move in ascending- and descending-scale progressions first, and then in short tunes. Do not skip. Melodies should be *stepwise* only and short. Begin with tunes containing repeated tones and going in one direction first; e.g.,

Sound pitch of: ↓	On ladder scale point to: ↓
G second line ⟶	*do do do re mi fa sol*
F first space ⟶	*do re mi fa sol sol sol*
C third space ⟶	*do ti la la sol sol sol*
B♭ third line ⟶	*do do ti ti la la sol*

Then go on to tunes that return to do:

A second space ⟶	*do ti la sol la ti do*
G second line ⟶	*do do re re mi re do*
D fourth line ⟶	*do ti ti la ti ti do*
E first line ⟶	*do re do re mi re do*

etc.

b. When the class has mastered the above, try writing the scale tones in a line approximating their related pitch levels:

do   ti   do   re   mi   re   do   do

The children will gain their music-reading independence a lot faster if you allow them to sing all their practice skills without giving vocal help. Any skill that involves the use of singing with syllables should be done by the children alone, except in very rare cases. One or two of these practice melodies each day should be sufficient. *Be sure to give the correct starting pitch in the right octave.* Check the silver side of the pitch pipe for the location of notes on the staff.

Games and Devices for Practice

a. Print the eight syllable names of the scale on eight individual **121** pieces of construction paper in large letters (one syllable name to each piece of paper). Pin these on the front of eight children. Have them line up in front of the class (low *do* on the left). As you hold your hand over the head of each child, the class sings the indicated syllable on correct pitch. Use tunes similar to those suggested for the ladder scale—stepwise only (no skips) and short.

b. The same procedure outlined in item *a* may be modified by substituting cut-out "lollipops" (on which the syllables are written) for the papers. The children can hold the lollipops up in front of them so that the class can see as you indicate which note they should sing.

c. Show a visual of a building with eight floors marked *do, re, mi*, etc., up to high *do*. Attach a cutout of an elevator to the pointer and take the children for a musical "ride." Adapt other visuals as desired.

THE STAFF

When the class is able to follow the pointer with ease on the ladder scale, singing the correct syllable names on the correct pitches without help, they are ready to be introduced to the *staff*. Present the staff one line at a time, beginning with the first line. Draw a line, tell the class that it is the "first line," and have the class repeat. Use the same procedure for the second, third, fourth, and fifth lines. Point to the spaces, tell the class the number of each space, and have the class repeat for all four spaces.

To help the class remember that the first line and first space of the staff are always on the *bottom*, liken them to the floors of a building, where the first floor is always on the lower level. It helps at this point if the teacher will draw all staves starting with the *first* line. When the staff has been completely drawn, print the word "staff" on the board and tell the class that this combination of lines and spaces on which we write music is called a "staff". Point to the vicinity of the fifth line and tell the class that when music is written up there, it usually sounds high. Point to the first line and tell the

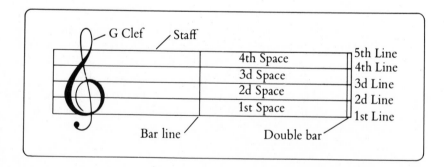

FIGURE 5–1 *Staff showing four spaces, five lines, a G clef, a bar line and a double bar.*

class that when music is written down there, it sounds lower. Show G clef (not G "cliff"!), bar line, and double bar. Identify each. NOTE: The use of the staff liner is not advised when the staff is first being introduced or for some time thereafter, especially at the primary level. It is much more desirable to draw one line at a time and provide for wide spaces between the lines.

The use of colored chalk for the G clef, bar lines, etc., adds interest. Incidentally, if you have difficulty drawing a G clef, start with a straight line and then, beginning at the top of the line, draw another line curving slightly to the right, then to the left, and then to the right and follow through with a circular motion.

Games and Devices for Practice

a. Using constructed pictures of clowns, animals, flowers, or whatever you choose, arrange a circle of Scotch tape on the back of each picture so that it will adhere to the board when pressed. Ask individual children to find the location of the various lines and spaces (by number, of course) and to put the picture in the proper place as you call off a certain line or space.
b. Use the procedure outlined in item *a* but on a flannel board or magnetic music board rather than the chalkboard.
c. Use large flash cards with the symbols for the G clef, staff, bar lines, etc., printed on them individually. Hold them up and ask children to identify them. The children also enjoy holding them up for other children to identify.
d. Using the left hand as a staff (palm facing the body, thumb up), point to different lines and spaces with the forefinger of the right hand. Indicate that *do* is on the first line or first space when first introducing this activity so that the children may easily see that

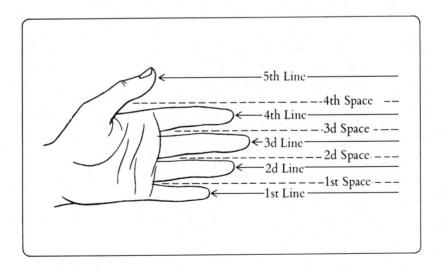

FIGURE 5–2 *The hand used as a staff.*

when *do* is on a *line*, for example, *mi* and *sol* above are also on *lines*—the next two lines above *do*. When *do* is on a *space*, *mi* and *sol* above *do* are located on the next two *spaces* above. This activity can be transferred immediately to the staff on the chalkboard, using note heads.

LOCATING DO

Tell the class that for now you will show the location of *do* on the staff by use of the letter "X". Place X's on various lines and spaces, one at a time, and ask individual children to indicate the number of the line or space on which *do* is located. A reminder to answer in complete sentences ("*Do* is on the second space," etc.) will help the children remember what they're looking for. It is important to change the position of *do* often so that the children will understand that *do* can be on *any* line or space.

SCALES ON THE STAFF

Put an X on any high *do* that will permit you to write the entire scale descending and still stay in range (fourth space, fourth line, fifth line, third space—any of these). Draw a note head beside the X and then draw the entire scale down in note heads. Give the proper pitch for high *do* and point to the descending note heads, one at a time, having the class sing:

Repeat the low *do* at the bottom of the staff and write the scale ascending in note heads. Tell the children that this is the way the scale looks when written on the staff. Call attention to the fact that there may be a *low do* as well as a *high do*. Point as before, having the class sing. Follow this procedure on other days by writing the scale descending and ascending as above, but from another location of *do*. Have the class sing as before. If board space is limited, use pre-prepared charts, but make certain that the location of *do* is changed often.

MELODIES ON THE STAFF (following a pointer)

Put a scale, descending only, on the staff in note heads, using an X to mark the location of *do*. Using the pointer, start with *do* and point to various notes, going in stepwise progression only—no skips—asking the children to sing each note as you point to it. Tell the class to watch closely, since it will not be simply a matter of going up and down the scale all the way. Begin with simple tunes going in one direction first; then go on to tunes that return to *do*. This is the same procedure that was used with the ladder scale (p. 121); thus the same

124

type of short stepwise tunes that were suggested previously (in connection with the introduction of the ladder scale) may be used here also. One or two of these each day is sufficient.

MELODIES ON THE STAFF (without pointer)

a. When the class is able to follow the pointer with ease, singing the correct syllable names as you point to each note head, try putting a whole melody on the staff at once, as follows:

Tell the class to study this for a few seconds, thinking the names of the syllables over to themselves and trying to hear how it might sound, and then inform them that they will be expected to sing it alone without pointing or other help from you. Give the correct indicated pitch (according to the location of the X) and have the class sing the melody unassisted. One or two of these a day is sufficient for practice.

b. When the class can sing many melodies similar to the foregoing with ease, they are ready for their first rhythmic skills.

Games and Devices for Practice

a. Place paper ball or bells of different colors (or use colored chalk or paint) corresponding to the colors of plastic Melodé bells (p. 179) on various lines and spaces indicated on the staff to make a tune. Then give each of eight children a bell and ask him to play when his color occurs on the staff. If the tune calls for a note to be played more than once, there must be as many balls as there are times for him to sound his note. For "Twinkle, Twinkle, Little Star" the balls on the staff might look like this (in colors, of course):

b. Place two sets of removable constructed pictures (any appropriate subject matter), one in ascending order and one in descending order, on two separate staves. Ask the class to listen while a simple tune is played or sung. The tune should go in either an up or a down direction. Have the class identify which set of pictures best fits the tune played.

125

c. Write the staff on the chalk board or use a flannel board or chart. Write in an ascending scale. Place a removable constructed paper animal next to low *do*. Place a picture of food appropriate for the animal next to high *do* (bunny, carrots; squirrel, nuts, etc.). Ask the children to watch the scale and listen while you play up the scale, one note at a time (representing the animal going to get his food). The children should determine how far the animal went by where you stopped playing. Have individual children come up and put the animal on the correct stopping note. You should stop on different notes each time.

d. Use large flash cards on which are written easy, stepwise, four- or five-note melodies for individual children to sing as the cards are held up.

e. Hold up flash cards showing a staff with two notes written on different pitches. Ask the children whether the second note of the two will sound higher or lower than the first when played or sung. After they have answered, play or sing the notes for them to hear and then have them sing.

f. Write two short tunes on two charts or flash cards. Ask the class to watch and listen while one of the tunes is played or sung and then have them try to identify which of the two tunes it was. In upper grades, the beginning measures of several familiar songs (melody only, no words) can be written on charts or flash cards, and the children can be asked to give the *names* of the songs.

SIMPLE RHYTHMS

In music, as in other areas of the curriculum, opportunities to relate new skills to familiar experiences should always be seized upon. In learning a new rhythm, for example, it is particularly helpful if a child can get the feel of it through some kind of body movement before he begins hearing facts about it and/or before he attempts to reproduce it correctly within some music-reading context.

According to the procedures suggested herein, a *quarter note* is the first rhythm a child learns. It is defined, for the present, as "one tone to one beat" and is sung slowly to facilitate accuracy in beginning music reading. A series of quarter notes, when properly executed, produces an even, steady series of sounds; thus before a child ever hears the term "quarter note" or sees a picture of one, he should be provided with some way to relate to it through "doing" experiences that will give him the feel of something even and steady in motion. The activity chosen should be one that is representative of an even beat and is within his range of experience. Once the child has physically experienced the characteristics of a given rhythm (or rhythm pattern), the teacher may then move on to defining it in its musical setting. It is at this teaching point that the following suggested procedures for teaching new rhythms to children should be started. Once the teacher becomes familiar with the characteristics of each succeeding new rhythm, he will undoubtedly originate many clever preparatory devices of his own.

1. Following the preparatory devices, inform the class that in music we have different kinds of notes—some long, some short—that help make our tunes more interesting. We can tell by looking at them how they would be sung or played.

2. Sing on a neutral syllable ("doo," "loo," "ta," etc.) or play on a melody instrument four quarter notes all on the same tone in a slow tempo. Have the class repeat. Draw a quarter note on the board (♩). Tell the class that it is a quarter note, and that the stems may go up or down (♪). For now, we shall say that it gets *one* beat. Write four quarter notes on the board as follows: ♩ ♩ ♩ ♩ . Sing or play for the class on a melody instrument. Have the class sing. (Use any comfortable pitch such as G, A♭, A, or B, for example.) Keep the tempo slow and *stress* each tone. Try four more with the stems going down: ♪ ♪ ♪ ♪ .

3. Put a simple melody on the board (stepwise only) using quarter notes:

Have the class study it for a few seconds. Give the indicated pitch of *do* and have the class sing. *Do not point and do not sing or play with the class.*

4. Have the class sing at least one new melody with quarter notes each day. Melodies should vary, of course, but they should remain *simple* and *stepwise*—no skips—at this level. Use an X to indicate the position of *do* and change the location of *do* with each new melody.

The Half Note

1. Ask the class to sing or chant four quarter notes from the board on a neutral syllable. ♩ ♩ ♩ ♩ .

2. Tie the quarter notes together in groups of two. Then sing or chant for the class, *pulsating* the second beat of each of the tied notes.

♩ ♩ ♩ ♩
loo-oo loo-oo

"Pulsating" means sounding the second beat on the extended syllable name of the first, e.g., "loo-oo" (or "ta-a"), the "oo" (or "a") being the pulsation of the second beat. This reinforces the feeling of the second beat and also allows you to hear immediately whether the note is receiving its required number of beats as the children sing. Telling the class, "You didn't *pulsate* the second beat" is a more immediate way of pointing up and correcting the error than saying, "You didn't sing the half note right."

3. Represent half notes directly under the ties:

Tell the children that these are half notes (some children will call them "half a note") and that they get two beats. When we sing a half note we pulsate the second beat. Sound a comfortable pitch and have the class sing, using a neutral syllable ("doo," "loo," etc.).

4. Use half notes in rhythm drills (*not on the staff*) in combination with quarter notes, such as the following. (One or two a day is sufficient. Sound a comfortable pitch—G, or A♭, for example—and have the class sing. *Do not point!*)

Rhythm Drills Using 𝅗𝅥 and 𝅘𝅥

5. Apply on the staff in simple melodies using quarter notes and half notes only. (Give the correct starting pitch as indicated for each melody.)

Simple Melodies Using 𝅗𝅥 and 𝅘𝅥

etc.

The Quarter Rest

1. Put four quarter notes on the board: ♩ ♩ ♩ ♩. Sound the pitch (G, A, A♭, or B, for example). Have the class sing on a neutral syllable.

2. Cross out the third note: ♩ ♩ ✗ ♩. Ask the class to sing again, remaining quiet on the third beat.

3. Tell the class that we do not cross out notes in music to indicate silence. We have "rests." A quarter rest gets one beat of quiet, just as a quarter note gets one beat of sound. Beats of quiet are counted in the same way as beats of sound.

4. Write on the board directly underneath the four notes above with the third beat as a rest: ♩ ♩ 𝄽 ♩. Have the class sing, saying "rest" softly when the rest occurs.

5. Put other eight-beat rhythm drills on the board, using quarter rests in combination with quarter notes and half notes. One or two a day is sufficient for practice. Sound a comfortable pitch. Have the class sing and keep the tempo slow.

a. ♩ 𝄽 ♩ 𝄽 ♩ ♩ 𝄽 𝄽   *c.* ♩ ♩ 𝄽 𝄽 ♩ 𝄽 ♩

b. 𝅗𝅥 𝅗𝅥 ♩ ♩ ♩ 𝄽   *d.* 𝅗𝅥 ♩ 𝄽 ♩ 𝄽 𝅗𝅥 etc.

6. Apply on the staff in simple melodies such as the following—at least one each day. Sound the starting pitch indicated for each melody. Insist that the children sing each melody without any help from you. Vary the melodies and change the location of *do* with each melody.

etc.

The Half Rest

1. Use the same procedure as with the quarter rest, having the children say "re-est" when the half rest occurs:

$$𝅗𝅥 \quad 𝅗𝅥.$$
$$𝅗𝅥 \quad ▬$$

2. Use the half rest in rhythm drills with quarter notes, half notes, and quarter rests (one or two a day for practice). Have the class sing, using neutral syllable. Pitch comfortably as before. *Do not point.* **129**

a. 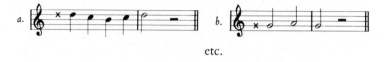   *d.*

b.

c.   etc.

3. Apply on the staff in simple melodies—at least one new one each day, sung without help from you. Sound the starting pitch indicated for each melody. Change the position of *do* often and vary the melodies.

a.   *b.*

etc.

The Dotted Half Note

1. Ask the class to sing or chant in quarter notes from the board:

2. Tie three together in two groups:

3. Sing or chant for the class, pulsating the second and third beats of each group. Have the class sing:

loo–oo–oo loo–oo–oo

4. Show dotted half note below each:

5. Tell the class that these are dotted half notes. They get three beats. When we sing them we pulsate the second and third beats. Have the class sing the dotted half notes. *Do not point.*

6. Use in rhythm drills, sung as before, with quarter notes and half notes:

a.   *d.*

b.   *e.*

c.   etc.

7. Apply in simple melodies on the staff, at least one new one each day, stepwise at first and then with skips, if and when skips are

introduced. Sound the starting pitch of *do* indicated for each melody. Have the class sing at least one or two each day for practice, without help from you.

etc.

The Whole Note

1. Put eight quarter notes on the board:

   Have the class sing on a neutral syllable.

2. Tie two groups of four together:

   loo-oo - oo - oo   loo-oo - oo - oo

   Sing or chant for the class, pulsating the second, third and fourth beats. Have the class sing. Show a whole note below each group:

3. Tell the class that this is a whole note. It gets four beats. When we sing this note we pulsate the second, third, and fourth beats. Have the class sing the whole notes.

4. Use in rhythm drills, as before, with quarter notes, half notes, dotted half notes, quarter rests, and half rests. Have the class sing. *Do not point.*

   a.   *b.*   *c.*   *d.*   *e.*   *f.*
   etc.

5. Apply on the staff in simple melodies—at least one new one each day, sung by the class without help from you. Sound the starting pitch indicated for each melody:

etc.

Games and Devices for Practice

a. Prepare large flash cards, each one showing a different kind of note. (Use various colors, if desired.) Have the class identify the notes by name and sing.
b. Prepare three- and four-beat (or longer) rhythm drills, combining the rhythms under study at the moment, as well as those previously learned. Write each drill in color on the flash cards and have the class sing. Vary by putting all the flash cards on the chalk rail, singing or playing one of the rhythms (or letting one of the children sing or play one), and asking the class to identify which rhythm was executed. Add new rhythms as they are taught.
c. Clap, beat, or chant rhythm rounds or canons such as those shown below. Divide the class into three groups and proceed in the same manner in which rounds are sung, with Group II performing Pattern 1 as Group I moves on to Pattern 2, etc.:

These may also be extended into longer patterns for each group.

TWO STAVES

Up to now, the children have been singing from one staff and have had no experience in leaving one staff and going on to another directly below it.

Introduce singing from two staves (or more) by pointing out that *do* is in the same place in *all* staves of any given song and that we find the name of the *first note* on the *second staff* from the *last note* on the *first staff*:

Questions such as, "Does the first note of the second staff go up or down from the last note of the first staff?" ought to clear up any minor difficulties almost immediately. Children generally have no trouble going from one staff to the next the first time, but it is still wise to point out the principle involved. (Singing from two staves is not to be confused with singing *two-part music* from separate staves, in which one voice sings from the upper staff while the other voice sings from the lower.)

PREPARING A SONG FOR MUSIC READING

As the music-reading experiences become more varied and increasingly more difficult, it is suggested that they be preceded by two devices that will provide needed practice in the melodic as well as the rhythmic problems that will be encountered in each new song. These preparatory devices are known as "rhythm drill" and "melody practice."

The teacher's use of melody practice and rhythm drill as preparatory practice devices for each new music-reading experience should ensure adequate melodic as well as rhythmic preparation for each song, since both devices are directly related to the given song. Their use is advocated here mainly because they require no singing on the teacher's part; rather, the responsibility is placed on the children. Furthermore, they move quickly and are musical in that each requires a *singing* response from the children rather than a *speaking* one.

USING RHYTHM DRILL AND MELODY PRACTICE AS PREPARATORY DEVICES FOR NEW MUSIC READING EXPERIENCES

The term "rhythm drill" should be familiar, for it was used extensively in previous sections to indicate a practice device for new rhythms. It refers to a line of notes (written *off* the staff) that may be chanted, clapped, tapped, or sung on a neutral syllable for the purpose of practice in learning the time values of various notes. The teacher simply sounds a pitch (if the rhythm drill is to be sung), establishes the tempo, gives the starting command, and has the class chant or sing the line of rhythm.

When rhythm drill is used as a preparatory device for a particular music-reading song, it should contain the rhythms that will be found in that song in order of their occurrence. The *tempo* established for singing the rhythm drill should be *no faster than that which will be used when the children sing the syllables of the song for the first time*. This may indicate a fairly slow tempo at the outset to ensure greater accuracy.

The term "melody practice" means just that—practice on the melody. It consists of putting a scale or portion of the scale on the board in the same key as the new music-reading song that is to be introduced with syllables that day. Using the pointer, the teacher points to *do* and sounds the correct pitch for the class to sing *do*. Following the pointer, the class then sings the notes as the teacher 133 moves from one note to another, sometimes stepwise and other times by skip, depending on the content of the music-reading song being prepared. In a tune such as the following, for example,

the rhythm drill would be:

and the melody practice scale would look like this:

The pointer would move *stepwise* only, since there are *no skips* in this particular song.

The technique of using melody practice is described in further detail in the following suggested procedure for introducing the *do–mi–sol* skips to the class.

INTRODUCING DO-MI-SOL (TONIC-CHORD) SKIPS

All the foregoing short melodies suggested for application of the various new skills were purposely made melodically simple so that the children might concentrate their attention on the new rhythmic problems that were to be introduced.

Now, however, in order to provide for musical growth, the melodic material must begin to increase in difficulty as the child prepares for music-reading experiences in his book. Where, previously, the melodies were in stepwise progression, they should now begin to contain simple skips such as *do–mi–sol*, often referred to as "tonic-chord" skips.

When the children are able to sing easy, stepwise melodies such as those given on pp. 128–132, using the rhythms of ♩, ♪, ♩., o, ♩, ♩ only, introduce the *do–mi–sol* skips through melody practice as follows:

1. Put an ascending scale on the board (use note heads only—no stems). Indicate the location of *do* with X:

2. Point to low *do* and sound the pitch. (This should be the pitch of whatever *do* is indicated on the staff. In the above example, the pitch of E should be blown because the X is on the first line of the staff.)
3. Ask the class to follow the pointer with their voices, singing as you point to this succession of notes. (Proceed rather quickly—don't drag.)

(For practice on *do-mi*) *do do do re mi mi mi re do do do*
  re mi mi mi re do mi do mi do mi do

(For practice on *mi-sol* with review on *do-mi* included) *do re mi fa sol sol sol fa mi mi mi*
  fa sol sol sol fa mi sol mi sol mi
  sol mi do mi sol mi do

The above may be done as one whole exercise without stopping. Note that each skip is approached "gradually," as it were, through singing the intervening tones, which act as "connectors"; thus in the *do-mi* skip, the connecting tone would be *re*; between the *mi-sol* skip, the connecting tone would be *fa*. In the case of a larger skip such as from *do* to *fa*, for example, there would naturally be more connecting tones, and each should be sung in succession as it occurs in order to facilitate reaching the upper tone (or lower, as the case may be) of the skip successfully. Once the sound of each note of the skip has been established by repetition (as indicated in the practice exercise above), using appropriate connecting tones to span the interval, then the skip itself is practiced by alternating between the two tones of the skip (*minus* the connecting tones) until the class is singing it with reasonable accuracy.

Change the position of *do* often when writing the scale on the staff for initial practice on this skip. (Watch the range!) Have the class practice singing the tonic-chord skips in many simple melodies from the board similar to the one shown below. The two preparatory devices of melody practice and rhythm drill appropriate for these melodies are shown to the right of each one. These should always *precede* the singing of the melody. Note that when the complete scale would fall out of range (see melody practice scale for melody 2), only the portion needed (for practicing the skips) is used.

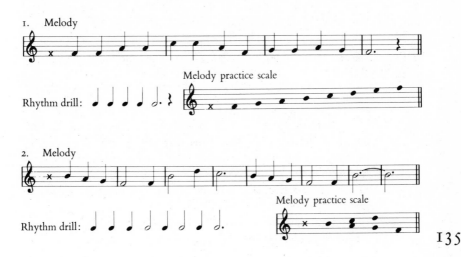

When the class has had sufficient practice in singing melodies from the board containing tonic-chord skips, they should attempt music-reading experiences from their *books* that contain these skips. Songs should be simple, with rhythms of ♩, ♩, ♩., ○, ♪, only, until other rhythms are introduced. (See "Reading Music from the Books," p. 143.) If sufficient material for practice is lacking in the books, the teacher might try creating more melodies of his own, similar to those suggested, or secure the necessary further practice material from another source. In either case, the preparatory procedures of melody practice and rhythm drill should always be carried out. It might be well to mention here that using the tonic-chord skips for reference when attempting to sing *any* new song with syllables can be a valuable aid to greater accuracy in music reading.

DEVICES FOR FURTHER PRACTICE ON TONIC-CHORD SKIPS

1. Point out that when *do* is in a space, *mi* and *sol* are in the two spaces above *do*. When *do* is on a line, *mi* and *sol* are on the two lines above *do*. Have the children go to the board and fill in *mi* and *sol* above a given *do* on the staff. Change the position of *do* often.
2. Using the hand as a staff (p. 123), point and sing tonic-chord skips from a designated *do*.
3. Have the class practice singing tonic-chord skips from any *do* sounded by you. Sound the pitch of *do*. The class sings *do* then sings *do-mi-sol*. (This need not be on the staff.) Change the pitch of *do* often, but watch the range so as not to go too high. Any note between B♭ below middle C to B♭ third line should be a reasonable *do* to sound.

STARTING SONGS ON TONES OTHER THAN DO

This should be attempted only when the children can sing the tonic-chord skips easily.

Songs usually begin on *do*, *mi*, or *sol* (sometimes *la* if the song is in the minor mode). When a song starts on some tone other than *do*, the children should be given practice in *thinking* up or down to the starting tone after hearing the *do* and then singing the starting tone. The following procedure is recommended:

1. Sound G (*do*) and ask the class to think *do* and then think up to *mi* by singing *do-re-mi* to themselves (not aloud). After waiting a few seconds, ask the class to sing *mi*. When first introducing this procedure you may help the class by moving your hand up silently (*do-re-mi*) while asking them to think up.
2. Sound A and ask the class to think *do* and then think down to the *sol* below and sing.
3. Using the same procedure, have the class try singing *do* below from the given pitch of high *do* (high D).

4. Using the same procedure, try having the class sing the *sol* above from the given pitch of *do* on F (first space).

Two or three of these a day is sufficient for practice. This may be followed by application on the board using the starting tones only:

Blow B♭. Say "Sing *mi*"   Blow G. Say "Sing *sol* below"

Blow G♭. Say "Sing *sol* above"   Blow *high* E♭. Say "Sing *mi* below"

If the class has not had experience in finding *do* with sharps and flats, use X to indicate the position of *do* and let the class find the name of the first note by themselves.

Apply in music-reading songs that start on tones other than *do*.

INTRODUCING SKIPS OTHER THAN DO-MI-SOL

When the children have mastered the tonic-chord skips so that they can sing them accurately at sight in their music-reading experiences, then additional skips, other than those contained in the tonic chord, should be introduced. It is important to remember here that whenever a new melodic problem (such as skips, for example) is being practiced, the rhythms contained in the practice melodies should be only those with which the class is already familiar. It is not wise to attempt to introduce new melodic as well as new rhythmic problems at the same time. Whenever one is under study at the moment, the other should be kept very simple in the practice material.

Skips other than those of the tonic chord may be introduced in the same manner as suggested for the tonic-chord skips, i.e., practiced in melody practice before being attempted within the context of any given song. As before, the rhythm of the song should be simple when a new skip is being introduced, and the same two preparatory devices—melody practice and rhythm drill—should precede all new music-reading experiences.

Try the following exercises just for practice. You may dictate the notes orally or from the ladder scale (see p. 121) on the board, using the pointer:

Ascending   1. Sound the pitch of *low D* (first space below the staff). Have the class sing: *do mi re fa mi sol fa la sol ti la do ti re do* (ends on high *do*).

Descending   2. Sound the pitch of *high D* (fourth line). Have the class sing: *do la ti sol la fa sol mi fa re mi do re ti do* (ends on low *do*).

Ascending   3. Sound *middle C* (first line below the staff). Have the class sing: *do re do mi do fa do sol do la do ti do* (high) *do* (low) *do* (high) *do* (low). All notes in exercise 3 are *above* the low *do* except where indicated.

137

Descending   4. Sound the pitch of C (third space). Have the class sing: *do ti do la do sol do fa do mi do re do* (high) *do* (low) *do* (high) *do* (low). All notes in exercise 4 are *below* the high *do* except where indicated.

The following melodies are examples of tunes containing skips other than those of the tonic chord. They may be used for practice in singing the skips as well as for using the two preparatory devices of melody practice and rhythm drill.

Rhythm drill for melody 1:

Melody practice scale for melody 1:

Practice skips: *do–sol–mi–do*
                   fa–re–ti
                   ti–sol
                   la–do

Rhythm drill for melody 2:

Melody practice scale for melody 2:

Practice skips: *do–mi–sol–do*
                   la–fa–re
                   re–la
                   do–la
                   sol–ti
                   do–sol

TEACHING METER (TIME) SIGNATURES

Meter, or time, signatures may be introduced in lower grades using colored construction paper as described below.

Place one sheet of a dark shade of paper on the chalk rail. Place a sheet of a lighter shade of the same color next to it. Repeat the patterns so that they will run dark, light, dark, light. Tell the class that when you point to the dark paper, they will clap and say the word "heavy." When you point to the light shade, they will clap a bit more softly and say the word "light." Demonstrate for the class. Have the whole class try it, and then individual children. Make sure that the beat is even and steady. Repeat the process, substituting the numbers "1" and "2" for the words "heavy" and "light." Every time the class sees the dark shade, they should be saying "1" and clapping heavily; on the lighter shade, they should be saying "2" and clapping lightly.

Show the following pattern on the board: | | | | | |. Clap as above, saying "1" on the long lines and "2" on the short, with heavy claps on 1 and light claps on 2.

Using another dark shade and lighter shades of the same hue, place one dark sheet and two light sheets on the chalk rail, in that order.

Ask the class whether they know what to say when they come to the dark sheet (either "heavy" or "1").

Q: What do we say on the first light sheet?
A: Light (or 2).
Q: What do we say on the second light sheet?
A: Light (or 3).
Q: How do we clap on 1?
A: Hard (or heavily).
Q: How do we clap on 2?
A: Lightly.
Q: How do we clap on 3?
A: Lightly.

Have the class try clapping 1-2-3, 1-2-3 without demonstrating first. All 1s should be heavy, and 2s and 3s should be light.

Put the following pattern on the board: | | | | | | | | | |.

Have the class clap and say "1-2-3," etc., aloud, accenting all the 1s. Tell them that they have been clapping in 3s.

Using still another color of construction paper, ask the class whether anyone thinks he could arrange the paper so that they could clap in 4s with no help from you.

Have another child draw the pattern for 4 on the board with no help from you | | | | | | |.

Have the class clap and say "1-2-3-4," etc., aloud, accenting and clapping hard on all 1s.

When the class has mastered the above, you may apply the knowledge in the upper figures of any time signatures by pointing out the relationship between the upper figures they see in their books (or from songs on board) and the clapping in 2s, 3s and 4s.

They will soon comprehend that if the upper figure of the time signature is 2, they clap in 2s—1-2, 1-2. If the upper figure is 3, they clap 1-2-3, 1-2-3, 1-2-3, etc.

Allow practice time for clapping music heard in various meter signatures.

Practice as follows: Clap or beat on the drum the three meters for the class to identify. Accented first beats should be fairly obvious in the beginning. The children answer orally or by going to the board and drawing the rhythm that you have clapped.

When the children are able to clap easily in 2s, 3s, and 4s, as suggested, have them clap first beats only and count the remaining beats softly to themselves, e.g., clap quiet, clap quiet (1, 2) or clap quiet quiet (1, 2, 3), etc.

Feeling for the 2-, 3-, and 4-beat meter may be enhanced through the use of body movement. (See Chapter 8, Experiences in Movement.)

IN UPPER GRADES

In teaching time signatures in the upper grades (as in the lower grades), the meaning of the *upper figure* is taught first.

Call attention to the numbers that resemble a fraction at the beginning of any piece of music. They are located to the right of the key signature. Just as the sharps and flats are known as the "key signature" and tell us where to find *do*, so the numbers are known as the "time signature" and tell us what kind of time the music is written in.

The upper figure of the meter (or time) signature tells us the number of beats that we may expect to find in each measure of the song, while the lower figure tells us what kind of note will get one beat. (Avoid pursuing the lower figure any further at this time.)

Write the following time signatures on the board:

$$\frac{2}{4} \quad \frac{3}{4} \quad \frac{4}{4} \quad \frac{6}{8} \quad \frac{9}{8} \quad \frac{3}{2}$$

Have individual children indicate which is the upper figure in each of the signatures.

Q: If 2 is the upper figure of the meter signature of a song, how many beats must there be in every measure of that song?
A: Two beats in every measure.
Q: If 3 is the upper figure in the meter signature of a song, how many beats must there be in every measure of the song?
A: Three beats in every measure.

Write the following on the board:

$$\frac{2}{4} \quad \text{♩ ♩ ♩ ♩ ♩ ♩ ♩ 𝄽}$$

Have a child come to the board and mark the bar lines in the correct places for two beats in each measure.

Repeat the process with the following samples and other similar ones using 3, 4, 6, and 2 for upper figures. (Use only 4 for the lower figure at present. In making up your own, be sure that there are no beats left over.)

$$\frac{3}{4} \quad \text{♩. ♩ ♩ ♩ ♩ ♩ ♩ 𝄽 ♩ — 𝄽}$$
$$\frac{4}{4} \quad \text{♩ ♩ ♩ ♩ — ♩. ♩ 𝅝}$$
$$\frac{6}{4} \quad \text{♩ ♩ ♩ ♩ 𝅝 ♩ ♩ — ♩ ♩ ♩ ♩ 𝄽 𝄽 ♩}$$

Ask such questions as, "Could we have a whole note in $\frac{2}{4}$ time?" "Why not?" (Too many beats.) "What other kind of a note could we not have in $\frac{2}{4}$ time" (Dotted half.)

Have individual children come to the board and write designated numbers of measures in a given time signature using any of the rhythms previously studied.

$$(\text{♩, ♩, ♩., 𝅝, 𝄽, —})$$

It should be pointed out to the children that many times a song starts on some beat other than the first beat, which results in what appears to be an incomplete measure at the beginning of the song and another incomplete measure at the end. This is not actually the case, however, for when they add the two "incomplete" measures together, they will find that they total the required number of beats for one full measure according to the given time signature in that song.

This is also the proper time to teach the whole rest. A whole rest hangs from the fourth line of the staff. It is used to indicate a *complete measure* of rest; thus the number of beats that it receives is dependent upon the upper figure of the time signature, since that is the figure which indicates the number of beats for each measure.

When the class is familiar with the upper figure of the meter (or time) signature, put several meter signatures on the board as follows:

$$\frac{2}{4} \quad \frac{3}{4} \quad \frac{4}{4} \quad \frac{6}{4}$$

Tell the class that the *lower* figure is the one on the *bottom* of the two figures. Have individual children indicate which is the lower figure in each of the above meter signatures.

Tell the class that the lower figure of a meter signature tells us what *kind* of note will receive 1 beat.

In the meter signature $\frac{4}{4}$ the quarter note will receive 1 beat because the lower figure is 4.

Q: If a quarter note receives 1 beat, how many beats will each of the following notes and rests receive?

$\textstyle\unicode{x1D15E}$ (2)

$\textstyle\unicode{x1D15D}$ (4)

$\textstyle\unicode{x1D15E}.$ (3)

━ (2)

𝄽 (1)

♪ ($\tfrac{1}{2}$)

Q: In the meter signature $\frac{6}{8}$, which is the lower figure?

A: 8.

Q: What does this tell us?

A: That the eighth note will receive 1 beat in this meter.

Q: If the eighth note receives 1 beat, how many beats will each of the following notes and rests receive?

$\textstyle\unicode{x1D15F}.$ (3)

$\textstyle\unicode{x1D15F}$ (2)

$\textstyle\unicode{x1D15E}.$ (6)

𝄽 (2)

𝄾 (1)

Q: What does the lower figure in the meter signature $\frac{3}{2}$ tell us?

A: That the half note receives 1 beat.

Q: If the half note receives 1 beat, how many beats will each of the following receive?

$\textstyle\unicode{x1D15F}$ ($\tfrac{1}{2}$)

$\textstyle\unicode{x1D15F}.$ ($1\tfrac{1}{2}$)

$\textstyle\unicode{x1D15D}$ (2)

━ (1)

𝄽 ($\tfrac{1}{2}$)

Q: Explain what each of the following meter signatures means:

$$\frac{3}{4} \qquad \frac{6}{8}$$

A: In $\frac{3}{4}$ time there are 3 beats in every measure of any song containing this upper figure in the meter signature. Every quarter note gets 1 beat. The time values of all the other notes are based on this lower figure.

In $\frac{6}{8}$ there are 6 beats in every measure of any song containing this upper figure in the meter signature. Every eighth note gets 1 beat. The time values of all other notes in the song are based on this lower figure.

Have the class practice singing or chanting (on "ta" or some other syllable) the following rhythm drills. Caution them to watch meter signatures.

READING MUSIC FROM THE BOOKS

When the class has mastered many of the foregoing skills, they should have had enough new music-reading experiences to prepare them for further experiences in their music books. It is assumed, of course, that they have previously become friendly with their music books, having used them to sing songs with words and to engage in other musical activities suggested by the authors, e.g., observing main themes while listening to a recording.

In selecting songs for music reading, care should be taken that the melodic and rhythmic problems contained in the song are appropriate for the class, depending not only on their grade level but also on the children's previous music-reading experience.

According to the procedures suggested in this text, music reading from the book may be done as early as the second grade (in the latter half of the school year). Although some companies publish books for first grade children to use as part of a "readiness" program, they are not appropriate for actual music-reading purposes as discussed here.

The amount of appropriate music-reading material varies with different books. Some publishers put in very little. Others provide for a great deal more at graded levels—depending upon the philosophy of the authors regarding music reading. A few of the many series published for children's use contain sections specifically designated "Music Reading."

Using the procedures suggested herein for the teaching of basic skills for music reading, a teacher would need to select carefully the songs suitable for   143 practice in the desired skills. This means that when children attempt their *first* music-reading experience from the book, it should be one that is totally within their achievement level at the time so that they may be successful. Thus the teacher should select the simplest song he can find in the book for this initial music-reading experience—preferably one that is stepwise or one with very few and very easy skips. Songs in the book that are unsuitable for *reading* may be used as *rote* songs.

As the class masters each new melodic and rhythmic skill designated for the grade level, the skill should be applied in a music-reading experience. Children have "mastered" a skill when they can sing it at sight with reasonable accuracy as it occurs in a new song. Mastery does not mean merely reciting facts about it. No song containing an unfamiliar rhythmic or melodic problem should be attempted as a music-reading experience until the class has had sufficient practice in the necessary skills. *Three new music-reading experiences per week* are suggested as adequate to ensure a child's continuing growth in the ability to read music. These three experiences may consist of either singing three new songs with syllables or learning any of the basic skills indicated for the grade level.

When a teacher finds that his present music book is lacking in enough suitable music-reading material to meet the need, his only recourse is to use whatever songs in the book that he can, supplemented by more songs from the board or other sources. Whatever the source, it should be a *new* music-reading experience for practice each time—not a repetition of something previously sung with syllables, and certainly not something already learned with words.

PROCEDURE

When a child looks at a new song to be sung with syllables for the first time, he should be encouraged to try to grasp a *general* picture of it with just a brief glance. At this time he should note like and unlike phrases, meter signature, tempo, approximate range of the melody, etc. Later, his attention may be concentrated on the specifics, such as the syllable names and rhythm patterns.

The procedure for preparing a song for music reading from the books is the same as that given for preparing a song for music reading from the board (p. 133), except that the actual song that is prepared will now be sung with syllables from the *books* rather than from the board. The two preparatory devices remain the same:

1. *Rhythm drill* (on the board) in the rhythm of the song in the book that is to be sung with syllables. As the class masters the singing of new rhythms, their music-reading experiences from the books should include these rhythms.
2. *Melody practice* (on the board) in the key of the song in the book that is to be sung with syllables. All skips that will occur in the song should be practiced at this point. The well-prepared teacher has

previously noted what skips the song contains; thus when he begins his melody practice, he knows exactly what skips to practice and how to present them. *He does not sing either with the class or for them*, nor does he play the tune of the song for them to hear.

Following rhythm drill and melody practice, the class should proceed directly to the new music-reading experience (new song in the book with syllables). The two preparatory devices (rhythm drill and melody practice) should be left on the board while the children are attempting their new song with syllables so that if and when they make mistakes in either the rhythm or the melody, the teacher may return immediately to the practice material. *Using a portion of the song as a practice device should be avoided because it requires a child to be concerned with both melodic and rhythmic problems at the same time.*

The melodies of the two songs given below are frequently found in children's music texts, although the words may differ from book to book. "Twinkle, Twinkle, Little Star" contains only two skips; thus it is a good choice for an initial music-reading experience in the books. Appropriate preparatory devices for this particular song would be:

Rhythm drill

Melody practice scale

Practice skips: *do* to *sol* above
re to *sol* above

Twinkle, Twinkle, Little Star

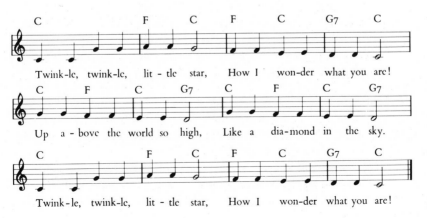

Twink-le, twink-le, lit-tle star, How I won-der what you are!

Up a-bove the world so high, Like a dia-mond in the sky.

Twink-le, twink-le, lit-tle star, How I won-der what you are!

Although "Vesper Hymn" contains more skips, they are simple ones, as are the rhythms. Appropriate preparatory devices for "Vesper Hymn" would be:

Rhythm drill

Melody practice scale

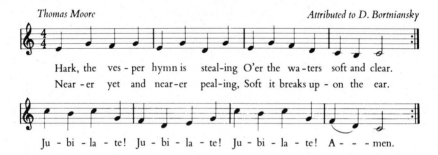

Practice skips: *mi–sol*
fa–re
re–sol
do–sol
do (low)—*do* (high)

Vesper Hymn

Thomas Moore   *Attributed to D. Bortniansky*

Hark, the ves - per hymn is steal-ing O'er the wa -ters soft and clear.
Near - er yet and near-er peal-ing, Soft it breaks up - on the ear.

Ju - bi - la - te! Ju - bi - la - te! Ju - bi - la - te! A - - - men.

CREDIT: From Musicianship for the Elementary Teacher, *by Anne Pierce and Neal Glenn. McGraw-Hill, © 1967. Used by permission.*

When rhythm drill and melody practice have been done and the proper page number of the song for the day has been given, the following may prove helpful in realizing a more successful music-reading experience:

1. Ask the children to put their books flat on their desks and their fingers under the notes and to keep their eyes on the books. It's harder to find a lost place in music than in word reading.

2. Tell class that *do* in their books is just where it was on the board. This requires that they find the line or space in their books that corresponds to the one on the board (melody practice) on which the X is placed. Once the class has learned to find *do* with sharps and flats, eliminate the X and use the appropriate key signature in the melody practice (i.e., key signature of the song in the book that they are going to sing with syllables). Avoid asking every time where *do* is; otherwise many children will not bother trying to find it for themselves, since they'll assume that eventually they'll be told anyway. When songs in the books do not start on *do*, help should be given in the form of well-directed questions to enable the children to discover the starting note for themselves. This may involve a few discussions when the problem is new, but it will ensure that the class gets started on the right syllable (as well as *independently*) in the future.

3. Have the class study. This could be the moment of truth for both you and the child. Has the child learned through all his previous experience in this area how to sum up a general total picture of a song mentally? Can he identify the starting note, estimate the range of the melody, deduce the meaning of the meter signature, recognize like phrases at a glance, and have some vague idea of which notes will be faster than others? Can he comprehend given symbols such as repeat signs, holds, etc., as they occur? "Study" means all these things, as well as trying to hear how the tune will sound as he thinks the names of the syllables over to himself, using the tonic-chord skips for reference.

It is helpful if you walk around the room to check progress while the children are studying. You should prepare yourself for a few surprises, however. One child will have the wrong page, another will have the right page but the wrong song, and still another will have the wrong book. He never heard that it was time for music.

Despite all the above verbosity, *the study period should be brief.*

4. Sound *do* with the pitch pipe, your voice, or a melody instrument. Have the class sing the *do*, give the command "Sing!" and have the class proceed to sing the whole song from the book. For songs not starting on *do*, see p. 136. If the song is excessively long, sing only a few lines.

5. If the singing with the syllables goes well, have the children hold their books in an upright position and try singing the words. Eventually, children in upper grades may be expected to sing the words and melody of any new song immediately, without first singing the syllables, if they have been "brought up" on the procedures suggested in this text. They simply learn to "think" the tune with syllables as they sing the words.

The above procedure is the same for all grade levels. Only the content of the songs will vary.

Under this plan there is no necessity for teaching the names of the lines and spaces and/or the names of keys unless the teacher plans to have the class play instruments or engage in some other musical activity that would require this knowledge—in which case there would be *application* for this information and a reason for teaching it. Of course, if a teacher feels strongly about teaching line and space names, he should certainly go ahead with it, provided that his class has met the minimal requirements for independent music reading at their grade level. The reason for the omission of this skill, especially in lower grades, is that children do not really understand what they are saying when they answer that a song is in the key of G or A or that the lines are E G B D F unless they are studying an instrument either privately or in the classroom. Without some kind of performance, there is simply no application, and teaching without application is not justifiable. Furthermore, there appears to be no valid proof that knowledge of line and space names contributes significantly to improved vocal music reading. When children sing syllables, they are not conscious of being in any particular key by letter name; rather, they feel only the general "tonality" of the song—how *do* should sound and how the other tones of the scale relate to the sound of *do*, for example.

Please do not talk a song to death before a child even has a chance to look at it. There is no need for children to give the name of the key, the number of sharps, the time signature, and the name of each note before they sing a song. This is unmusical and time consuming, as well as tedious. Occasional games for more practice in basic skills are very acceptable and may often serve a purpose. Otherwise, children will learn much more about these things through *singing* than through *talking* about them.

Reminder: Please limit the music-reading and skills practice to five to seven minutes in any given twenty-minute music period.

The following devices have been found helpful in this area:

1. Using flash cards for desired practice material:
   Ex: Locating *do* with X.

   Ex: Individual singing of simple melodies by pupils.

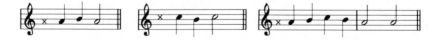

   Progress to more difficult skips and rhythms as they are introduced.
2. Having the children draw pictures of tunes that you play or sing. These should be short (five or six tones only) and may be represented by either straight lines or curved lines to show their direction. (These need not be on the staff at first, but they may be transposed to the staff eventually to show the children that when a tune goes higher, it moves toward the *top* of the staff.)
3. Putting syllables to simple tunes that you play or sing. These should start on *do* and proceed stepwise at first. Later they may be expanded

to include skips as they are introduced. Keep these very short—four or five tones.

4. Giving melodic dictation in upper grades, if desired. (See Chapter 4, Ear Training Experiences.)

TEACHING FINDING DO WITH SHARPS

1. Tell class that as they look at some of their songs, they often see a group of symbols just to the right of the G clef. These symbols may be either sharps (show sharp symbol ♯) or flats (show flat symbol ♭). For now, we shall be concerned only with the sharps.

2. There may be as few as *one* sharp (show key signature with one sharp)

 or as many as seven sharps (show key signature of seven

sharps) by adding to the previous signature of

one sharp until there are seven in all.

NOTE TO TEACHER: Place the sharps on the treble clef in the following order (each sharp placed slightly to the right of the previous one). Any other order is incorrect:

  a. F (fifth line)
  b. C (third space)
  c. G (first space above the staff)
  d. D (fourth line)
  e. A (second space)
  f. E (fourth space)
  g. B (third line)

On the bass clef, the letter names remain the same, but the line and space locations will differ accordingly. (See Appendix A, p. 331.)

3. Tell class that this group of sharps is known as a *key signature*. It tells us many things about the song, including where to find *do*.

4. Ask class to look at the sharp way over to the right, the one that is the farthest from the G clef. This is known as the *last* sharp and is the one which will serve as our signpost on the road to finding *do*.

5. Have the class practice finding the location of the last sharp (by ("third line," "fourth space," etc., *not* by letter name of the line or space) in selected key signatures. This may be done by erasing one sharp at a time from the seven-sharp signature shown in step 2 or by using prepared flash cards containing selected sharp key signatures.

6. Tell the class that the last sharp is always on *ti*. Have them practice finding *ti* using selected sharp signatures. The sharps that were previously erased in the seven-sharp signature in step 2 may now be replaced one at a time to facilitate this practice, or prepared flash cards may again be used.

7. When finding *ti* has been mastered, point out that *do* always lies immediately above *ti* on either a line or space, depending on the location of *ti*. Illustrate with an example showing the position of *do* when *ti* is on a *line*, then with another example showing the position of *do* when *ti* is on a *space*.

8. Practice finding *do* from the board or flash cards using selected key signatures.

   NOTE TO TEACHER: When signatures of one and three sharps are shown, proceed as above, showing *do* in its proper place immediately *above ti*. However, indicate to the children that since they will seldom be singing notes that are written above the staff, it is better to locate the *do* on the staff. Thus, when finding *do* in these two key signatures, suggest that they count *down* from *ti* to locate *do* on the staff. Remind them that they must be sure to include all the notes of the *descending scale* from *ti* (*la, sol, fa* etc.) when counting down to *do*. In the signature

   of three sharps, for example 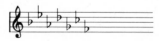 *do* would fall on the second

   space when counted *down* correctly from *ti*.

9. Tell class that when they see no key signature at all next to the G clef, they have to remember that *do* is on the third space (or on the first line below the staff, if you prefer).

   Once the children have learned to find *do* with sharps, their music-reading experiences should be chosen, whenever possible, from those which contain sharps in the key signature.

   In music-reading experiences written in sharp keys, eliminate the use of the X for locating *do* in the melody practice scale (see p. 147) and substitute the sharp key signature appropriate for the song.

   There is no necessity for asking children to locate *do* by the letter name of the line or space, nor of expecting them to name the *keys*.

TEACHING FINDING DO WITH FLATS

The procedure is the same as for finding *do* with sharps, with the following exceptions:

1. The *placement* of the flats on the treble clef. The following order should be observed. Any other order is incorrect.

   a. B (third line)
   b. E (fourth space)
   c. A (second space)
   d. D (fourth line)
   e. G (second line)
   f. C (third space)
   g. F (first space)

On the bass clef, the letter names remain the same, but the line and space location will differ accordingly. (See Appendix A, p. 331.)

2. The *name* of the last flat. The last flat is always on *fa*, which makes it easy to remember because it begins with the same letter as the word "flat."

3. The *counting direction*. We count *down* (*fa, mi, re, do*) from the last flat. (Some flat key signatures lend themselves to counting either up *or* down, but children should be reminded that if they choose to count *up*, the progression must be *fa-sol-la-ti-do*, the *ascending* scale progression. Many children make the mistake of using the same syllables to count up as they use to count down.)

Once the children have learned to find *do* with flats, their music-reading experiences should be chosen, whenever possible, from those which contain flats in the key signature. In music-reading experiences written in flat keys, eliminate the use of the X for locating *do* in the melody practice scale (see p. 147) and substitute the flat key signature appropriate for the song.

There is no necessity for asking children to locate *do* by the letter name of the line or space, nor of expecting them to name the *keys*.

TEACHING MINOR AND MAJOR MODES

A "mode" in music is simply a specified arrangement of whole and half steps. The "major" mode has one arrangement, while the "minor" mode has another. (There are other modes besides these, of course, but the discussion here will be limited to just the major and minor modes.) As these different arrangements are utilized in various musical compositions, the resulting sounds enable an experienced listener to designate the composition heard as "major" or "minor."

It is often said that all minor music sounds sad. There are too many exceptions, however, for this statement to stand as a generalization, although it is true that we are conscious of a different feeling when we listen to music in the minor mode. Children sometimes say that it sounds "darker."

There are several ways of introducing the minor mode to children. It is up to the teacher to choose the best way for his particular class and to determine which is the "teachable" moment. If the children happen to be singing a song (with syllables) that end on *la*, skillful questioning by the teacher will help them discover that:

1. There is something different about the song.
2. The difference occurs in the melody.
3. The difference in the melody occurs at the end of the song.
4. The ending note is *la* instead of the usual *do, mi,* or *sol*.

When a song ends on *la*, we say that it is in the minor mode—as opposed to songs in the major mode, which usually end on *do, mi,* or *sol*. Children can

151

find minor songs for themselves by sight merely by looking in their textbooks for those which end on *la*. Sometimes they will also discover that the chromatic syllables *fi* and *si* (see "Introducing Chromatic Tones," p. 163) occur in many songs, indicating that the song is in a special *kind* of minor. (See "Minor Scales," Appendix A, p. 338.)

The minor mode may also be discovered by sound. If the teacher is familiar with major and minor chords on the piano, he might play them for the class, asking them to try to discover the difference in the sound of the two modes. (Any major chord may be converted to a minor chord simply by *lowering* the *third* of the chord a half step. See "Piano Chording," p. 214.) If there is no piano available or if the teacher feels more comfortable with the Autoharp, this is an excellent way to demonstrate major and minor chords to children. The chord names on the bars of the Autoharp indicate whether the chords are major or minor.

As the children's ears become somewhat more attuned to the sounds that characterize the differences between the two modes, they will enjoy identifying major and minor compositions in whole or in part from records.

They will also enjoy singing minor songs—many of which have strong appeal for children. "Hey, Ho! Nobody Home,"★ "Coventry Carol" (*Making Music Your Own*, Book 6, Silver Burdett), "Fum Fum Fum" (*Music around the World*, Silver Burdett), and "Minka" (*Making Music Your Own*, Book 6) are but a few of the favorites. Choices of listening selections in the minor include "In the Hall of the Mountain King" (Grieg), "March of the Three Kings" (Bizet), and "Wild Horseman" (Schumann).

Children should be reminded that a large musical work may often include the word "major" or "minor" as part of its title.

INTRODUCING EIGHTH NOTES

NOTE: Do not introduce eighth notes until the class has mastered music-reading songs containing ♩, ♩, ♩., 𝅝, 𝄽, ▬ .

Eighth notes may be introduced in any one of the several ways (or combinations thereof) listed below. Whichever one seems most appropriate for the class and/or most comfortable for the teacher should be chosen. Whatever method of introduction is used, the eventual outcomes should be the same:

1. The ability to recognize eighth notes by sight and sound.
2. The ability to sing *independently* many songs at sight containing eighth notes, with syllables and words.

USING LINE NOTATION

1. Draw long lines on the board to represent quarter notes, and short lines to represent eighth notes:

_____   _____   ___ ___   _____

★ See Song Index.

2. Have the children chant, "long, long, short, short, long", etc., giving proper relative time values to long and short lines. (Long lines are sung twice as long as short lines.)

3. Put two eighth notes on the board (♪ ♪). Tell the class that:

    a. These are eighth notes. Each eighth note has a stem and one flag. When there is more than one note they are sometimes written with a bar instead of a flag (♫).

    b. The stems may go up or down (♪ ♪ ♪ ♪ ♫ ♫)

    c. *Two* eighth notes must be sung in the time it ordinarily takes to sing *one* quarter note; thus we must sing eighth notes *twice* as fast as we sing quarter notes.

4. Have the class discover what kind of notes (eighths or quarters) should be placed over the long and short lines to correspond to the time value; then indicate them as follows:

Have the class say the words "quarter, quarter, eighth, eighth, quarter" as they occur over the lines.

5. Remove the lines and have the class chant from notes only, "quarter, quarter, eighth, eighth, quarter."

6. Have the class chant the rhythm of the quarter note on "ta" or another similar syllable and the eighth notes on a different word, such as "tee," for example.

7. Have the class sing the rhythm on "doo," "loo," or another neutral syllable. Be sure to establish tempo and a steady beat by counting at least one measure out loud (1-2-3-4) before beginning the first line. Some teachers find it helpful to have the children beat the meter quietly with one hand or tap it quietly with one foot while speaking or singing the rhythms indicated. Each tap of the foot or beat of the hand would represent a quarter note or *one* beat.

8. Try other combinations of long and short lines such as the following, using the same chanting and singing procedure as above:

    a. ―――― ―― ―― ―――― ――――
    b. ―――― ―――― ―― ―― ―― ――
    c. ―― ―― ―――― ―― ―― ――――.

9. Apply in rhythm drill (see p. 155). These may be first translated into long and short lines for preliminary practice.

10. Apply in new music-reading experiences containing eighth notes, in simple board melodies first (see p. 156) and then in books.

USING WORD PATTERNS

1. Remind the children that spoken language may be rhythmical (as well as musical) and that it is often possible to fit musical rhythms to

word patterns. These word patterns sometimes help us to remember what the rhythm sounds like when we meet it. When choosing suitable subject matter for word patterns, the closest to home, of course, is the child's name; however, there are many other possibilities, depending on what happens to be under study in some other area of the curriculum at the moment. A few examples are listed below.

2. Once the names have been clapped and then translated into long and short sounds, they may be put on the board in the proper notation of quarter and eighth notes. For variety, the teacher or a child can clap the name of another child in the class to see whether the others can guess what it is. This might be followed by having the children try to think of others in the class whose names have the same succession of sounds. It is also helpful to incorporate body movement into this activity, as well as to use homemade rhythm instruments (shakers and beaters) to sound the patterns of the names before they are notated, and then to read them from notation:

	♫ ♩	♩ ♩	♫ ♫	♩ ♫
Names:	Mary Ann	John Blake	Judy Jacobs	Joy Harris
Places:	Riverbed	Swanee	Mississippi	Grand Canyon
Food:	Apple pie	Hot dog	Maple walnut	Black coffee
Flowers:	Daffodils	Sweet peas	Lady slipper	White orchid

3. For our purposes, the longer sounds will be represented by quarter notes, and the shorter sounds by eighth notes, as previously suggested. At this point, proceed as was suggested in item 3 under "Using Line Notation," p. 152.

4. Apply in various rhythm drills (see p. 155). These may be translated into word notation for preliminary practice. The children may choose the word phrases they feel will help them remember best.

5. Apply in new music-reading experiences containing eighth notes in simple melodies first (see p. 156) and then in books.

6. For practice, clap (or have individual children clap) four-beat patterns for the class to identify:

Pattern clapped: ♩ ♩ ♪ ♪ ♩

Answer: Quarter, quarter, eighth, eighth, quarter.

OTHER APPROACHES

1. If desired, pictured objects in large and small sizes may be used to introduce long and short sounds, e.g.,

The class may clap or chant on "ta," or other similar sound, the rhythm pattern shown by the order of the pictures—long sound for large size, short sound for small size, etc. Use any appropriate subject matter for drawings. Translate the pictures into long and short lines and then proceed as in item 3 under "Using Line Notation," p. 152. This is known as "picture notation."

2. If you prefer, simply sing, chant, or play the rhythm of a group of eighth notes for the class, taking care to *stress* the first note of each group of two eighth notes:

Then have the class sing the rhythm played and respond with facts about it (two equal tones to one beat, etc.). Then you may proceed as in item 3 under "Using Line Notation" (p. 152), through rhythm drills, simple melodies from the board, and music reading from the books.

Rhythm Drills for Eighth Notes

Pitch on Bb, G, or A. Have the class sing or chant on "doo" or "ta."

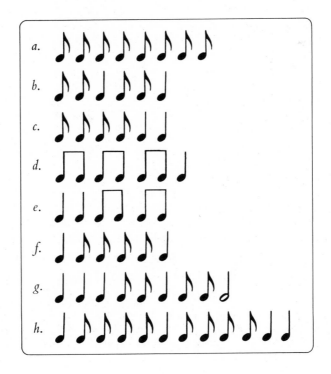

Simple Melodies Using Eighth Notes*

(Arranged in order of difficulty)

When first introducing music-reading experiences containing eighth notes in the book, use melodically simple songs such as the following (be sure to prepare each song as suggested above—through rhythm drill and melody practice appropriate for the given song):

---

* Precede each melody with rhythm drill in the rhythm of the melody and melody practice in the key of the melody (see p. 153). The singing of these and other similar practice melodies should *precede* any music-reading experiences in the book with eighth notes.

Taffy

Traditional

Taf-fy was a Welsh-man, Taf-fy was a thief, Taf-fy came to our house and

stole a leg of beef; I went to Taf-fy's house, Taf-fy was in bed,

I took a mar-row bone and hit him on the head. (*Thump*)

CREDIT: *By special permission of the publishers, Holt, Rinehart and Winston. From Book 1, Exploring Music series,* © *1966.*

Rhythm drill for "Taffy":

Melody practice scale for "Taffy":

Practice skip: high *do* to low *do*

INTRODUCING DOTTED QUARTER AND EIGHTH NOTES

NOTE: Do not introduce dotted quarter and eighth notes until the class has mastered:

1. Have the class sing the first line of "America."
2. Write "'tis of thee" on the board.
   In a slow tempo sing or chant just these three words, stressing the pulsation on the last part of the word "'tis." Have class repeat, also stressing the pulsation.
3. Show proper notation over the words:

'tis of thee

157

4. Sing again for class, pointing to each note as it is sung, again stressing the pulsation on " 'tis" when. pointing to the dot. Have the class repeat, while you point as before.

5. Ask if anyone knows the word for what you were doing to the dot when singing the word " 'tis." (Class should be familiar with the term "pulsate" from previous experience with other notes (p. 127); thus they should have no difficulty in making this identification.

6. Point out that this pulsation, however, is of shorter duration than the others which they have been used to singing in the past (on the half note, dotted half note and whole note). It is, in fact, of the same duration as an eighth note. Put the following on the board:

Have class sing or chant on a neutral syllable ("doo", "loo," "ta," etc.). Have them recall the number of beats which each eighth note should receive.

7. Tie the first two notes together:

Sing or chant it for them, stressing the pulsation on the tied eighth note. Have class repeat. Ask them to deduce how long the pulsation should have been. ($\frac{1}{2}$ beat.)

8. Write the dotted quarter and eighth note rhythm pattern below the appropriate tied notes as follows:

Tell class that the dot will substitute for the tied eighth note; thus the time value as well as the sound will be the same. Have class sing the rhythm pattern above, pulsating the dot as it occurs.

9. Go back to the words " 'tis of thee" with the rhythm pattern shown over them (step 3). Have class sing.

10. Ask class if they can think of other portions of the song "America" which have a similar sounding rhythm pattern ("liberty," "fathers died," "Pilgrim's pride," "mountainside"). Write out each with proper notation over the syllables as shown in " 'tis of thee."

11. Tell class that this rhythm is made up of a dotted quarter note and an eighth note. It equals two beats altogether. Because the tones are *unequal* (one long, the other short) the rhythm is classed as an "uneven" rhythm, as opposed to two eighth notes, for example, which are *equal* and therefore classed as an "even" rhythm.

12. Use this rhythm in combination with other familiar rhythms in rhythm drills as follows:

Rhythm Drills for Dotted Quarter and Eighth Notes

Pitch on B♭, G, or A. Have the class sing on "doo," "loo," "ta," or a similar sound.

13. Use the rhythm in simple melodies such as the following:

Simple Melodies Using Dotted Quarter and Eighth Notes*
(Arranged in order of difficulty)

14. Apply in books in music-reading songs containing the dotted quarter and eighth note rhythm pattern. Use melodically simple songs at first. NOTE TO TEACHER: You may feel that this is an appropriate place to discuss the way in which the time value of any given note can be increased through the addition of a dot. (See Appendix A, Review of Fundamentals, pp. 341–342.)

---

* Precede each melody with rhythm drill in the rhythm of the melody and melody practice in the key of the melody (see p. 133). The singing of these and other similar melodies should precede any music-reading experiences from the book containing the dotted quarter and eighth note rhythm pattern.

INTRODUCING SIXTEENTH NOTES

Sixteenth notes are less frequently found in children's music texts than other rhythms; however, since they do occur, it might be helpful to be prepared to give children some practice with them.

The procedures suggested for teaching eighth notes may be applied to the teaching of sixteenth notes also, with variations to accommodate the speed and the number of notes, of course:

1. Assuming that the unit of beat is the quarter note, in the study of eighth notes it was found that *one* beat should accommodate *two* tones of equal time value. When singing sixteenth notes, one beat must now accommodate *four* tones of equal time value. Obviously, this means that the notes must go still faster and will be divided into four equal parts. If the *line notation* is used as it was with eighth notes, then the short lines to represent the sixteenth notes will be even shorter than those used to represent the eighth notes—half the size, to be exact.

2. When word patterns are used, new word combinations must be created as aids in remembering. Get a steady beat going with the hand or foot, set the tempo, and then chant the following word phrases:

a. teeny-weeny alligator

b. elevator   escalator

c. Cinerama

d. radiator

Combining sixteenth notes with quarter notes and eighth notes will help establish the time relationship:

e. alligator   hedgehog

f. Tom Sawyer Huckleberry Finn

160

g. elevator   door

3. Whatever the approach used to introduce sixteenth notes, the outcomes should be the same:
   a. The children should know how sixteenth notes sound and that they are *four equal tones to one beat.*
   b. The children should know how sixteenth notes look (two flags or sometimes two bars across when there is more than one note).
   c. The children should be able to sing them independently as they occur in any given music-reading experience.
4. Sixteenth notes do not always appear in groups of four. They are sometimes combined with eighth notes in patterns such as:

   Each of these combinations totals one beat—divided into one long tone and two short, but *equal,* tones.
5. A sixteenth note may also follow a dotted eighth note to produce an *uneven* skipping rhythm in which the first tone is longer than the second:

   Together the two notes equal *one* beat.
6. Use sixteenth notes in rhythm drills as follows: Pitch B♭, G, or A. Set the tempo by a steady beat with the hand or foot and then chant or sing.

Rhythm Drills Using Sixteenth Notes

etc.

7. Apply in simple melodies such as the following:

Simple Practice Melodies Using Sixteenth Notes*

etc.

8. Apply in books in music-reading songs containing sixteenth notes. Use melodically simple songs at first.
9. Try "Talkin' Blues" for fun and practice on this rhythm. Strum chords on the Autoharp or guitar or use for accompaniment, if desired.

Talkin' Blues

Most blues are slow, melancholy jazz songs; but this is a "talkin' blues." The words are chanted in a rhythmic "sing-song" while chords are strummed on a guitar or banjo.

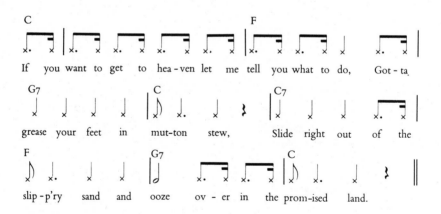

CREDIT: *By special permission of the publishers, Holt, Rinehart and Winston. From Book 6, Exploring Music series, © 1966.*

---

* Precede each melody with rhythm drill in the rhythm of the melody and melody practice in the key of the melody (see p. 133). The singing of these and other similar melodies should precede any music-reading experiences from the books containing sixteenth notes.

INTRODUCING CHROMATIC TONES

NOTE TO TEACHERS: The length of this portion of music-reading experiences requires that it be divided into several lessons. Furthermore, the nature of the material is such that it may require more time for presentation than is evident at first glance. Hopefully, when covering this material, some misconceptions regarding chromatic tones may be dispelled: (1) that all the black keys on the piano are chromatic tones (this is true *only* in the key of C), and (2) that the notes which are sharped or flatted in a key signature are chromatic tones. (Since *chromatic tones* are defined as those which *do not belong to a given key or scale*, the notes which are sharped or flatted in the key signature are *not* chromatic tones because they *do belong* to the given key.)

There is very little music-reading material in the children's books which is simple enough for beginning practice on chromatic tones. Thus it becomes necessary to supplement from other sources if sufficient practice on each of the skills is to be provided.

PROCEDURES

1. *Chromatic Tones a Half Step Higher*

   a. At some time previous to the presentation of this lesson, ask your class to express their ideas on the place of *color* in their total environment.
   b. At the time chromatic tones are to be introduced, recall the color discussion and relate it to music by telling the class that music also needs touches of color. One of the ways in which we achieve color in music is through the use of "chromatic tones." These chromatic tones serve to make a piece of music more interesting melodically, just as variations in rhythm make music more interesting rhythmically. A "chromatic tone" may be defined as one which is not native to a given scale or key.* The notes of the major scale are *do-re-mi-fa-sol-la-ti* and, as such, are called "scale tones." When we see a plain, unadorned note on any line or space within the text of a song, we can safely assume that it is a scale tone and will be called by one of the scale tone names. *Chromatic tones*, on the other hand, are frequently identified by the presence of an accompanying symbol known as a "chromatic sign." These chromatic signs may be any one of the following:

   ♯   a sharp
   ♭   a flat
   ♮   a natural (also called a "cancel")

   c. The presence of any one of these three signs before a note is our clue that the note is being altered in some way. Whether the

---

* Notes which are sharped or flatted in a key signature are *not* chromatic tones because they *do* belong to the given key.

163

alteration results in the scale tone being sounded a half step higher
or a half step lower, is determined by two factors:

1. Which chromatic sign is used.
2. Whether the note which the chromatic sign affects is
   sharped or flatted (or neither) in the key signature of the
   given song.

d. Put the following on the board and have the class sing:

Ask whether they think the notes in the melody should be called
scale tones or chromatic tones. Place a sharp immediately before
fa as shown in the following melody.

e. Tell the class that the addition of the sharp before *fa* changes the
    scale tone *fa* into a chromatic tone a half step higher, since in this
    melody *fa* was neither sharped nor flatted in the key signature.
    The presence of a chromatic sign before a note not only alters the
    sound of the note, but also changes the syllable name by which it
    is called. In the melody above, placing the sharp before *fa* will
    change its name to *fi*. The name *fi* is obtained by taking the first
    letter of the scale tone *fa* and adding an *i* (pronounced "ee"),
    making *fi* (pronounced "fee"). Have the class sing the melody.

f. Try a few other melodies in different sharp keys, using *fi* in simple
    chromatic progressions such as the following:

g. Write the following melody on the board and ask the class what
    they will call the third note in the melody when they come to it.
    (*Fi*):

Point out that the fourth note has no sharp directly before it, but
that we call it *fi*, nevertheless, because it is affected by the sharp of
the previous note, which is on the same space in the same measure.
The fourth note would *not* be affected if it were in a different
measure or on a different line or space than the third note. Have
class sing the melody above.

164

h. Write the following melody on the board:

Inform the class that when we see a natural sign (♮) in front of this note when it reoccurs in the same measure, we know that it has returned to its original state of being a scale tone, and we must call it *fa* again when we sing it. A natural sign occurring in this way removes the effect of the previous chromatic sign, which was a *sharp* in this case. Have class sing the melody above.

i. For practice in singing *fi* in sharp key signatures, and the natural of the same, try a few melodies such as the following:

j. Although the children will rarely encounter a double sharp in their music books, it may be shown here, if desired:

1. Tell class that when *fa* is already sharped in the key signature, the chromatic tone *fi* a half step higher is indicated through the use of a double sharp (✗). Show the following melody. Have class sing:

2. A natural and a sharp must be used to make it *fa* again. Show the following melody. Have class sing:

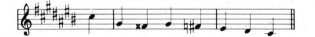

k. Tell the class that a sharp is not the only chromatic sign which will transform a scale tone into a chromatic tone a half step higher. Write the following on the board:

Remind the class that when they see a chromatic sign before a note in a song, they should refer back to the key signature of that song to see whether the note has been sharped or flatted (or neither) in the key signature. Call attention to the key signature of the melody above. Note that one of the flats falls on the *fa* space. Tell class that when this occurs, the chromatic tone a half step higher is indicated not by a sharp, as before, but by a natural sign (♮). **165**

l. Write the following melody on the board:

Have class name the third note correctly (*fi*) and sing the melody.

m. Tell class that like other chromatic signs, the natural sign affects all the notes that follow within the given measure that are on the same line or space as the chromatic tone. Write the following melodies on the board and have the class sing:

n. If, however, we see a flat in front of the note when it reoccurs in the same measure (as in the melodies below), we know that it has returned to its original state of being a scale tone. Write the following melodies on the board and have the class sing:

o. For practice in singing *fi* in flat key signatures, try a few melodies such as the following:

p. Ask class to recall how the chromatic tone *fi* got its name. (Add *i* to first letter of scale tone *fa*.)
Tell class that all chromatic tones a half step higher than the scale tones are named in the same manner—by simply taking the first letter of the scale tone and adding *i* (pronounced "ee"). Thus, *re*,

for example, altered to sound a half step higher would become the chromatic tone *ri*. Have the class name the others (see Naming Chromatic Tones, p. 171). Have class practice identifying and singing chromatic tones a half step higher in melodies such as the following:

The following progressions may be used for practice also. Have class sing first from the notes as written below, then from notation on the staff:

Starting pitch D   *do re mi ri mi fa mi fa sol fi sol la si la ti li ti do*
(1st space below staff)   *ti do re di re do*

Starting pitch D   *do ti do ti li ti la si la sol fi sol fa mi fa mi ri mi re di re do*
(fourth line)

Starting pitch Middle C   *do di re ri mi fa fi sol si la li ti do*

2. *Chromatic Tones a Half Step Lower*

   NOTE: It is suggested that the teaching of Chromatic Tones a Half Step Higher (pp. 163–167) precede the teaching of those a half step lower; thus, we may assume that children are already familiar with certain facts concerning chromatic tones in general. It is upon this assumption that the procedures which follow are based.

   a. Put the following melody on the board:

   Ask the class if they can identify these notes as scale tones or chromatic tones.

   b. Place a flat immediately before *ti* as shown in the melody below:

   Tell the class that the addition of the flat before *ti* changes the scale tone into a chromatic tone a half step *lower*, because in this melody *ti* was neither sharped nor flatted in the key signature. **167**

The presence of the chromatic sign before *ti* here not only alters its sound, but also changes the syllable name by which it is called. In the melody above, placing the flat before *ti* will change its name to *te*. The name *te* is obtained by taking the first letter of the scale tone *ti* and adding an *e* (pronounced "ay"), making *te* (pronounced "tay"). Have class sing the melody.

c. Try a few other melodies with simple chromatic progressions using *te*, such as the following:

d. Put the following melody on the board:

Ask the class to look at the third measure and indicate what they would call the second note in that measure (*te*). Point out that the fourth note in that measure has no flat directly before it, but that we must call it *te*, nevertheless, because it is affected by the flat of the *second* note which is on the same space in the same measure. The fourth note would *not* be affected if it were in a different measure or on a different line or space than the second note. Have the class sing the melody above, noting *te* in the second measure also.

e. Put the following melody on the board:

Inform the class that if we should see a natural sign (♮) in front of this same note when it reoccurs in the same measure, then we know that it has returned to its original state of being a scale tone and we must call it *ti* again when we sing it. A natural sign occurring in this way removes the effect of the previous chromatic sign—which was a flat, in this case. Have class sing the melody above.

f. For practice in singing *te* in flat key signatures and the natural of the same, try a few melodies such as the following:

168

g. Although the children will rarely encounter a double flat in their music books, it may be shown here, if desired:

  1. Tell class that when *ti* is already flatted in the key signature, the chromatic *te* a half step lower is indicated through the use of a double flat (♭♭).

  2. A natural and a flat must be used to make the note *ti* again.

h. Tell class that a flat is not the only sign which will convert a scale tone into a chromatic tone a half step lower. Write the following melody on the board:

Remind the class that when they see a chromatic sign before a note in a song, they should always refer back to the key signature of the song to see whether the note has been sharped or flatted (or neither) in the key signature. Call attention to the key signature in this melody. Note that one of the sharps falls on the *ti* space. Tell the class that when this occurs, the chromatic tone a half step lower is indicated not by a flat, but by a natural sign (♮).

i. Write the following melody on the board:

Have class give correct name of chromatic tones and sing the melody.

j. Like other chromatic signs, the natural affects all the notes that follow in the given measure that are on the same line or space as the chromatic tone. Write the following melody on the board and have the class sing.

k. If, however, we see a *sharp* in front of the note when it reoccurs in the same measure (as in the melody below), we know that it has returned to its original state of being a scale tone, and we must call it *ti* again. Have class sing the following:

l. Have class practice a few melodies containing *te* in sharp key signatures such as the following:

m. Ask the class to recall how *te* got its name. (Add *e* to first letter of scale tone *ti*.) Tell the class that all chromatic tones a half step lower than the scale tone are named in the same manner. We simply take the first letter of the scale tone and add *e* (pronounced "ay"). Thus *mi* altered to sound a half step lower would become the chromatic tone *me* (pronounced "may"). Have the class name the others (see Naming Chromatic Tones, p. 171). Note that since *re* already has the "ay" sound, it becomes "rah".

n. Have class practice identifying and singing chromatic tones a half step lower in melodies such as the following:

o. For additional practice, have the class sing the following progressions, first from the notes as written below, then from notation on the staff:

Starting pitch low E♭   *do re mi fa sol le sol la te la ti do ti do*

Starting pitch high E♭   *do ti la te la te la sol le sol fa mi re do*

Starting pitch D fourth line   *do ti te la le sol se fa mi me re rah do*

	SCALE TONE	CHROMATIC TONES A HALF STEP LOWER (Read *down*)
	do	↓
li	*ti*	→ *te*
si	*la*	→ *le*
fi	*sol*	→ *se*
	fa	
ri	*mi*	→ *me*
di	*re*	→ *rah*
	do	

(Read *up*)

CHROMATIC TONES
A HALF STEP
HIGHER

Ascending progression: *do di re ri mi fa fi sol si la li ti do*

Descending progression *do ti te la le sol se fa mi me re rah do*

CHROMATIC SUMMARY

CHROMATIC TONES A HALF STEP HIGHER

1. The *left-hand* column in the chart below indicates what has (or has not) been done to any given note in the key signature of a given song.
2. The *middle* column indicates what chromatic sign would be required to represent a chromatic tone a half step *above* the note.
3. The *right-hand* column indicates what sign would be needed to erase the effect of the previous chromatic sign.

a. If the note in the key signature has been:	*b.* The chromatic tone a half step above will be indicated by:	*c.* The effect of the chromatic sign would be erased by:
1. Unaltered in any way	→ ♯ (sharp)	→ ♮ (natural)
2. ♭ (flatted)	→ ♮ (natural)	→ ♭ (flat)
3. ♯ (sharped)	→ 𝄪 (double sharp)	→ ♮♯ (natural *and* sharp)

CHROMATIC TONES A HALF STEP LOWER

1. The *left-hand* column in the chart below indicates what has (or has not) been done to any given note in the key signature of a given song.

171

2. The *middle column* indicates what chromatic sign would be needed to represent a chromatic tone a half step *below* the note.
3. The *right-hand* column indicates what sign would be needed to erase the effect of the previous chromatic sign.

a. If the note in the key signature has been:	*b.* The chromatic tone a half step below will be indicated by:	*c.* The effect of the chromatic sign would be erased by
A. Unaltered in any way ——→	♭ (flat) ————————→	♮ (natural)
B. ♯ (sharped) ——→	♮ (natural) ————————→	♯ (sharp)
C. ♭ (flatted) ——→	♭♭ (double flat) ——→	♮♭ (natural *and* flat)

Upon completion of the foregoing material on chromatic tones with the children, it is hoped that they would:

1. Know the meaning of the word "chromatic tone."
2. Recognize a tone as being *chromatic* when it occurs in the text of a given song.
3. Be able to call the chromatic tone by its proper name.
4. Be able to sing the chromatic tone correctly.

Preparation for music-reading songs which contain chromatic tones is the same as for other songs, that is with *rhythm drill* and *melody practice*. The melody practice scale, however, must contain not only the notes of the scale in the appropriate key (according to the song that is being prepared) but also any *chromatic* tones which the song contains. For example, should the skip *ri–la* occur within the text of the song chosen for music reading, then the melody practice scale must of necessity include the chromatic tone *ri* so that the skip may be practiced:

As stated previously, sufficient music-reading material for practice on chromatics is rare in children's music books. This does not mean, however, that the children should be denied the opportunity of becoming familiar with chromatic tones.

Vocabulary

Listed below are some musical terms with which children should become familiar in the course of music-reading experiences at various grade levels. The degree of familiarity, of course, will be determined by the frequency of their occurrence and by their meaningful use in the child's musical experience.

staff	meter (or time) signature
bar lines	*Fine*
double bar	key signature
G clef	chromatic tones
measure	chromatic scale
accent	syncopation
pulsate	triplet
rest	quarter note
tie	half note
slur	dotted half note
leger lines	whole note
repeat sign	eighth note
Dal segno	sixteenth note
Da capo	dotted notes
hold	half step
phrase	whole step
sharp	major scale
flat	whole-tone scale
first and second endings	pentatonic scale

Materials for Music Reading

For the teacher (See also Appendix A, Review of Fundamentals)

Pace, Robert: *Music Essentials for Classroom Teachers*. Wadsworth Publishing Co., Belmont, Calif., 1961.

Pierce, Ann E. and Neal E. Glenn: *Musicianship for the Elementary Teacher: Theory and Skill through Songs*. McGraw-Hill Book Company, New York, 1967.

Winslow, Robert, and Leon Dallin: *Music Skills for Classroom Teachers*, 2d ed. Wm. C. Brown Co., Dubuque, Iowa, 1964.

Filmstrips for the classroom

Developing Skills in Music
Group 1: Rhythms, note values, time signatures, accents.
Group 2: Lines and space names of staff, scales, key signatures, intervals, phrases.
Published by Society for Visual Education, 1345 Diversey Parkway, Chicago, Ill., 60614.

Introduction to Music Reading (filmstrip and record). Published by Classroom Materials, Inc., Great Neck, N.Y.

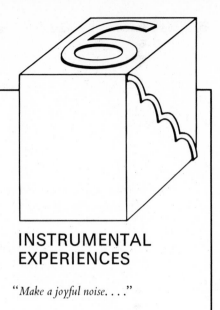

INSTRUMENTAL EXPERIENCES

"Make a joyful noise. . . ."

Classroom Instruments

SMALL WINDS

These plastic melody instruments (tonette, song flute, melody flute, etc.) are known by many different names, but basically they are very similar, and are all played in much the same manner. The thumb of the left hand covers the hole on the back side of the instrument, while the fingers of the left hand are used for the upper set of holes on the front side. The thumb of the right hand rests on the thumb guide located on the back of the instrument, while the fingers of the right hand are used for the lower set of holes on the front.

FIGURE 6–1 *Small winds. From left to right; tonette, flutaphone, song flute. (Courtesy of Peripole, Inc., Far Rockaway, N.Y.)*

The range of these small winds is usually a ninth:

The instruction books that come with the instruments almost always contain fairly adequate directions for holding and playing. In addition, it is most important to stress the following to the children when introducing any new classroom wind instrument:

1. Blow gently. (Children have the tendency to blow hard, much as they would blow a whistle. This distorts the tone of wind instruments.
2. Say "too" as you blow. This puts the tongue in the right position for producing a clearer sound.
3. Cover the holes firmly with the cushion part of the fingertip. Make certain that no air is escaping from anywhere around the hole; otherwise the sound will be more like a whistle than a musical tone.

A few pros and cons regarding the use of these instruments are presented here as an aid to the teacher in deciding whether or not to try them with his class.

On the *minus* side:

1. When played incorrectly, these small winds can emit a rather disagreeable sound.
2. This type of instrument is not always in tune as it comes from the manufacturer. Although it is possible to make some adjustment of the mouthpiece to correct this condition, the adjustment is not always completely accurate.
3. There is frequently a danger of overuse of these instruments, to the exclusion of other musical activities in the classroom.

On the *plus* side:

1. These instruments are enjoyed by the children, are inexpensive, and may be used another year since the mouthpieces can be sterilized.
2. They provide a means for immediate application of certain basic skills that a teacher may wish to present to his class.
3. Some teachers consider them an aid to music reading.
4. They may be used by children and teacher alike in executing some of the activities suggested in Chapter 4, Ear Training Experiences, (p. 108).

So use them—along with singing, music reading, rhythm instruments, or whatever you wish—but mostly with discretion.

RECORDERS

The works of Shakespeare and of other writers of his time often include mention of the recorder, whose history dates back many centuries. Early

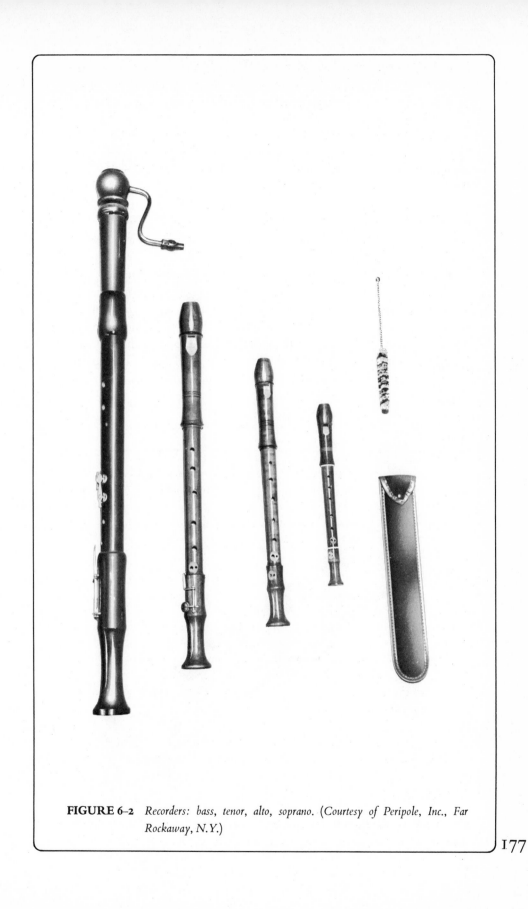

FIGURE 6–2 *Recorders: bass, tenor, alto, soprano. (Courtesy of Peripole, Inc., Far Rockaway, N.Y.)*

orchestral works of Purcell, Scarlatti, and Bach included recorder parts in the scores; however, with the development of larger orchestras, the use of the recorder gradually diminished. Its recent revival is manifested in its increased use in school classrooms as well as in the advent of numerous recorder groups across the country who play simply for enjoyment.

Recorders are available in different sizes, from very small to large, the most common of which are the soprano, alto, tenor, and bass shown in Fig. 6-2. A fifth, the sopranino, is smaller and sounds higher than the soprano. The soprano (sometimes called the "descant" recorder) is the one most often selected for classroom use.

In the past, recorders were usually made of wood and were more expensive than the smaller plastic small wind instruments; however, recorders are now available in plastic as well, thus reducing their cost somewhat.

The recorder is played in much the same manner as the small winds, except that there is no thumb guide, as such, located on the back of the instrument. The points previously mentioned regarding breathing, covering the holes, etc., in connection with the small winds also apply to the recorder. The recorder range is much greater than that of the small winds, for it covers about two octaves. In the soprano recorder, for example, the range is:

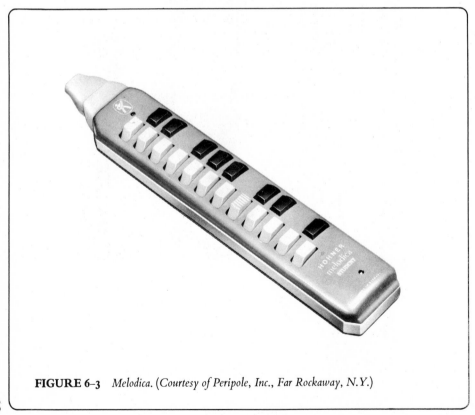

FIGURE 6-3 *Melodica. (Courtesy of Peripole, Inc., Far Rockaway, N.Y.)*

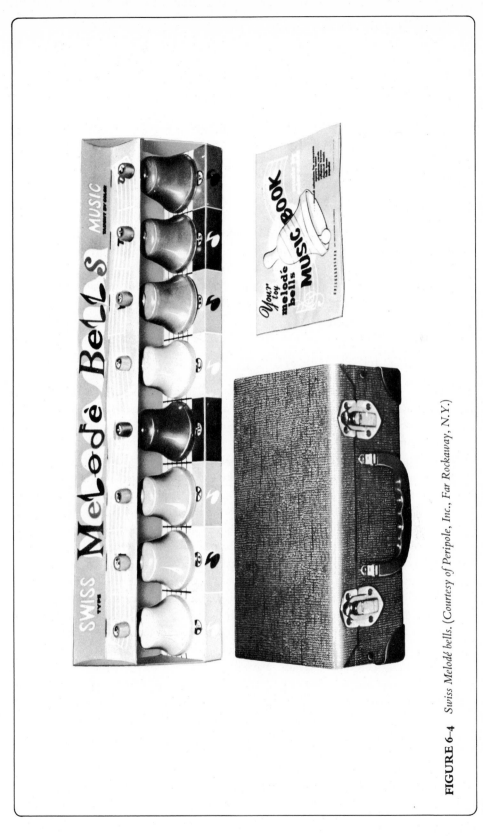

FIGURE 6-4 *Swiss Melodé bells. (Courtesy of Peripole, Inc., Far Rockaway, N.Y.)*

MELODICA

The melodica is one of the many instruments contrived mainly for classroom use. It is a sort of combination keyboard and wind instrument; it resembles a very small piano keyboard, with black and white keys located in the appropriate positions, but the sound is produced by blowing on a mouthpiece located at the top end of the instrument. Single tones as well as chords may be played. There are several different models, varying in size, range, and price.

SWISS MELODÉ BELLS

These come in a set of eight tuned (F to F) colored plastic bells played by holding a small handle at the top and shaking the bell to make the clapper hit against the side of the bell. They may be used in pre-music-reading experiences (through the use of color coding) as well as in later music reading and in other musical areas such as ear training (p. 108) and basic skills (pp. 120–132).

NOVELTY INSTRUMENTS

Ocarinas, sometimes known as "sweet potatoes" (because of their shape), are played by covering the holes much as they are covered in playing other small wind instruments. They are available in soprano, alto, and bass models, with corresponding ranges.

The *Guitaro* is a combination Autoharp and guitar, in that it is held in the same manner as a guitar, but is played like an Autoharp by pressing buttons for chords.

The *kazoo-type* instruments are simply hummed into to make a sound and are very inexpensive. They are available in various shapes, resembling a clarinet, cornet, slide trombone, or "submarine," but they may also be attached to other objects for a single novelty number in a program. One PTA group attached kazoos to kitchen utensils such as egg beaters, potato mashers, etc., and made a "kitchen band." The drum major wore an inverted colander on his head with a dishmop waving merrily at the top. The conductor used a long wooden spoon for a baton. A few other "instruments" were added, mostly of the percussion type—an old dishpan for a drum, two pot covers for cymbals, etc. This unique group "played" several selections in harmony.

The *jaw harp* is a very small harp-shaped piece of metal, held at the mouth and "twanged" with the fingers.

A glissando effect can be achieved on the *slide whistle* by blowing in the mouthpiece and moving the plunger (at the opposite end) back and forth. With practice, it is also possible to play tunes on this instrument.

The *fife* is held to the side and played by blowing *over* the hole at one end (like a flute) and covering the other holes with the fingers. Fifes are available in keys of B♭ and C and are usually made of metal.

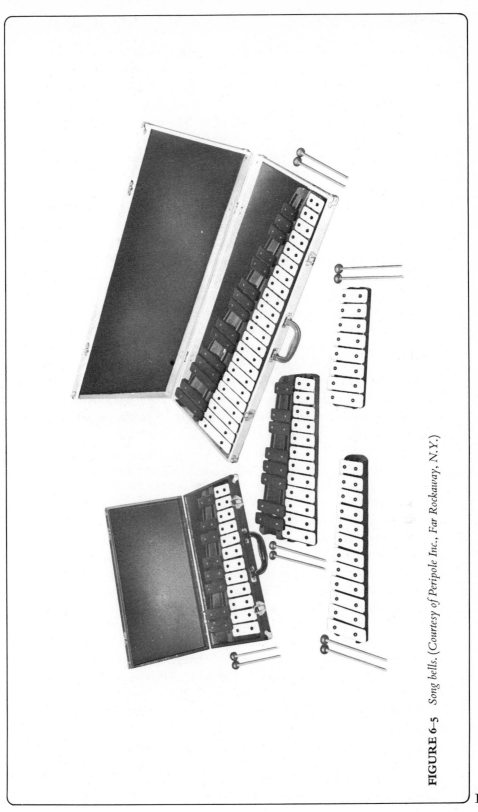

FIGURE 6-5 *Song bells. (Courtesy of Peripole Inc., Far Rockaway, N.Y.)*

SONG BELLS, STEP BELLS, AND RESONATOR BELLS

Song bells are sets of attached, graduated metal bars constructed so as to produce different pitches when struck with a wooden or rubber-tipped mallet. The white bars represent the white keys on the piano and the black bars the black keys. They are arranged in the same order as on the keyboard.

Song bells are available in various sizes. The most desirable size for classroom use has been found to be the $1\frac{1}{2}$-octave chromatic song bells. These provide an adequate range of tones, are easy to handle, and may be played by the children as well as the teacher.

On all song bells the name of the note is indicated on each key. This is most helpful when one is first learning to read music. Although it is possible for children to play the song bells without learning the letter names of the lines and spaces (by using color coding and by simply being shown which notes to strike), they must learn the letter names if they wish to work out new tunes independently. In such cases, there is a valid reason for teaching the letter names, for immediate application of the learning would be possible.

Song bells are usually considered a *melody* instrument, primarily because they are played one note at a time, as a rule. Of course, it is possible to use more mallets to strike several notes at once, but this is not considered to be their primary function. As a melody instrument, song bells are an aid to teaching the melody of a song where a teacher feels that he needs support for his voice or where he feels that he cannot carry the tune at all. The song bells may also be used in tone-matching games and scale practice, if desired, as well as in sounding tones for ear training (see p. 108), since a wide range of intervals is possible.

Descants and other harmonizing parts may be played on the song bells while the class sings the melody of a given song. Special effects, such as small chimes, are also possible on the song bells.

Step bells are merely song bells arranged in a staircase order.

The term "resonator bells" or "tone bells" covers a wide range. Even song bells as described above are sometimes referred to as resonator bells. In this text, however, the term "resonator bells" is used to describe a set of thick, rectangular blocks of wood with a small metal bar attached over the top of a hole in the center of each. Unlike song bells, resonator bells may be handled and played separately, since they are not all attached together as song bells are.

The sound is produced by striking the metal bar with a wooden or rubber-tipped mallet. Each resonator bell produces a different pitch, and it is usually true that the larger the bell, the lower the pitch. When used in the classroom, they may be arranged in scale order so that a child can play them much as he plays song bells, or they may be passed out individually to be struck at prescribed times.

Chord accompaniments using the three principal chords (I, IV, V7) are possible by having various children strike their bells simultaneously to produce a chord. For example, one child might have the C bell, another the E bell, and a third the G bell. When struck together, they would produce the C chord.

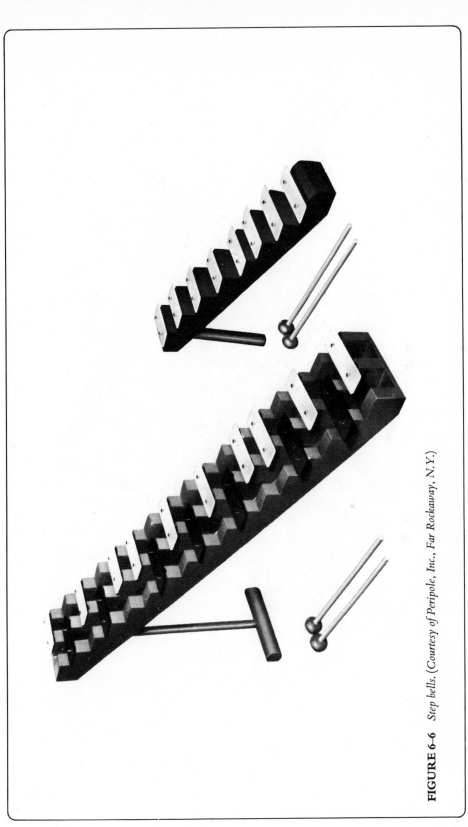

FIGURE 6-6 Step bells. (*Courtesy of Peripole, Inc., Far Rockaway, N.Y.*)

FIGURE 6-7 *Resonator bells. (Courtesy of Peripole, Inc., Far Rockaway, N.Y.)*

FIGURE 6-8 *Autoharp. (Courtesy of Peripole, Inc., Far Rockaway, N.Y.)*

Having the children lay out the bells in a random order (rather than in the usual scale order) and playing them as they occur can produce some interesting results.

PLAYING THE AUTOHARP

An Autoharp can provide a great deal of enjoyment for the children as well as a satisfying accompaniment for many of the songs. Furthermore, it is simple enough to play so that the children can do their own accompanying also.

Autoharps are available in many different models—the difference, for the most part, being in the number of bars on each instrument that must be pressed down to sound the chords. The twelve-bar Autoharp has been found most adequate for the average classroom, the key bars of which are arranged as shown in Fig. 6-9.

The chord letter names on the bars correspond to the chord letter names found in the music texts. If there is a *G major* chord written above a measure of a given song, the teacher simply presses the *G major* button on the Autoharp and strums. The felt on the bottom of the bar silences all other strings except the ones contained in the G major chord. If the song calls for an *A minor* chord, the teacher simply presses the *A minor* button and strums.

There is no need to be concerned about putting the right fingers on the proper keys, as in playing the piano. If the children cannot read letters, the

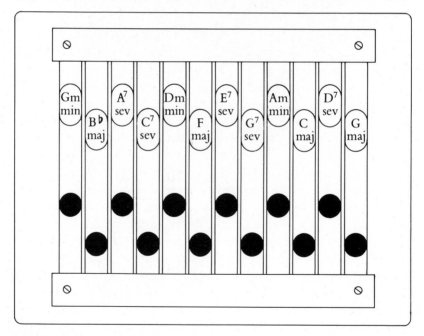

FIGURE 6–9 *Diagram of Autoharp bars.*

buttons may be color-coded to the song (four red circles on the song chart mean to press the bar with the red circle on it and strum four times, etc.), and a child may simply be shown which button to press and when to change.

Note that the three principal chords of *each* of the keys C, F, and G are arranged conveniently close together so that they may be manipulated easily with the fingers of the left hand. While the left hand presses the designated bars down *firmly*, the right hand reaches over across the left hand and strums the strings, beginning the strum from the low strings of the instrument to the high. A plastic or felt pick may be used, or the player may simply prefer to use his hand. Whatever device is used for strumming, the strum should be a firm one, encompassing all the strings so that the sound is full and resonant. Placing the Autoharp on top of the closed carrying case has been found to enhance the sound. A banjo-type sound is produced by strumming on the section of the strings located to the right of the bars.

The learning of accent and meter can often be reinforced through different types of strumming on the Autoharp. In $\frac{3}{4}$ time, for example, a teacher might wish to strum one long strum on the first beat and two short ones on the second and third beats. Children may move their hands in strumming motions in the air—one long strum and two short ones—to get the feeling of the meter.

The strings may be plucked as well as strummed, using the picks provided with each Autoharp. When used in combination with the strumming, this produces a very delightful sound, but it does take practice! (Incidentally, Autoharps that may be amplified electrically are also available.)

Charts of the Autoharp showing the key bars, etc., may be purchased in sets, so that every child can have his own chart at his desk for practice in locating chords as well as in pressing the left-hand fingers firmly while strumming with the right hand.

Tuning the Autoharp is actually a simple process. It should be done with the pitch pipe to be accurate, but if it is to be used with the piano or some other instrument such as the song bells, then tune to the instrument, by all means. Some people prefer to tune each string separately, starting with the lowest and proceeding to the highest, blowing the pitch for each one as they go along. Others prefer to tune by octaves—all the C's first, then all the D's, etc.—and still others tune by listening to the sound of individual chords.

Strings may be tightened to make them sound higher or loosened to make them sound lower, using a little wrench that comes as part of the standard equipment with all Autoharps. The inside of the wrench is hollow and fits over the silver pins that hold each string at the top of the instrument. Simply fit the wrench over the pin and turn in the desired direction. Take heart if you're not sure which *is* the desired direction. This comes with practice and advancing age, like many other good things in life.

TEACHING THE HARMONICA

"Play now—learn later!" is a most appropriate slogan for the harmonica. Of all the instruments suitable for classroom use, certainly this little gem is the front-runner when it comes to making "instant music". The results produced by merely breathing in and out are immediate and usually quite satisfying to a nonmusician. In addition to the pleasure the harmonica provides in school and out, it makes possible many musical learnings.

Obviously, not much technique will be developed in class time. Rather, in the short time devoted to teaching the harmonica, the most we can hope for is that the class, as a whole, will grasp the blow-and-draw breathing procedure so that it may be executed with ease, minus the explosions of air that are so common to beginning harmonica players. In addition, practice in moving the mouth back and forth on the correct numbers is required in order to develop a smoother progression so that the player doesn't have to take his mouth off the instrument every time a note or the breathing is changed.

The following suggestions are offered as an introductory aid to the formation of a beginning school harmonica group.

PREPARATION

Before presenting the idea of playing harmonicas to the children, find a music store or similar establishment that will agree to give a better price on the purchase of a quantity of harmonicas than on one or two. Select harmonicas of metal construction, in preference to plastic, with ten holes in the top. The numbers 1 to 10 should be indicated over the corresponding holes. Request that all harmonicas be in the key of C. Harmonicas come in different keys, but if the children are to play them together, they must all be in the same key. C is as good as any for a beginning.

Have an understanding with the store that if any of the harmonicas sound off pitch, they may be returned for replacement. This is most important and is mentioned here because it happens often enough to be an issue. It is impossible for a group to produce an acceptable sound if one or two of the instruments are slightly off. Usually the problem is due to a defect in manufacture. Sometimes off-pitch sounds appear later on as a result of mishandling of the instrument, such as dropping it, exposing it to dampness, or allowing debris to become lodged in the holes. Obviously, the dealer or manufacturer is not responsible in such cases. Children should be cautioned to carry their harmonicas in the box in which they came (or in another container), avoid dropping them, refrain from taking them into the bathtub, and, in general, treat them with care. It is advisable also, when first passing out the new harmonicas to the children, to check the key of each instrument to ensure that they are all in the key ordered. Dissonant sounds can also result when one instrument is in another key.

Since the cost is nominal, some schools prefer to buy their own harmonicas, either through the parents' groups or with school funds; however, harmonicas cannot be sterilized and therefore cannot be kept from year to year. It follows, then, that each child should keep his own harmonica whether he or the school pays for it. With a minimum of direction in class, plus the opportunity to explore further the playing possibilities of the instrument outside of class as a solitary pastime, many children develop a truly fine technique of their own and also learn to play many songs by ear. A child really needs his own harmonica to keep if it is to be more than a "sometime" thing to him. With a harmonica in his pocket, he soon discovers that he is never quite alone.

PROCEDURE

1. When all the children have their harmonicas at their desks (and all have been checked to ensure their being in the proper key), ask them to hold their harmonicas in their left hand, embracing them from the side with the thumb on the front and the forefinger on the back and with the numbers 1 to 10 reading from left to right.
2. Have the class find the 4 and blow gently on this hole. Now tell them to draw the breath in. Blow again. Draw. Be sure that they do not move to another hole when they are alternating drawing and blowing.
3. Have the class slide up one hole (without removing their harmonicas from their mouths) to the 5. Tell them to blow. Draw. Blow.
4. Have the class move back to the 4. Blow. Move to the 5. Blow. Draw. Blow.
5. Put these numbers on the board: 4 5 6 7. Tell the class that when they are first learning a piece of music, they will play from numbers like these. *A plain number means to blow.* Have the class play the number on the board, blowing on each one.

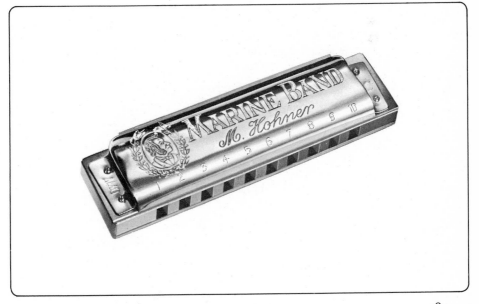

FIGURE 6–10 *Harmonica. (Courtesy of M. Hohner, Inc.)*

6. Put these numbers on the board, circled as shown:

(4) (5) (6) (7)

Tell the class that a circled number means to draw the breath in. Have them play the circled numbers as shown, drawing on each one.

7. Put the following on the board:

4 4 6 6 (6)(6) 6
(5)(5) 5 5 (4)(4) 4

8. Since the children will have no idea what the tune is or what the time should be, point to each number in the proper rhythm of the song, which, incidentally, is "Twinkle, Twinkle, Little Star." Have the class play the two lines as you point to each number; then add the remaining numbers of the song. When completed, it will look as follows:

"Twinkle, Twinkle, Little Star"

4 4 6 6 (6)(6) 6
(5)(5) 5 5 (4)(4) 4
6 6 (5)(5) 5 5 (4)
6 6 (5)(5) 5 5 (4)
4 4 6 6 (6)(6) 6
(5)(5) 5 5 (4)(4) 4

9. Then try "Are You Sleeping, Brother John?" and others, in the suggested following order:

"Are You Sleeping, Brother John?"

4 (4) 5 4   4 (4) 5 4
5 (5) 6   5 (5) 6
6 (6) 6 (5) 5 4   6 (6) 6 (5) 5 4
4 2 4   4 2 4

"London Bridge"

6 (6) 6 (5) 5 (5) 6
(4) 5 (5) 5 (5) 6
6 (6) 6 (5) 5 (5) 6
(4) 6 5 4

190

10. Show the class that the scale played on the C harmonica looks like this:

do	re	mi	fa	sol	la	ti	do
4	④	5	⑤	6	⑥	⑦	7

NOTE: It is also possible on a ten-hole harmonica to play the following note *above* high *do* when required:

⑧ 8 ⑨ 9

Although the scale (as well as the extra notes shown above) was written in the key of C to accommodate the harmonicas in C that are being used here, the pattern for blowing and drawing the scale is the *same in any key*. For example, to play the scale of (or songs in) the key of D, one would need to have a harmonica manufactured in the key of D. Properly numbered for harmonica, the key-of-D scale would look like this:

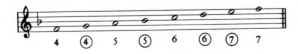

4 ④ 5 ⑤ 6 ⑥ ⑦ 7

To play the scale of (or songs in) the key of F, an F harmonica is required:

4 ④ 5 ⑤ 6 ⑥ ⑦ 7

Note that the numbered sequence remains the same in all keys. **191**

11. Have the children deduce the proper numbers for such simple note patterns as:

♪ *mi–re–do*	*do–re–mi*	*mi–fa–sol*
do–mi–do	*do–re–do*	*mi–fa–mi*

Write these patterns on the staff in the key of C; then try playing them from notation.

12. Have the children play longer simple melodies in the key of C from the board and then from their textbooks if any can be found in the proper key. Eventually, children should be able to translate songs written in the key of C into numbers, blows, draws, etc. Appropriate songs *not* in the key of C may be *transposed* into the key of C and then played on the harmonica.

13. Individual children should be encouraged to work out songs of their own by ear and play them for the class. Also, specialized techniques for producing more varied sounds on the harmonica can be demonstrated either by children who have learned them or by a visiting friend or parent who plays the instrument exceptionally well and is willing to play for the class. A deft use of the tongue and hands can produce an almost unbelievably full sound of melody and chordal accompaniment in rhythm, even on a small harmonica.

Since the harmonica has appeared on the concert stage and has been scored for in serious music, opportunities to view professional players (or to hear them on recordings) should certainly be afforded the children. In addition, children should also be shown various types of harmonicas such as the chromatic harmonica, bass harmonica, etc. These are available at most music dealers or from M. Hohner, Inc., Hicksville, Long Island, N.Y., along with instruction books that provide detailed instructions for playing all types of harmonicas. (See "Instructional Materials," p. 239.)

USING THE DRUMSTICKS

The inclusion of this activity here should not be interpreted as meaning that a teacher must teach the rudiments of drumming to his class. Rather, it represents simply another possible musical area for children to explore. Some children achieve a degree of success great enough to encourage them to study percussion instruments privately. For others, the use of the drumsticks will prove to be a pleasurable activity as well as a possible motivating factor in the learning of selected basic rhythms.

Lightweight drumsticks (the most desirable type for this purpose) may be purchased from any dealer in musical instruments. Dowels from the lumberyard may be substituted for drumsticks when funds are low; however, they should be as close to the drumstick size as possible so that the child can hold them easily in his hand.

The following diagram shows the proper holding position for each
192 hand. The sticks should be held in the fingers loosely and freely enough to

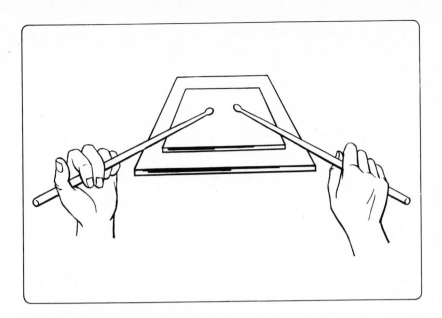

FIGURE 6–11 *Two hands holding drumsticks and practice pad.*

allow them to bounce as they hit the practice pad. Drumming practice pads can be made from a square of plywood or other wood, covered with a piece of linoleum, rubber, or similar material.

The teacher may compose rhythm patterns for the children to play, selecting those which will provide practice in the basic rhythms appropriate for the grade level, as well as other rhythm patterns for accompanying records or songs. Children can originate simple patterns of their own to repeat throughout a given song, or they may wish to create a more difficult drum score for selected pieces of their choice.

Below are a few sample beginning rhythm patterns for practice. The left hand is indicated by L, and the right hand by R. Have the children count one measure aloud before beginning so as to ensure a steady beat. Add music when the beat has been established, if desired.

1. L L L L   R R R R

2. L L R R   L L R R

3. L R L R   L R L R

4. L L L L   R R R R

5. ♩ ♫ ♫ ♩ ♩ ♫ ♫ ♩ :‖
    L   L   R   R   L   L   R   R

6. ♪ ♪ ♪ ♪ ♪ ♪ ♪ ♪ :‖
    L R L R   L R L R

7. ♪ ♪ ♩   ♪ ♪ ♩ :‖
    L L R   L L R

8. ♩ ♪ ♪   ♩ ♪ ♪ :‖
    L R R   L R R

A very simple score for "Oh, Susanna" might shape up something like this:

♫ ♩ │ ♩ ♫ ♩ │ ♩ ♫ ♩ │ ♩ ♫ ♩ │ ♩ ♫ ♩ ♩ │ ♩ ♩ ♫ │
L L │ R L L │ R L L │ R L L │ R L L │ R L L R L L │ R L L R L R L L │

♩ ♫ ♩ ♫ │ ♩ ♫ ♩ ♫ │ ♩ ♩ ♩ ♩ │ ♩ ♩ :‖
R L L R L L │ R L L R L L │ R L R L │ R

A demonstration of drumming and of the use of other percussion instruments by a child in the school who is taking lessons or by someone else in the community would be most helpful.

Further information and instructions may be found in drum methods books, which are available at most music dealers. (See "Instructional Materials," p. 239.)

PLAYING THE UKULELE

The ukulele is sometimes referred to as a "social" or "recreational" instrument. By any name at all it's still great fun to play and may be used by the children as well as the teacher for accompanying song material. It is considered principally a harmony instrument, as opposed to a melody instrument such as the song bells or recorder.

Many children's music texts show ukulele tablature (diagrams indicating where the fingers go on the strings to make various chords) in selected songs throughout the books. Such tablature is also included here (see p. 213), along with further information designed to inspire the teacher to try playing and teaching the ukulele to his class. Fifth and sixth grade children (sometimes even fourth grade) can manage to play it very well and absorb with pleasure many musical learnings in the process.

Although the initial cost of a ukulele is somewhat more than that of the harmonica or a plastic recorder, a set of ukuleles may be used over again each year since there is no health problem involved such as the sterilization of mouthpieces.

TUNING

The ukulele has four strings, tuned in certain intervals. It may be tuned to play in several different keys; however, through the use of various finger positions, it is possible to play in more than one key without retuning. The size of the interval between each string remains the same regardless of what key the ukulele is tuned in. The two most common tunings are for the key of G and the key of F (instructions below). Before attempting to tune the ukulele, hold it as shown in the diagram below—with the long neck of the instrument to your left and the back pressed flat against your body. Steady the body of the instrument with the inside part of the right forearm. The steadying must be done from this end in order to enable the left hand to move freely from one chord position to another. The fingers of the left hand press down on various strings simultaneously, while the right hand is used to strum. There is a series of small ridges along the whole length of the neck of the ukulele. The spaces between these ridges are known as "frets." It is most important when pressing the strings that the fingers remain within the confines of the appropriate fret for the desired chord and do not spill over into a neighbouring fret. The space between each fret and the next is a half-step interval. The white dots are merely markers for locating selected frets.

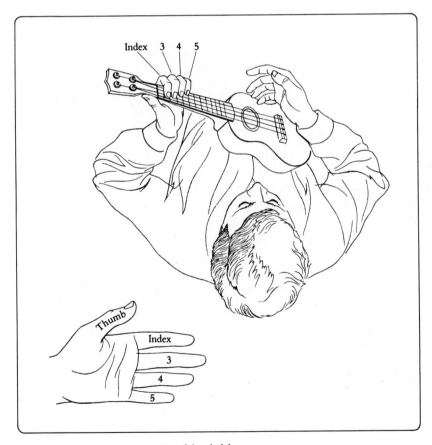

FIGURE 6–12 *Holding position of the ukulele.*

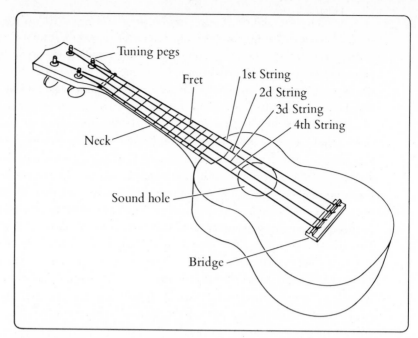

FIGURE 6–13 *Parts of the ukulele.*

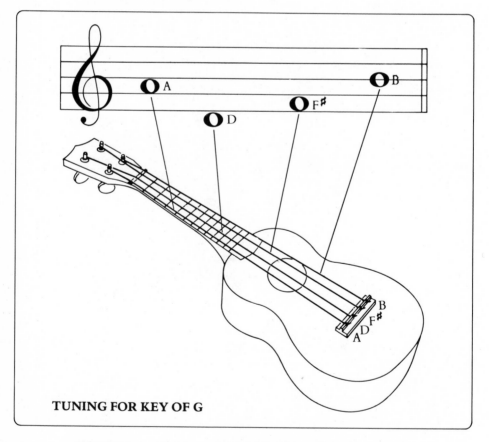

TUNING FOR KEY OF G

FIGURE 6–14 *Ukulele—tuning A D F♯ B from staff.*

Holding the ukulele in the position suggested in Fig. 6-12, tune the string closest to your chin first. This is the *fourth* string. Tuning may be done from a pitch pipe, the piano, or some other melody instrument. If you intend to use the ukulele to play along with another instrument such as the piano, then tune from that instrument. Sound the pitch from the instrument, pluck the ukulele string, and determine whether to tighten it (using the tuning peg) to make it higher or loosen it to make it lower. If the peg has a tendency to slip, tighten the tiny screw on the underside of the handle of the peg. If your tuning pegs have no screws, try pushing the peg into the hole a little more tightly. When proper pitch is attained, go on to the next string below (this is the *third* string) and then to the remaining two in order. For our present purposes, let's tune to the key of G, using the following pitches for the strings in the order suggested above: A D F♯ B.

PLAYING THE G CHORD (Tonic I)

In order to sound the G (I or tonic) chord, place the *index* finger of the left hand on the *first* fret on top of the second string (remember that the *first* string is on the bottom when the ukulele is held in the correct position) and the *third* finger of the left hand on the *second* fret on top of the fourth string. Press down firmly with the cushion tips of the fingers, taking care not to cover or touch any of the strings in between. The fingers on the left hand should be curved.

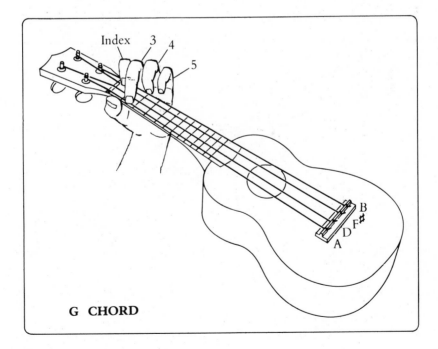

FIGURE 6–15   *G chord with fingers.*

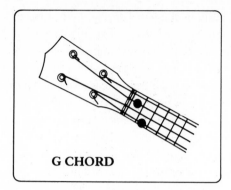

G CHORD

FIGURE 6–16 *G-chord tablature.*

STRUMMING

Strum with the right hand (while holding the left hand firmly in the chord position), starting from the top fourth string. Brush all the strings in a *downward* motion, using either a pick (felt or plastic—it comes with the ukulele) or the fingers. Some people prefer to strum down and up (like shaking water from the hand), making a "plunka-plunka" sound. You'll soon develop your own style. Either way is fine.

PLAYING THE D7 CHORD (Dominant seventh V7)

To sound the D7 chord, roll the wrist back from the G position, keeping the index finger close enough to the string to ease it gently onto the first fret of the *first* string. All other strings are played in "open" (uncovered) position for this chord:

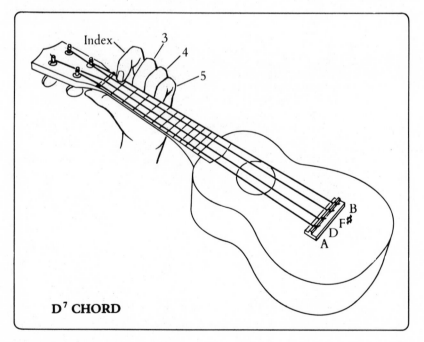

D⁷ CHORD

FIGURE 6–17 *D7 chord with fingers.*

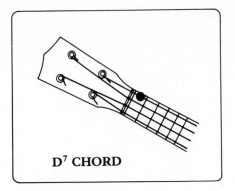

D⁷ CHORD

FIGURE 6-18 *D7-chord tablature.*

Try this song using the chords just practiced.

Down in the Valley

Folk Song

1. Down in the val - ley, the val - ley so low, Hang your head
2. Build me a cas - tle, for - ty feet high, So I can

o - ver, hear the winds blow. Hear the winds blow, dear, hear the winds
see him, as he rides by. As he rides by, dear, as he rides

blow, Hang your head o - ver, hear the winds blow.
by, So I can see him, as he rides by.

Tune Ukulele: A D F♯ B

G (I) chord   D7 (V7) chord

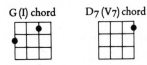

199

PLAYING THE C CHORD (Subdominant IV)

The C chord will seem a little awkward to play at first because the index finger must cover *both* the first and second strings at once, while the third and fourth fingers reach over to successively lower frets on the third and fourth strings:

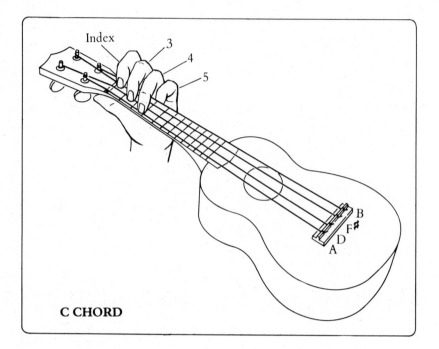

C CHORD

FIGURE 6–19 *C chord with fingers.*

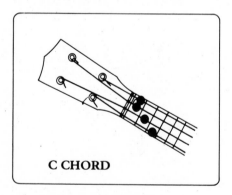

C CHORD

FIGURE 6–20 *C-chord tablature.*

The following song is a favorite at all levels. Makes a delightful program song, using actions and ukuleles.

Hawaiian Rainbows

Describing a scene with a dance.
Dance directions.

In Hawaii a beautiful rainbow may appear behind the fleecy white clouds even on a sunny day. People of the Islands use their hands and arms to | tell | about the rainbow.

Children kneel and sit low on their heels. They stretch both arms out to the left, with fingers pointing up and palms facing out.

G   **C**

Ha - wai - ian rain - bows,

Slowly swing arms over the head from left to right to show the shape of a rainbow.

White clouds roll by;

Swing arms back from right to left. At the same time, roll one hand over the other to show clouds.

G   **D7**   **G**

You show your col - ors

Swing arms from left to right. At the same time, make a rippling motion with the fingers as if pointing to all the colors of the rainbow.

A - gainst the sky.

Raise both hands high to the right (palms up). Move the left hand "across the sky" to the left side.

G   **C**

Ha - wai - ian rain - bows,

Slowly swing arms over the head from left to right to show the shape of a rainbow.

It seems to me,

Place the right hand under the left elbow and point the index finger of the left hand toward the chest ("it seems to me").

G   **D7**   **G**

Reach from the moun - tain

Raise both hands high to the left.

Down to the sea.

Slowly lower hands toward the right knee and continue moving them out to the right ("Down to the sea").

Tune Ukulele: A D F♯ B

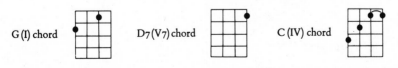

G (I) chord   D7 (V7) chord   C (IV) chord

CREDIT: *From* Making Music Your Own, *Book 3, Teacher's Edition,* © *1968, General Learning Corporation. Dance directions from* Growth through Physical Education, *by A. K. Chang, published by Department of Education, Honolulu, Hawaii. Used by permission of Silver Burdett Company.*

PLAYING THE A7 CHORD (Dominant seventh of the dominant—V7 of V)

The A7 chord may also seem a little difficult to execute at first try; however, keeping the wrist out and up and the fingers in a position resembling a triangle may help. Note that two fingers are used on the same fret, but on different strings. This necessitates some maneuvering with the wrist as well as the hand. (Try not to let the wrist "sag in" toward the ukulele when playing any chord.)

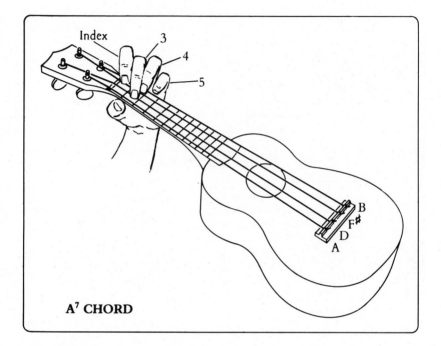

FIGURE 6–21 *A7 chord with fingers.*

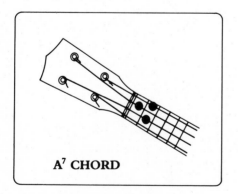

FIGURE 6–22 *A7-chord tablature.*

PLAYING THE D CHORD (Dominant V)

The chord shown in Figs. 6–23 and 6–24 is a simple D chord in this tuning, played by pressing the third fret of the first string with the fourth finger of the left hand. The D chord is included here because when used in combination with other of the above chords, it enables a player to play in a key other than G without retuning the ukulele. For example, recalling *chord structure* for a moment (p. 96), remember that everything can be calculated in a relative

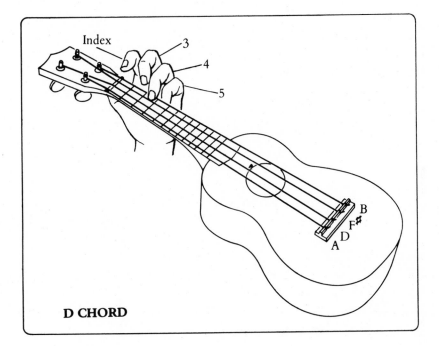

FIGURE 6–23 *D chord with fingers.*

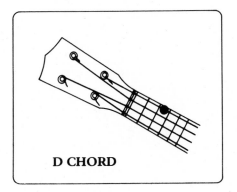

FIGURE 6–24 *D-chord tablature.*

manner alphabetically and numerically. When we are in the key of G, G is the I, or tonic, chord. D then becomes the V chord, C the IV chord, etc., because when we count by the musical alphabet, D is 5 away from G, C is 4 away from G, etc. If we decide to play in a key other than G, then of course the letter name of the I, or tonic, chord must change to correspond to the letter name of the new key. Let's try the key of D.

PLAYING IN THE KEY OF D

In the key of D, D is the I, or tonic, chord and is played in the position shown for D in Figs. 6–23 and 6–24. The V_7 of D (count up 5 from D) is A_7, which, happily, is a chord that we already know how to play (Figs. 6–21 and 6–22). The IV chord in the key of D is G (count up 4 from D), which is also a familiar chord position (Figs. 6–15 and 6–16). Thus, simply by using some familiar chord fingering positions, we find that we can play in the key of D as well as in the key of G without retuning.

Michael Row the Boat Ashore

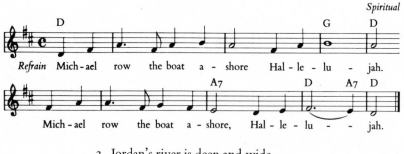

2. Jordan's river is deep and wide . . .
    Milk and honey on the other side . . .
3. Jordan's river is chilly and cold . . .
    Chills the body but not the soul . . .

Tune Ukulele: A D F♯ B

Play in the key of D:

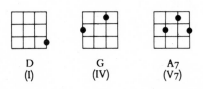

D (I)   G (IV)   A7 (V7)

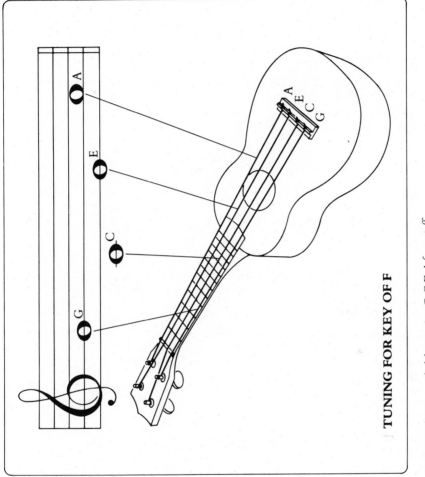

TUNING FOR KEY OF F

FIGURE 6-25 *Ukulele—tuning G C E A from staff.*

All the foregoing chords were based on the tuning for the key of G. Now let's try tuning to the key of F, using the pitches G C E A for the strings 4, 3, 2, 1 in that order. Playing in the key of F, the finger positions will be the same as they were in the key of G. Only the chord *names* will differ, since we are in a different key.

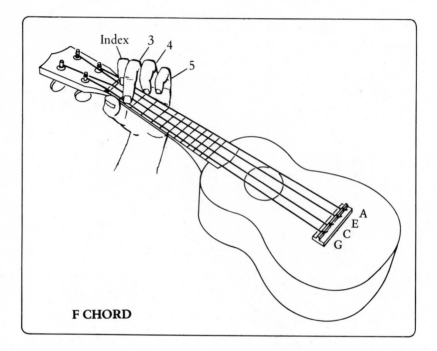

FIGURE 6–26 *F chord with fingers.*

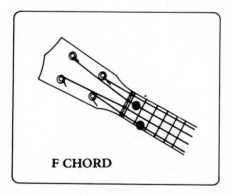

FIGURE 6–27 *F-chord tablature.*

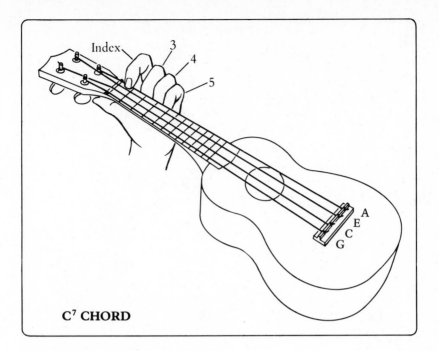

C⁷ CHORD

FIGURE 6–28 *C7 chord with fingers.*

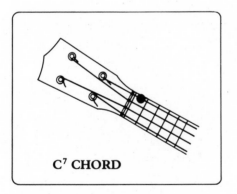

C⁷ CHORD

FIGURE 6–29 *C7-chord tablature.*

207

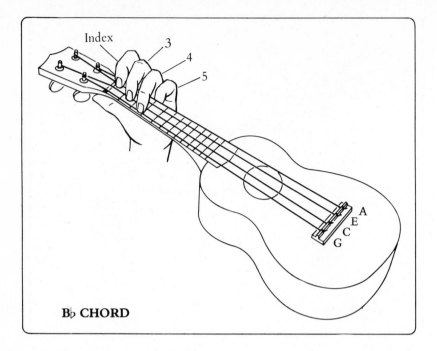

FIGURE 6–30 *B♭ chord with fingers.*

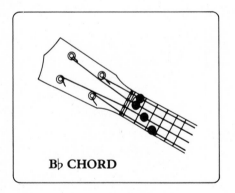

FIGURE 6–31 *B♭-chord tablature.*

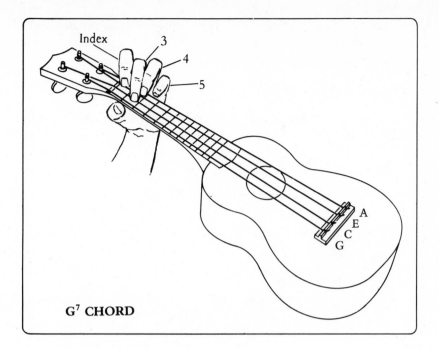

FIGURE 6–32 *G7 chord with fingers.*

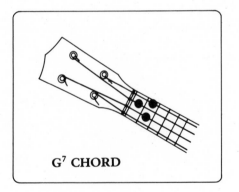

FIGURE 6–33 *G7-chord tablature.*

209

You've probably already figured out that when you are tuned in the key of F, you can also play in the key of C without retuning by using the same procedure suggested for the key of D.

PLAYING IN THE KEY OF C

Using the V (dominant) chord position (which was D when we were tuned in the key of G and which is now C since we are tuned in the key of F),

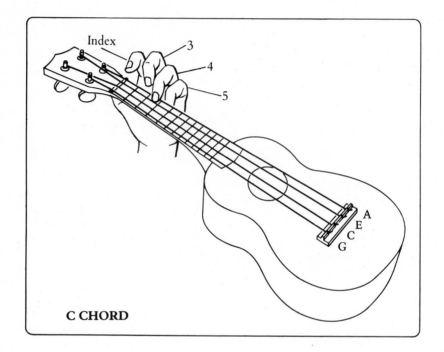

FIGURE 6–34 *C chord with fingers.*

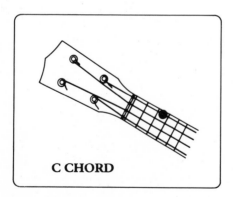

FIGURE 6–35 *C-chord tablature.*

we find that the remaining chords are played in the same familiar positions that they were in the key of D—only their letter names will differ.

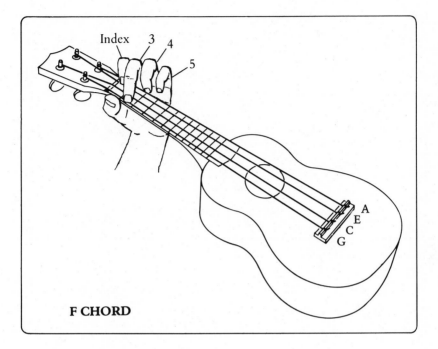

FIGURE 6–36 *F chord with fingers.*

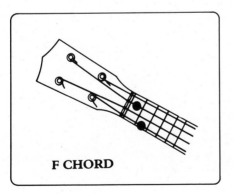

FIGURE 6–37 *F-chord tablature.*

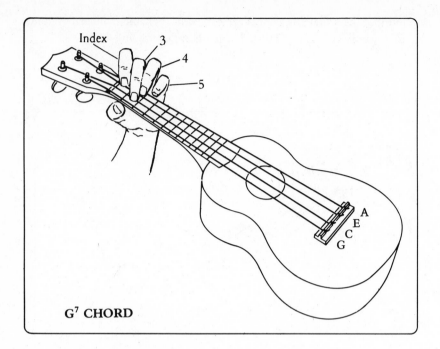

FIGURE 6–38 *G7 chord with fingers.*

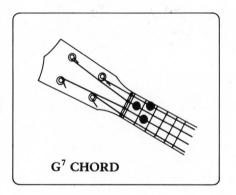

FIGURE 6–39 *G7-chord tablature.*

Be brave. Try "On Top of Old Smoky" (p. 81).

Being familiar with the chords makes the use of diagrams or tablature unnecessary except when the chords of the song become other than I, IV, or V7. After a little practice, you can simply look at the chord letter name (which is indicated in most songbooks) and play the chords directly from that.

In summary, then:

When the ukulele is tuned to A D F♯ B, we can play in the key of

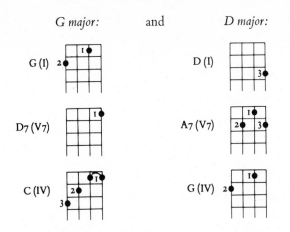

G major: and *D major:*

When the ukulele is tuned to G C E A, we can play in the key of

F major: and *C major:*

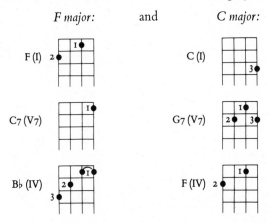

There are many other possible chords, of course. In the few given below, note that the names of the chords differ according to which tuning is used but that the tablature remains the same.

Key-of-G Tuning (A D F♯ B)   *Key-of-F Tuning (G C E A)*

Chord	Tablature	Chord
B minor		A minor
E7		D7
E minor		D minor

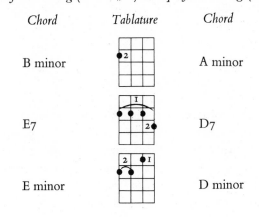

213

Chord	Tablature	Chord
F♯7		E7
B7		A7

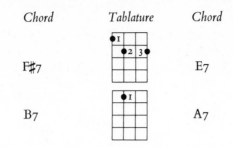

COLOR CODING FINGER POSITIONS

When teaching finger positions to children, try using circles of colored self-sticking tape pressed on to the proper frets (not the *strings*, please), e.g., two red circles showing the position of the index and third fingers for the I chord or one green circle showing the position of the index finger for the V7 chord.

BARITONE UKULELE

Some teachers may wish to try playing a baritone ukulele. It resembles the standard ukulele in shape, but is somewhat larger and has a deeper sound. Because of ease in learning and handling, some people prefer baritone ukuleles to guitars.

GUITAR

Those teachers who have already taken up the guitar and have used it in the classroom will probably agree that it makes a fine accompanying instrument whose sound always seems to appeal to children.

The guitar has a much wider chord range than is possible on the Auto-harp and a richer sound than a ukulele and it is certainly more portable than a piano.

There are six strings, as opposed to four on the ukulele, the top four of which are tuned to the same intervals as on the ukulele, although not in the same octave. (The guitar sounds an octave lower than the notation written for it on the treble staff.)

Piano Chording

The piano keyboard consists of eighty-eight black and white keys arranged in a successively repeated pattern.

A commonly used reference point when first learning to locate notes is *middle C*, situated approximately in the center of the keyboard about 21 inches from the left, immediately to the left of a group of two black keys (see Fig. 6-40).

214

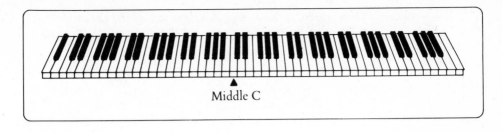

Middle C

FIGURE 6–40 *Entire keyboard showing position of middle C.*

Note that the black keys throughout the entire keyboard are arranged in alternate patterns of twos and threes; therefore, the white key located immediately to the left of every group of *two black keys* is always C. (The term "middle C" refers only to that C shown in the location noted in the diagram above.) Similarly, the white key located immediately to the left of every group of *three black keys* is always F. *Which* of these F's or C's one is supposed to play is determined by where the notation is placed on the staff

as well as by what clef—bass $\left(\begin{array}{c}\mathbf{\mathcal{9}:}\end{array}\right)$ or treble $\left(\begin{array}{c}\mathbf{\&}\end{array}\right)$ —is indicated.

In children's music texts, seldom does a melody go any lower than G below middle C:

Through the use of leger lines (lines added above or below the staff), this G, as shown, may be written on the treble or G clef and played with the right hand. It is usually expected that melodies or chords written on the treble or G clef will be played with the right hand, while those written on the bass clef will be played with the left hand.

It is not the intent here to try to teach piano, by any means, but simply to provide a few simple guidelines and to point out that with a little practice and a lot of patience, a teacher can acquire enough keyboard facility to pick out the tunes of songs, play simple main themes from listening selections, and provide a reasonably adequate accompaniment for many songs in the basic music texts. In this latter connection, the method suggested below for executing simple chord progressions has proved to be the most painless one for nonmusicians to learn to play with two hands *immediately*. (NOTE: It would be most helpful to gain some familiarity with the structure of chords before attempting the following piano chording with the left hand. See "Chord Structure," p. 96.)

The following diagrams show left-hand positions and fingering for the tonic (I), subdominant (IV), and dominant seventh (V7) chords on the bass clef in the keys of C, F, and G major. Note the positions of the chords. Not all the chords are in their *root positions* (with the root written in the lowest **215** position). Some are in an *inverted position*, and yet all the chord tones that belong are still contained within each chord. Inverting chords facilitates fingering and promotes a smoother progression from one chord to another. Note also that whereas the dominant seventh chord usually contains four tones here it contains only three. It is possible to eliminate the fifth of the dominant seventh chord and still get the "feeling" of dominant seventh harmony. This elimination of the fifth of the chord is done here also for the sake of ease in fingering when first learning to play chords.

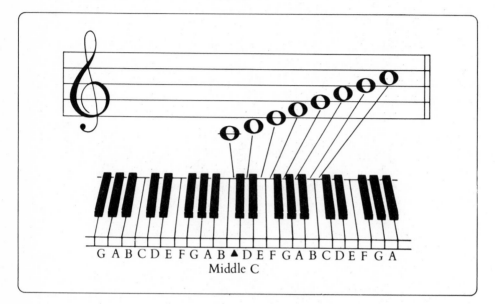

FIGURE 6–41 *Piano keyboard showing location of middle C and staff.*

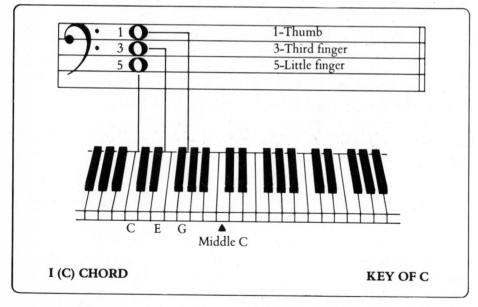

FIGURE 6–42 *Piano keyboard: C chord with left hand; staff (key of C).*

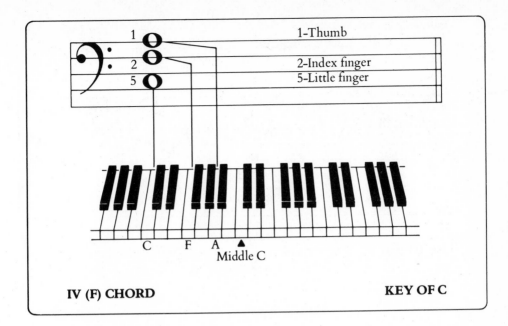

FIGURE 6-43 *Piano keyboard and staff: F chord with left hand (key of C).*

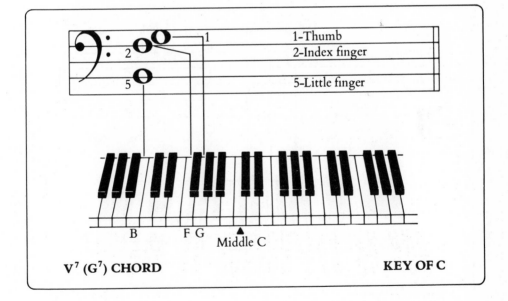

FIGURE 6-44 *Piano keyboard and staff: G7 chord with left hand (key of C).*

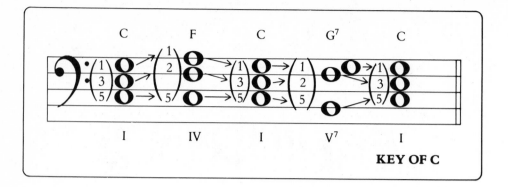

FIGURE 6–45 *Chord progressions I IV I V7 I (key of C). 1= thumb; 2= index finger; 3= third finger; 5= little finger.*

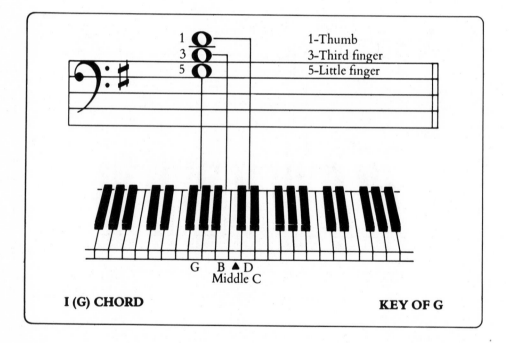

FIGURE 6–46 *Piano keyboard and staff: G chord (key of G).*

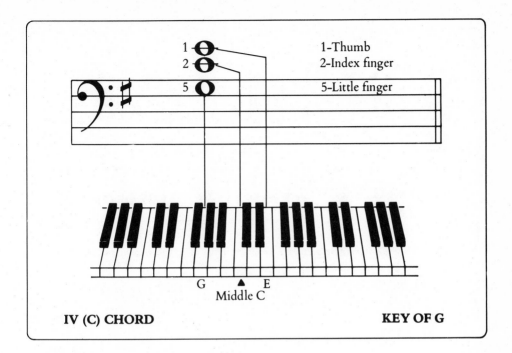

FIGURE 6–47 *Piano keyboard and staff: C chord (key of G).*

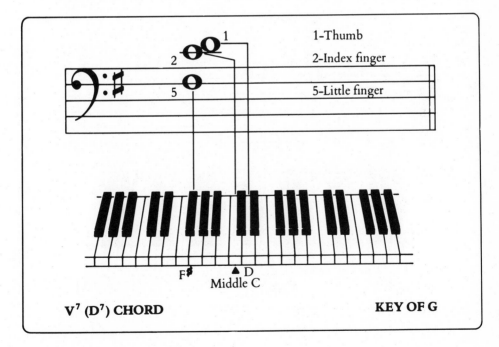

FIGURE 6–48 *Piano keyboard and staff: D7 chord (key of G.)*

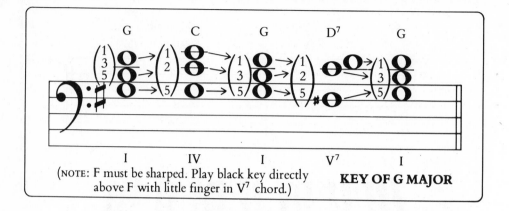

(NOTE: F must be sharped. Play black key directly above F with little finger in V⁷ chord.) **KEY OF G MAJOR**

FIGURE 6–49 *Chord progressions I IV I V7 I (key of G). 1=thumb; 2=index finger; 3=third finger; 5=little finger.*

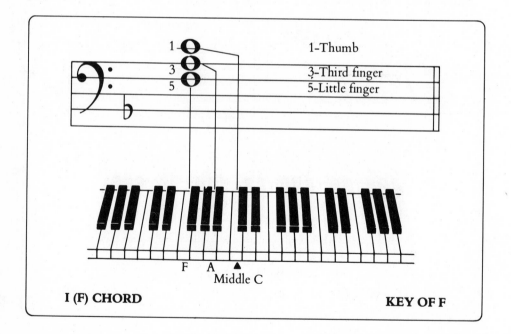

FIGURE 6–50 *Piano keyboard: F chord (key of F); also staff.*

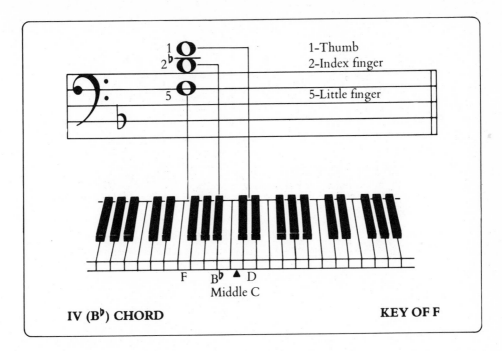

FIGURE 6–51 *Piano keyboard and staff: B♭ chord (key of F).*

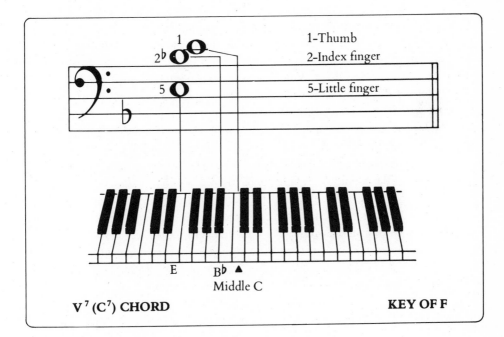

FIGURE 6–52 *Piano keyboard and staff: C7 chord (key of F).*

221

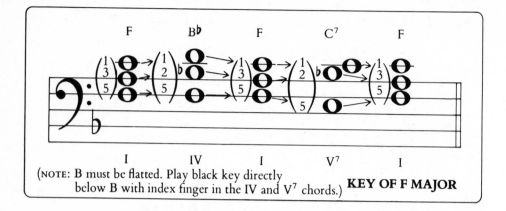

FIGURE 6–53 *Chord progressions I IV I V7 I (key of F). 1= thumb; 2= index finger; 3= third finger; 5= little finger.*

Examination of the finger movements in the foregoing figures will reveal that the same fingers move in the same manner to and from the given progressions regardless of key. For example, in the progression I to IV, the little finger remains where it is, while the thumb and index finger move upward. In the progression I to V7, it is the thumb that remains in place, while the little finger moves down and the index finger moves up. From IV to V7, the index finger remains stationary, while the outside fingers (thumb and little finger) move down.

These movements may be practiced even without a piano keyboard just for the "feel," much as one practices typing skills without actually having a typewriter at hand all the time. Once the progression from one chord to another becomes an automatic movement, the player need not even look at his left hand in order to strike the proper notes going from one progression to another. This enables him to devote his entire attention to reading and playing the notes of the melody with his right hand.

In most music texts the proper chord letter names are indicated in the songs (usually above the staff) to enable the teacher to accompany on some chording instrument such as the piano, an Autoharp, a ukulele, etc.; however, if no chords are indicated, it is helpful to know how to determine what chords could be used. This means writing one's own accompaniment, as it were. (See "Selecting Appropriate Chords for Accompaniment," p. 104.)

Obviously, any harmonization limited to three chords only does not always produce great harmonic variety or the most exciting sounds possible, but it is a start from which a teacher may go on to greater heights when he wishes. Furthermore, many of the songs in the basic music texts do not require any more than the use of the I, IV, and V7 chords to provide a reasonably satisfactory accompaniment.

Rhythm Instruments

The term "rhythm instruments," as it is used in this book, refers to those instruments from which sound is produced by striking, shaking, or hitting and which are played by children in the elementary classrooms. Some teachers prefer to call them "percussion instruments," which, indeed, is their rightful instrumental classification (as opposed to woodwinds, brass, etc.). Many of these same instruments (some on a larger scale, of course) are commonly used in symphony orchestras and bands to produce certain musical effects. In the classroom they provide one more avenue for possible musical achievement by the children.

For many years, rhythm instruments were considered by many educators to be suitable only for the early primary grades. More recently, however, because of increased interest and expanded possibilities for more creative experiences with the instruments, they have come into their own, as it were, and are being used successfully in all grades.

The following list contains the names of rhythm instruments most commonly used in the classroom. Some are in use more than others. The suggested number of each instrument that would produce a fairly good balance when all are playing together is indicated at the right. These numbers are not inflexible, by any means.

Rhythm sticks	six pairs
Triangles (include striker and holder when ordering)	four
Bells (jingle type)	four
Cymbals	two pairs
Tambourines	four
Finger cymbals	two pairs
Drums (include mallet for beating when ordering)	two
Sandblocks	two pairs
Castanets on a stick	one pair
Woodblocks (sometimes referred to as "tone blocks")	two
Jingle clogs (optional)	two pairs

Some companies issue sets or kits of rhythm instruments. These offer no choice as to the type of instrument or the number of each—they must be bought "as is." It is the author's feeling that instruments should be purchased individually in order to avoid "wasting" instruments and be assured of better quality.

Other so-called melodic percussion instruments are often included with rhythm instruments of the nonmelodic type such as those listed above. A "melodic percussion" instrument is one upon which it is possible to play a melody, e.g., the xylophone, which consists of a series of graduated wooden bars, and the glockenspiel, metallophone, and song bells, which consist of a series of graduated metal bars. Larger melodic percussion instruments such as

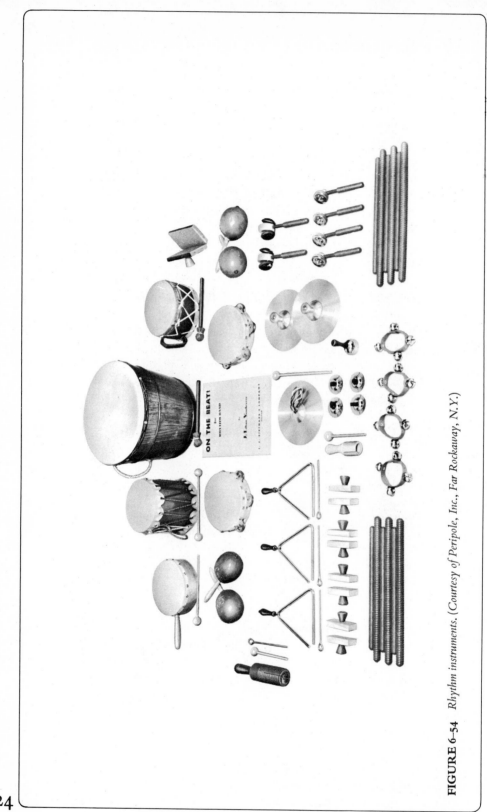

FIGURE 6-54 *Rhythm instruments. (Courtesy of Peripole, Inc., Far Rockaway, N.Y.)*

FIGURE 6-55 *Calypso instruments. (Courtesy of Peripole, Inc., Far Rockaway, N.Y.)*

the marimba and vibraharp are not usually found in the elementary classroom, but children should certainly be afforded an opportunity to see and hear them whenever possible; a sound film may be shown, or, better still, an artist or a parent who plays can be invited to visit the classroom. The Orff method of teaching music to children, as introduced by the German composer Carl Orff in Germany, makes extensive use of the melodic percussion as well as other selected percussion instruments (including the body!). This method seeks to make the elements of music more meaningful to the child through providing extensive creative participation in playing, speaking, and moving, using such simple beginnings as children's calls, nursery games, and pentatonic-scale intervals. The Orff method is gradually becoming more widely known in this country through the efforts of various interested music educators who are attempting to adapt it for American classroom use. (Further references dealing with the Orff system are included at the end of this chapter.)

Also appropriate for classroom use are lummi sticks, calypso instruments (conga drum, bongo drums, cowbell, maracas, guiro), and Hawaiian instruments ('I Pu—a gourd drum; 'Illi-Ili—volcanic rocks; Pu'ili—fringed bamboo sticks). In most cases, they are more appropriate for use in the intermediate grades.

Many songbooks provide rhythm patterns written especially for use with percussion instruments to accompany given songs, especially those of calypso and Latin-American origin. Children can often read these from notation at upper-grade levels or, if they are too difficult, they may learn them by rote.

When commercial instruments are not available (and even when they are!), children can make simple instruments of their own similar to the following:

Sticks	$\frac{1}{2}$- or $\frac{1}{4}$-inch dowels cut to 12-inch lengths.
Triangles	A large nail suspended on a string, or a horseshoe suspended on a string.
Cymbals	Pot covers.
Tambourines	Metal disks or flattened bottle caps attached around paper or aluminum plates.
Sand blocks	Small blocks of wood with sandpaper attached to the bottom and sides and a knob (of the drawer-pull type) attached to the top.
Large drums	Nail kegs or barrels.
Small drums	Oatmeal, cornmeal, or salt boxes. Metal coffee, shortening, or other cannister-type cans with plastic covers. When a plastic cover is unavailable, use old tire rubber stretched and laced or attached in some other way over the top (or over both ends if desired). Wooden bowls with rubber stretched over the top. Skin may be purchased from an instrumental supply dealer and used instead of rubber, if desired. Ice-cream cartons. Large, round plastic containers often found in delicatessen shops.

Shakers	Dried gourds. Paper cups placed mouth to mouth, taped together with masking tape, and filled with rice. Fruit-juice or other small cans (attach handle), paper plates taped or sewed together with yarn, small milk cartons, and small boxes all may be filled with dried beans, peas, rice, etc. A large light bulb can be covered with papier-mâché, decorated as desired, and then struck hard enough to break the globe inside.
Jingle clogs	Metal disks or flattened bottle caps attached to a flat stick at one end.

More sophisticated melodic percussion instruments can be made from graduated pieces of pipe suspended and hit with a tack hammer for a chime effect, while wooden bars of varying lengths attached to a frame and struck with a mallet can make a very acceptable xylophone.

Even graduated sizes of flower pots produce various pitches when suspended by a large knot through the bottom hole of the pot and struck with a wooden mallet. Water glasses may be tuned to different pitches by filling them with water to various levels; they are sounded by hitting a silver knife or spoon against the side of the glass. Simple tunes can be played in this manner. Tuned bottles are another possibility. (See "Bottle Bands," p. 235.) All the above home-made instruments can be decorated or not, as desired. There are many other possibilities, of course. Have the children suggest a few.

In cases where it is not feasible for the children to try to make their own instruments, help has been known to emerge from the custodial or maintenance staff, or even the junior high woodworking class!

Philosophies vary among educators as to how rhythm instruments should be used. Some advocate total class participation immediately, with everyone having an instrument. Others feel that a gradual introduction of the instruments—perhaps one or two at a time—is more desirable. Successful results are possible either way; however, it is the author's feeling that teachers know their own classes better than anyone else. Therefore, no set prescription is offered here, but rather a general array of possible uses from which a teacher may choose whatever he deems appropriate for his group.

INTRODUCING THE INSTRUMENTS

Before a child handles any instrument, he should become familiar, through teacher demonstration, with the proper way to hold it, the way in which it is played, and the kind of sound it makes. Some instruments make different sounds when played in different ways. A tambourine, for example, may be rapped vigorously, tapped lightly, or shaken. A less common way of playing the tambourine is to run the fingers lightly around the edge of the metal disks or to rub the knuckles (including the fingernails) back and forth over the head of the instrument. A nice glissando effect may be produced on the xylophone or song bells by sweeping the mallet over all the bars instead of striking each one separately.

Equally important for a child to learn is how *not* to play an instrument. Cymbals are played in a brushing, up-and-down motion—not clanged together the way we "pop" a blown-up paper bag. Individually, they may also be struck lightly with a mallet. Triangles must hang freely from the holder—not clutched into soundless oblivion.

When the instruments are first introduced, it is fitting that the children also be made aware of two ground rules regarding their use:

1. Handle with care.
2. Play only when directed.

Failure to comply with the rules should result in a child's having to give up his instrument for that lesson. This is painful for the teacher as well as the child, but it does help to reduce the confusion (more like chaos!) that often ensues when no limits are set. Once the children understand that the rules will be enforced, further problems of this nature can be more easily avoided.

USING THE INSTRUMENTS

Now that everyone is instructed in the care and handling of the instruments, to what musical uses may the teacher put them? The many and varied possibilities extend far beyond the few suggested below:

I. Using rhythm instruments with songs.
    A. Check the children's songbooks for songs using individual instruments. These are usually classified under "Playing Our Instruments," "Playing in the Band," or a similar heading. The song indicates the instrument to be used and where it is to be played.
    B. Have the children originate some words about rhythm instruments set to familiar tunes such as the following:
        TUNE: "Did You Ever See a Lassie?"
            Did you ever see a triangle, etc.?
        TUNE: "The Farmer in the Dell"
            The leader of the band, etc.; The drum takes the sticks, etc.
        TUNE: "Old MacDonald Had a Farm"
            Old MacDonald had a band [substitute instruments for animals], etc.
        TUNE: "Hokey Pokey"
            You tap your tambourine in,
            You tap your tambourine out, etc.
        TUNE: "The Bus"
            The cymbals in the band go bang, bang, bang, etc.
        TUNE: "Row, Row, Row, Your Boat"
            Beat, beat, beat, your drum, etc.

TUNE: "Rig a Jig Jig"

> As I was walking down the street,
> Heigh ho, heigh ho, heigh ho, heigh ho,
> A pair of sticks I chanced to meet, etc.
> (Play sticks on chorus.)

C. In rounds such as "Are You Sleeping, Brother John?" have the class suggest a different instrument to play while singing each line.

D. In counting songs such as "Ten Little Indians" and "Angel Band," use a different instrument for each number as it occurs. All play on chorus.

II. Building discrimination and increased awareness of the quality of sound.

A. Add instrumental sound effects as suggested by the children to a familiar piece, e.g.

Eensy weensy spider went up the water spout.
(Sound woodblock on each beat.)
Down came the rain and washed the spider out.
(Shake tambourine throughout the line and rap on "out.")
Out came the sun and dried up all the rain.
(Strike triangle on each beat.)
And eensy weensy spider went up the spout again.
(Sound woodblock on each beat.)
(Try humming through the second time with the instruments. The third time through, think the tune in time, but play the instruments only.) Other songs that lend themselves to this type of activity are "Down by the Station," "Six Little Ducks," and "Hush Little Baby."

B. After a brief discussion of how different instruments can produce different effects, play a vigorous march and ask the class, "What instrument would you choose to play with this piece of music?" "Why?"

In contrast, play a soft lullaby or a light waltz and ask the same questions. Play a selection in which the rhythm of the song is somewhat representative of an activity, such as a cowboy song, for example. Ask the class, "What *two* instruments might be appropriate for this song?" "How shall we play them?"

C. Have the class choose instruments to heighten dramatic effects in nursery rhymes and selected poems. Care should be exercised not to use too many instruments too often in the course of the poem, otherwise the effect will be lost.

D. Have the class choose instruments to heighten dramatic effects in favorite stories, using discretion as suggested in item *C* above. Have a child or a chorus narrate the story, while the others play instruments. For example, in "The Three Little Pigs," simple sound effects might be added in the following ways:

229

First little pig's straw house	sand blocks
Second little pig's stick house	tambourine
Third little pig's brick house	woodblocks
Pigs running	sticks
Wolf blowing house down	drum

For younger children, stories such as "Chicken Little," "The Gingerbread Boy," "The Three Billy Goats Gruff," etc., adapt very well to this activity. For older children, favorite fairy tales and humorous stories such as the story of *Ferdinand*, in addition to their selections, are a challenge to the imagination.

E. Recite a familiar nursery rhyme using instruments only.

F. Hold up either a brilliant or a pastel color. Ask the children, "Which instrument do you think best describes this color?" Play one of three selected instruments and have the class decide which is best suited to the color.

G. Hold up a design—either busy or simple. Ask the children, "Which instrument do you think best describes this design?" Play one of three selected instruments.

H. Use the procedure outlined above in selecting instruments that best describe certain patterns or colors of clothes the children are wearing; the sound of a train or a clock for example; and various scenes. For the latter, hold up a picture of a scene and ask the children to choose the instrument or combination of instruments that best describes it.

I. Put some words such as the following on the board: "boom," "marshmallow," "avocado," "ticktock," "shiver," "jingle," "rap," "swish," "ting," "sassafrass," "clock," "bang" "clang." Ask the class, "What instrument would you choose to represent the sound of each of these words?" Reverse the procedure by asking, "What words do you think best describe the sound of this instrument?"

J. Describe a familiar scene, using instruments only—no narration.

K. Describe a recent class trip, using instruments only.

L. Originate a story or situation, letting each character or happening be represented by a different instrument or combination of instruments. Tell the story, using instruments only—no narration. Suggested topics might include "A Day in Town," "A Day at School," "A Pony Express Ride," "A Hometown Ball Game," "A Visit to the Circus," etc.

III. Playing instruments by rote. If the children are to have the experience of playing together as a total group, but have not as yet learned to read from a score, it will be necessary for the teacher to teach the orchestration by rote. If such an activity is to provide for the children's musical growth, it should consist of more than simply having everyone pound out all the beats at the same time. Using a little imagination, orchestrations can be made very interesting to play and to hear. They do require, however, that the children be able to count (at least up to 4) and that they be able to play or be quiet (as the piece requires) on any or all beats of a given measure or measures. Practice for this may be done through clapping, long before the instruments are introduced:

A. Using music (either the piano or a record) in strong $\frac{4}{4}$ or $\frac{3}{4}$ time, you might say, "Clap all the beats while you count 1–2–3, 1–2–3 (or 1–2–3–4, etc.)."

B. Ask the class to find the 1s and clap only on them, being quiet on the remaining beats in each measure.

C. Ask the class to clap on just 1s and 3s, being quiet on the 2s and 4s. When this type of activity is adapted to the instruments, the drums and cymbals might play the 1s, and the triangles play the remaining beats; the tambourines could rap on the 1s and shake on the remaining beats, etc.

Simple orchestrations suitable for teaching by rote are suggested in many of the albums prepared especially for use with rhythm instruments. (See listings at the end of this chapter.) As the children progress, they will enjoy playing more complicated orchestrations with longer pieces, such as Leroy Anderson's "Syncopated Clock" or Gounod's "Funeral March of a Marionette." Once the children are fairly familiar with the orchestration, they often enjoy having another child conduct them. It is quite surprising how very young children can familiarize themselves with the arrangement of a given selection to the point where they can cue, conduct, and command the attention of the players nearly as well as many professional conductors. In turn, the class also learns much about the real function of a conductor in a situation to which they can easily relate. (Some educators frown on this, but the children seem to enjoy it.)

IV. Reading from a score.

A. As an introduction to score reading, put a simple score on a chart or on the chalkboard, using drawings (in color, if possible) of the instruments to indicate the number of times they are to play in each measure, as below.

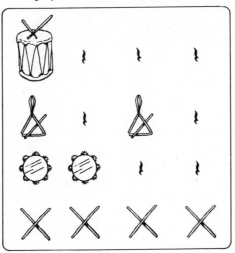

B. When the children have learned to identify quarter notes, half notes, dotted half notes, whole notes, quarter rests, and half rests, they will enjoy executing combinations of these rhythms from written notation using the instruments. In any short piece in $\frac{4}{4}$ time, for example, the notation might look something like this:

Picture or name of
instrument here, such as: Rhythm pattern here:

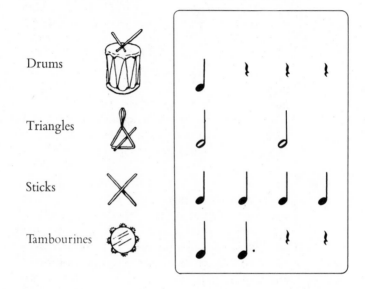

Drums

Triangles

Sticks

Tambourines

The same pattern is played over and over again throughout the piece.

C. In the following score, which is typical of many that are printed in children's songbooks, the rhythm patterns are varied. The method of playing such a score depends largely on the grade level and the previous experience of the children. The teacher may present the orchestration by rote by simply telling each child when and how many times he is to play, if the class is familiar with notation. If they have learned to read music, such a score provides a most desirable means of practice in the basic rhythms.

Note that the instrument indicated above the line in each row corresponds to the notes with the stems going up, whereas the instrument indicated below the line corresponds to the notes with the stems going down. A score of this type is read line by line; thus, the sticks and woodblocks will play the first line and the second line, but will stop and allow the bells and triangles to continue, beginning on the third line. Also note that the cymbals play only on the notes where the X is indicated. The double lines through the stems of the notes indicate that the tambourine is to be shaken rather than tapped on these notes.

Surprise Symphony

(From the Second Movement)

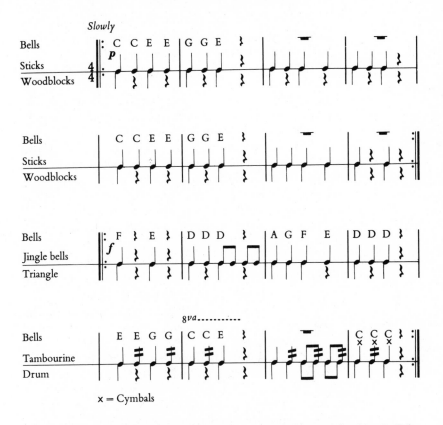

CREDIT: *From* This Is Music, Book III, *by William R. Sur, William R. Fisher, Mary R. Tolbert, and Adeline McCall. Copyright 1967 and 1961, by Allyn and Bacon, Inc. Used by permission.*

In scores such as the foregoing, not only is the child getting practice in basic rhythmic skills through reading the suggested notation, but he is also being afforded the opportunity to hear fine music. When his actual participation is required, he cannot help but listen more intently. Such listening, hopefully, should result in a more acute awareness of a feeling for the form, mood, dynamics, and beauty of the music than the child might otherwise have experienced.

As the children become more familiar with such scores, they should be encouraged to originate their own scores for use with other musical selections of their choice. This will require them to decide on appropriate instrumentation, create suitable rhythm patterns in sound (after listening carefully to the music), and be able to translate the sounds of their rhythm patterns into music notation for others to read.

V. Reinforcing a feeling for musical elements such as:

A. *Tempo* and *dynamics.* Have the children listen to a selected piece or pieces in which there are contrasting fast and slow sections or contrasting soft and loud sections. Ask the children to suggest appropriate instrumentation for each of the sections and to play when that section is heard.

B. *Mood.* Have the children select appropriate instruments for pieces of different moods or for pieces that contain contrasting moods and have them play. Judgment should be exercised as to whether the whole selection or merely certain portions of it are adaptable to the use of rhythm instruments.

C. *Form.* Have the children listen to a selected piece in AB, ABA, or rondo form. Ask them to suggest an appropriate instrument to play with the A theme every time it is heard. Do the same with the B theme (and others, according to the form of the piece). Assign selected instruments to various children. Careful listening is required to ensure playing at the proper time.

VI. Using rhythm instruments with body movement:

A. Rhythm instruments may be used to designate a change of movement and a direction or level of the movement:
   1. "Start walking while the drum beats the rhythm. When you hear the sound of the bells, run. At the sound of the tambourine, skip."
   2. "Start walking while the drum beats the rhythm. When the triangle sounds, walk on tiptoe; when the cymbals clash, stoop way down."
   3. "Start walking while the drum beats the rhythm. When you hear the bells, change the direction of your walk."
   4. "Skip in time to the drumbeat. When you hear the cymbals, freeze like a statue at whatever level you wish (high, medium or low)."

B. Quality in the sound of the rhythm instrument may be related to the quality of the body movement:
   1. Have a child show a movement that he would like the class to try. Have everyone do the movement. Ask, "Which of (three) instruments do you think is best suited to accompany that movement?"
   2. Choose a child to play the instrument and have him accompany while the class does the movement.
   3. Ask for another suggestion in movement. Encourage a different kind of movement. Proceed as above.
   4. If desired, the two movements can be done by two groups, using the appropriate instruments to accompany the groups. The number of times that each movement is to be executed should be stipulated in advance so that one may follow the other without interruption.

C. *Form* may be expressed in body movement as well as in music. Using one combination of body movement and rhythm instruments for an A, B, or C section, for example, requires attentive listening on the part of the child in order that he may make his response at the appropriate time. Harl McDonald's *Children's Symphony*★ is particularly adaptable to this type of exercise because the themes are familiar children's songs and are easily identifiable. Furthermore, such an activity could also help to heighten the child's awareness of various kinds of form, as well as provide an aid to better understanding of such terms as "development" and "symphony."

VII. Using rhythm instruments as a motivational device with tone-matching games. (See "Tone Matching Using Instruments," p. 12.)

Bottle Bands

Many instruments suitable for school use involve an expenditure of money, but the bottle band does not. In addition, it is fun, musical, and full of learning possibilities. The following suggestions are basic for beginners. They may, of course, be enlarged and improved upon through the use of bottles of various sizes.

1. Have each child bring to class a small soft-drink bottle of a specified kind. When a class is playing together, it is important that all the bottles be alike, i.e., the same brand of drink and the same size—especially when this activity is being attempted for the first time.

2. Producing an acceptable sound from a bottle is slightly more difficult than it might seem. The following suggestions might prove helpful in getting the children started correctly:
   a. Have the child press the bottle rim against the lower part of his lower lip and then blow across the top of the bottle in such a manner that the column of air is directed down as well as across. This is best accomplished by bringing the upper lip out and over just a bit, thus directing the air downward. The breath should be expelled evenly and easily—not in great explosions.
   b. Have the children practice at home. (Encourage them to teach their families too!)

3. Choose eight children from the class and "tune up" a scale as follows:
   a. Let the first empty bottle (on your left) be *do*. (Never mind what key you're in.)
   b. Add ½ to 1 inch of water in the next bottle—enough to produce the sound of *re* when blown.
   c. Add enough water to the third bottle to produce the sound of *mi* when blown.
   d. Add enough water to the fourth bottle to produce the sound of *fa*. Let the children discover that less water is needed for this interval

---

★ *Adventures in Music*, Grade two, RCA Victor.

from *mi* to *fa* (because it is only half step). The same will be true of the interval from *ti* to *do*.

    e. Add enough water to each of the remaining bottles to produce the sounds of *sol*, *la*, *ti*, and *do*, in that order.

4. When the eight bottles have been tuned, have the children stand in order of their scale tones from left to right so that—as you face the group—the low *do* is on your left, *re* is to the right of *do*, *mi* is to the right of *re*, etc., up to high *do* on your right. Show the class that they can play simple tunes merely by blowing when you point to them individually. Try an easy tune at first, something like "Twinkle, Twinkle, Little Star."

Point to the children individually as follows:

("*Twinkle, Twinkle, Little Star*")

Do do sol sol la la sol—
Fa fa mi mi re re do—
Do do sol sol la la sol—
Fa fa mi mi re re do—
Sol sol fa fa mi mi re—
Sol sol fa fa mi mi re—
Do do sol sol la la sol—
Fa fa mi mi re re do

or ("*Mary Had a Little Lamb*")

Mi re do re mi mi mi—
Re re re—mi sol sol—
Mi re do re mi mi mi
Mi re re mi re do

or ("*London Bridge*")

Sol la sol fa mi fa sol—
Re mi fa—mi fa sol—
Sol la sol fa mi fa sol—
Re—sol—mi do

Once the children have become familiar with the technique of blowing the bottles and have played the tunes by being pointed to individually, they should go on to reading their own music from notation, which is possible through the use of color:

a. Assign each scale tone a color. Low *do* might be red; *re*, blue; etc. It is helpful to have each child color his bottle (up to the water level) the color of the note he is to play.

b. Using colored inks, write out the tunes to be played on the staff on poster board. Using the colors previously suggested, every *do* would be a red note, every *re* a blue note, etc. If you don't care what key you're in, then just notate the song in its proper key and play from that notation. (For the moment, avoid accompanying on any other tuned instrument.) If you feel strongly about playing in a particular key, then first determine what key the bottles are actually in by blowing the empty one and finding the matching pitch on the piano. That will be *do*, of course, which means that whatever that note turns out to be is the name of the key. Simply write the tune in that key. The third alternative, obviously, is simply to tune the bottles by adding or subtracting water to arrive at whatever key you wish, using the piano, pitch pipe, or song bells.

Tunes which go below low *do* or above high *do* or which contain tones other than those in the major scale (chromatic tones) may be played merely by adding more bottles tuned to the desired pitches. In the case of the tones *below* the low *do*, however, it may be necessary to increase the size of the bottle, since otherwise it would be impossible to go any lower than the tone of the empty bottle that was originally used for *do*. The larger the bottle, the lower the pitch; the more water that is added, the higher the pitch.

If desired, the *entire* class may play all at once by tuning multiple bottles to the eight pitches. This will mean that within one class there may be several bottles tuned to the *do*, several to the *re*, etc., so that everyone is tuned to some scale tone. It is well to spread them as evenly as possible.

Chords may also be played with tuned bottles by blowing the selected notes simultaneously. For example,

Do–mi–sol played together produces a I chord.

Fa–la–do played together produces a IV chord.

Sol–ti–re–fa played together produces a V7 chord.

(More information on chords may be found under "Chord Structure," p. 96.)

Chording for "Twinkle, Twinkle, Little Star" might look something like this:

I	I	IV	I
Twinkle	Twinkle	Little	Star
IV	I	V7	I
How I	wonder	what you	are

When a few children have learned to play the tune without the teacher's help, they may be accompanied by the rest of the class playing chords through "cues" from the teacher—holding one finger up for I chord, four fingers for the IV chord, and five fingers for the V7 chord. Children soon learn who is to play on the I chord (when one finger is held up) and who is to play on the IV and V7 chords. The playing of chords is also possible through the same type of color coding that was suggested for playing melodies (p. 236), using the three proper note colors for a three-tone chord.

Chording for other songs may be easily worked out either by ear or by translating given lettered Autoharp chords (found in music textbooks) into number I, IV, or V7 accordingly, depending on the key of the song.

Accompaniments by the bottles may be varied through the use of the "oom-pah" rhythm—having the root of the chord played alone on the first beat, or "oom," followed by the remaining notes of the chord played on the remaining beats, either "pah" or "pah pah," depending on the time signature.

The addition of other "instruments" such as large gallon jugs, washboards, spoons, and a "one-string bass" (combination of broomstick, string, and washtub) produces what is commonly referred to as a "jug band."

Materials for Playing Classroom Instruments

MUSIC TO PLAY BY

The following selections provide good listening experiences as well as opportunities for creative uses of rhythm instruments.

"Andante" from *Symphony No. 94* ("Surprise")   Haydn
"Funeral March of a Marionette"   Gounod
"Minuet" from *Don Juan*   Mozart
"Minuet" from *Eine kleine Nachtmusik*   Mozart
"Norwegian Dance No. 2"   Greig
Toy Symphony   Haydn
"Waltz" from *Coppélia*   Delibes

RECORDS

Calypso Music for Children, AS–25 American Book Company. Audio Education Division, 55 Fifth Avenue, New York.

First Listening Experiences. Classroom Materials, Inc., 93 Myrtle Drive, Great Neck, N.Y.

Introducing Rhythm Instruments. Classroom Materials, Inc., 93 Myrtle Drive, Great Neck, N.Y.

Introduction to Rhythm Instruments. Lyons Band Instrument Company, 223 West Lake Street, Chicago, Ill.

Let's Have a Rhythm Band. Columbia Records, Inc., Educational Division, 799 Seventh Avenue, New York.

Little Indian Drum. Young People's Records, The Greystone Corporation, 100 Sixth Avenue, New York.

Music for Children. Orff and Keetman, Angel 3582B.

Music for Rhythm Bands. RCA Victor Basic Record Library for Elementary Schools.

Rhythm Band Patterns, vols. I and II, AS–28. American Book Company, 55 Fifth Avenue, New York.

Rhythm Instruments. Ruth White: Rhythms Productions, 1107 El Centro Avenue, Hollywood, Calif.

Strike Up the Band. Young People's Records, The Greystone Corporation, 100 Sixth Avenue, New York.

Toy Symphony (Haydn). Young People's Records, The Greystone Corporation, 100 Sixth Avenue, New York.

FILMS

Music for Children. Carl Orff: National Film Board of Canada, Contemporary Films, 267 West Twenty-fifth Street, New York.

Music with Children (four films dealing with adaptation of Orff concepts). Grace Nash: Box 476, Scottsdale, Ariz.

Percussion: The Pulse of Music. NET Film Service, Indiana University, Bloomington, Ind., 1957.

Rhythm: Instruments and Movements. Encyclopaedia Brittanica, 1150 Wilmette Avenue, Wilmette, Ill., 1959.

INSTRUCTIONAL MATERIALS

RECORDER

Enjoy Your Recorder. The Trapp Family Singers New Complete Method of Instruction for the Recorder. Magnamusic Distributors, Inc., Sharon, Conn. 1957.

Goodyear, Stephen: *The New Recorder Tutor Books.* Mills Music, Inc., New York, 1956.

Nash, Grace: *Recorder for Beginners.* Swartwout Enterprises, Scottsdale, Ariz.

Nitka, Arthur: *Your Popular Hits for Recorder.* Edward B. Marks Music Corporation, New York.

SMALL WINDS

Beckman, Frederick: *Classroom Method for Melody Flute.* Melody Flute Co., Laurel, Md.

Buchtel, Forrest L.: *Melody Fun for Singing and Playing the Tonette.* Neil A. Kjos Company, Park Ridge, Ill., 1939.

Van Pelt and Ruddick: *Flutophone Classroom Method*, rev. ed. Trophy Products Co., Cleveland, Ohio.

HARMONICA

How to Play the Harmonica. M. Hohner, Inc., Hicksville, N.Y.

Let's Play the Harmonica. M. Hohner, Inc., Hicksville, N.Y. (Books of songs for playing with the harmonica also available from the same company).

UKULELE

Breen, May Singhi: *Self Teaching Method—Islander Uke.* Mastro Industries, Inc., New York.

Keen, Laura J.: *Sing and Play the Ukulele.* Carl Van Roy Co., Far Rockaway, N.Y.

Reser, Harry: *Picture Chords for Standard Ukulele*. Remick Music Corporation, New York.

Smiths' Simplified Illustrated Baritone Ukulele Method and Song Folio. Wm. J. Smith Music Co., New York.

Waikiki Ukulele Method. Carl Fischer, Inc., New York.

MELODICA

Playing the Hohner Melodica. M. Hohner, Inc., Hicksville, N.Y.

Popular Favorites. M. Hohner, Inc., Hicksville, N.Y. (Song collections for playing with the melodica also available from the same company.)

GUITAR

Silverman, Jerry: *Beginning the Folk Guitar*. Folkways, New York. (Record available with this book.)

DRUMS

Christie, Thomas: *Beat Easy Drum Method*. Wm. J. Smith Music Co., New York.

Kessler, William: *Simplified Modern Drum Technique*. Carl Van Roy Co., Far Rockaway, N.Y.

AUTOHARP

Instructor for the Autoharp. Oscar Schmidt–International, Inc., Union, N.J.

Learn to Play the Autoharp (film strip and record). Bowmar Records.

OTHERS

Hall, Doreen: *Music for Children* (Orff method). Associated Music Publishers, Inc., New York, 1960.

Krugman, Lillian D., and Alice Jeanne Ludwig: *Little Calypsos*. Carl Van Roy Co., Far Rockaway, N.Y.

Lesinksy, Adam: *Fife Jug and Bottle Book*. Belwin, Inc., New York.

Nash, Grace: *Music with Children* (adaptation of Orff method). Swartout Enterprises, Box 476, Arizona.

Staples, R. J.: *Classroom Teacher's Guide and Score for the Musical Fun Books*. Follett Publishing Company, Chicago, 1956.

———: *Fun with Keyboard*. Follet Publishing Company, Chicago.

———: *Fun with Melody Bells*. Follett Publishing Company, Chicago.

———: *Fun with the Rhythm Instruments*. Follett Publishing Company, Chicago, 1955.

Vandevere, Lillian: *Sound Sketches for Rhythm Instruments*. Carl Van Roy Co., Far Rockaway, N.Y.

Further material relating to the playing of classroom instruments may also be found throughout various children's music texts as well as in selected chapters in the professional literature. (See "Professional Reading," p. 7.)

INSTRUMENTS

Children's Music Center, 5373 West Pico Boulevard, Los Angeles, Calif.

Conn Corporation, 1101 East Beardsley Street, Elkhart, Ind.

Educational Music Bureau, 434 South Wabash Avenue, Chicago, Ill.

M. Hohner, Inc., Hicksville, N.Y. (harmonicas, melodicas, recorders).

Kitching Educational, 505 Shawmut, LaGrange, Ill.

Lyons Band Instrument Co., 223 West Lake Street, Chicago.

Melody Flute Company, Laurel, Md.

Oscar Schmidt–International, Inc., Union, N.J. (Autoharps and guitars).

Peripole, Inc., 51–17 Rockaway Beach Boulevard, Far Rockaway, N.Y.

Scientific Music Industries, Inc., 1255 South Wabash Avenue, Chicago. (Swiss Melodé bells).

Walberg and Auge, 31 Mercantile Street, Worcester, Mass.

LISTENING
EXPERIENCES

"Whether you listen to Mozart or Duke Ellington, you can deepen your understanding of music only by being a more conscious and aware listener—not someone who is just listening, but someone who is listening *for* something."*

The above statement, made by one of America's foremost composers, embodies much of what is at the heart of a successful listening lesson—providing the children with something specific to listen *for*.

Without a focus there is no involvement—the child's listening becomes passive rather than active, and what he hears becomes simply another sound in his already sound-full environment. He becomes "tuned out" rather than "turned on."

As suggested in Chapter 4, Ear Training Experiences (p. 108), children need to be aided in the art of listening in general, and various procedures for accomplishing this were outlined there. In addition to those procedures, the following might be helpful before attempting any formal listening experiences:

1. Have the children close their eyes, keep very still, and listen to all the sounds inside and outside the room. (You can make some of your own if you wish.) If there are enough interesting sounds, divide the class into groups and assign each group a sound to reproduce.
2. Alert the children to listen for sounds in the environment by asking, "What did you hear on the way to school today?" (Try again tomorrow. Since they didn't know you were going to ask, they probably won't have heard a thing today.) As the children indicate some of the sounds they heard, list them on the board. Depending on the level and previous musical experience of the class, try having them categorize the sounds according to whether they were:

   High or low
   Soft or loud
   Fast or slow
   Long or short

   Of course, some sounds will be none of these. Others will seem to have pitch (brakes, teakettles, whistles, bells, sirens, horns, etc.), while others will have a definite rhythmic sound (trains, washing machines, cement mixers, windshield wipers).**
3. Help the children to discover that "pitch" (in this context) refers to the highness or lowness of a sound and that "rhythm" refers to the regular recurrence of something and is present not only in their immediate environment but in nature and the universe as well (heartbeat, breathing, the seasons, the tides, day and night, etc.).
4. Ask the children to try to translate these definitions of pitch and

* Aaron Copland, *What to Listen for in Music*. McGraw-Hill Book Company, New York, 1957.

** Folkways record *Rhythms of the World* (FC 7340) is excellent for this.

rhythm into musical terms; e.g., pitch refers to the highness or lowness of a tone, and rhythm is the regular recurrence of accent. (It might be pertinent to mention here that both of these terms are often the subject of spirited discussions among musicians whose opinions differ widely as to how each should be defined. The very simple definitions given above were used because they have been found to be within the children's understanding and adequate for teaching purposes.) If the science of sound is under study in the curriculum at any given time, then further information relating to vibrations and air columns as they affect pitch could enrich both the science and the music experience.

Scheduling

Optimally, a teacher should set aside at least one music period weekly to be devoted to a carefully planned listening experience. This would ensure continuity in the total year's listening program as well as progress in the children's musical growth. This is not to imply that a child never hears a record at any other time than during the scheduled period. Rather, the object here is to try to avoid the loss of an integral part of a child's musical education.

Time Allotment

Budgeting of time is most important in planning a listening activity. The time devoted to listening should not exceed that devoted to any regular music period and certainly should be no longer than thirty minutes. Even less is preferable—mandatory in lower grades. Indeed, in lower grades the teacher may need to resort to "serializing," that is, playing a short installment each time. In upper grades, too, it would be unwise to attempt to play a whole symphony in one sitting, for example. There may be many instances where more than one period is necessary for the purpose of completing a "total" listening experience. In others, a teacher may wish to play more than one musical selection in the course of a single music period, depending upon the original purpose of the lesson.

Equipment and Environment

Providing the children with an aesthetic experience requires attention not only to the musical material itself but also to such mundane matters as proper equipment and environment. Souls are not exalted when distortions emanate from worn records and phonographs in need of repair. Children deserve only the best equipment and environment for listening. This implies:

1. A good-quality multispeed phonograph—either monaural or stereo.
2. A proper needle, also in good condition, designed for playing monaural or stereo records (depending on the phonograph) and varying speeds.
3. Unscratched recordings appropriate to the type of phonograph used—monaural or stereo. Today most records are issued in both monaural and stereo. Choice must be specified when ordering.
   NOTE: Some machines require a slight needle adjustment on the tone arm when the record is 78 rpm, as opposed to slower. It is imperative that this adjustment be made when called for; otherwise many records will quickly deteriorate in quality.
4. A well-ventilated, adequately lighted room, reasonably free from outside noise, at least for the time the listening is planned. (A Halloween parade in the hall or a play period outside the window is hardly conducive to a successful listening experience.)
5. An orderly arrangement of the materials to be used, e.g., theme charts or other visual materials, as well as sufficient usable chalkboard space when required.

Levels of aggravation may be reduced if the teacher remembers to set up and check out all equipment beforehand. Failure to do so could result in putting the needle down during a moment of hushed expectancy and having nothing come out. (And who among us hasn't had *that* happen at least once?) Furthermore, a teacher can't afford to waste minutes of designated listening time dashing about to find an extension cord or looking for double plugs. When the plans include the use of a filmstrip projector or any other piece of equipment that requires electricity, it is even more imperative that everything be in proved working order before the lesson begins.

While we are on the subject of equipment, a tape recorder, when available, is most helpful for programming lessons. This provides a means of isolating main themes as well as other significant musical elements to which the teacher may wish to call attention before the class listens to the whole composition. It also enables the teacher to replay these elements as many times as he feels necessary. Trying to find just the right place to put a needle down on a record for this purpose can prove most frustrating.

A "listening station" is also a valuable addition to any class room. This consists of a record player adapted to the use of several sets of earphones so that the children may enjoy hearing previous classroom listening experiences, as well as discovering new ones. A tape recorder may also be adapted to the use of earphones in the same manner.

245

In order for listening experiences to result in children's musical enrichment and growth, it is vital that the teacher pay careful attention to the planning of each of the listening lessons.

Good planning requires a clear statement of what it is hoped will be accomplished, plus some specific measures for attaining these goals, keeping ever in mind, of course, the reasons why we are teaching music in the classroom in the first place. Stated in more specific terms, a suggested skeletal framework for planning a listening experience might shape up something like this:

1. Teacher Preparation
   a. General background information
   b. Familiarity with specific selection(s) to be played
   c. Materials and equipment needed
2. Definition of objectives
3. Procedures:
   a. Getting children to listen
   b. Questions and comments designed to direct the listening
   c. Providing opportunities for creative expression and/or possible related activities for reinforcing learnings
4. Related additional listening experiences
5. Evaluation

Since the foregoing outline is brief, further information and suggestions relative to some of the items are given in the following paragraphs.

Teacher Preparation

GENERAL

In the beginning of the year it might be helpful for the teacher to indicate to his class that he intends to bring them a wide variety of musical listening experiences so that they may become familiar with all kinds of music. Actually, there are only two kinds of music—good and bad—and children should be made aware of this. It is only through being provided with a variety of listening experiences and opportunities to develop their discriminatory powers that children will become better able to distinguish, at least in part, between what is good music and what is less than good.

Teachers frequently voice concern over finding ways to bridge the "gap" between what children hear pounded incessantly on the "outside" and what it would be nice to expose them to "inside." There needn't be such a dichotomy here. If a teacher is sincere in his desire to have his children become selective and discriminating consumers, then he is committed to allowing into appraisal setting *all* types of music, including that of the current idiom. What better place for a good, close look at this product of a subculture than in the classroom, where valid evaluative criteria may be discussed and refined? If we refuse to allow any of today's music into the classroom, we are in effect denying its existence. This is not to say that all the classroom musical listening experiences will consist of this type of music or that it will be played indiscriminately and without purpose. Rather we can draw upon this music occasionally as one more source of musical material to illustrate certain elements or qualities in music that may be under study at the moment, just as we draw upon musical examples from the past. Counterpoint, for example, did not die with Bach. It is still very much alive today in Brubeck. A lesson involving music in the modern idiom may well require even greater skill in planning in order to achieve the desired objectives or outcomes. This could conceivably be considered one way of bridging the so-called gap—another is through the use of highly rhythmical ethnic music, which is very appealing to children and provides many learning possibilities.

Young children are interested in music that is more descriptive, highly expressive, and/or emotional in content; thus "program" music (dealing with stories, scenes, ideas, etc.) should constitute a large part of the younger child's listening experiences. This is not to say that music for young children must always be *about* something. They frequently find beauty and satisfaction in listening to some of the more "abstract" pieces. As a child matures, so do his discriminatory powers; thus an older child is more capable of grasping subtleties in the music than a younger child. The older child will find beauty not only in the sound but also in the design and form of the music. Since it is possible for him to derive intellectual enjoyment from listening, the implication here is that we may enlarge his listening experiences to include more music of the "absolute" or nondescriptive type.

The stereotyped approach of starting with music of the baroque or classical period and proceeding through the romantic period, etc., has little appeal for children, nor have long, date-filled biographies of composers. Information about periods and composers, when pertinent, should emerge logically and be explored only when it serves to enhance the child's listening experience and make it more meaningful.

With older children it is possible to study a composer's music in terms of him as a person—subject to the joys, frustrations, and needs common to all human beings. Perhaps his music expresses some of these. Perhaps he may have felt it necessary, because of the times in which he lived, to say musically what could not then be said in oratory; maybe a love for his country or a cause to which he felt committed shines through in his music.

Children should not be led to believe that all composers must be divinely inspired before they can write music. In the past, composers had jobs to do, such as composing music for certain occasions—celebrations, funerals, church services, etc. There simply was no time to sit and wait for the spirit to move them. Incidentally, understanding the purpose for which a piece of music was

247

written provides a child with the opportunity to decide whether he thinks the piece is appropriate for that purpose.

Children should also be made aware of the fact that music, along with the other arts, has been subjected to many influences through the ages—social, political, and economic pressures as well as the individual composer's own personal pressures—and that the effects of these influences are evident not only in the *kind* of music that grew out of each period but also in the amount and quality of it. (Some of the basic music textbooks contain what are termed "time lines,"[*] which often prove useful in this connection, for they show familiar historical events that occurred during a given composer's lifetime.) Evidence of the effects of the aforementioned influences may also be pointed out in terms of the other art forms. Showing paintings by famous artists while playing selected musical compositions of the same period is one way of illustrating parallel similarities in the two art forms. This activity might also be used as a springboard to provoke some thoughtful discussion among the children as to the effect modern social, political, and economic factors are having, or could have in the future, on music and the other arts.

There seems to be a general feeling that children have difficulty finding *do* in their lives today, just as we often experience difficulty finding *do* in much of today's music. Similarly, in the realm of art we don't always know which way to hang the picture, for in many cases we can't identify the "up" side. Both art forms seem to be steeped in a kind of contemporary unrest that isn't evident in a Hadyn symphony or a Gilbert Stuart painting, for example. As a child begins to sense the apparent pattern of direction, he may wish to speculate on the kind of music he may conceivably expect to hear in the future. Such a discussion, it would seem, is far more significant, because of the challenge it presents to a child's thinking, than the keeping of voluminous notes on the lives of numerous composers.

In the process of bringing many kinds of music to the children, the teacher should always exercise care and not attempt to impose his own personal tastes on them, for the child's first impulse is to reject the teacher's values in order to maintain respect for his own. In many classrooms where the teacher-pupil relationship abounds with respect on both sides, the children seem willing to listen with open minds to anything the teacher chooses to play for them. After a decent period of exposure, whether they like the piece or not should be an entirely personal matter for them.

SPECIFIC

The more familiar the teacher is with the recording, the better able he is to select the musical qualities for which he wishes his class to listen. Also, the broader the teacher's background of listening experiences and the more related information he has about the music, the better equipped he is to make more

---

[*]*Exploring Music.* Holt, Rinehart and Winston, Inc., New York, 1966; *Discovering Music Together.* Follett Publishing Company, Chicago, 1966; *Making Music Your Own.* Silver Burdett Company, Morristown, N.J., 1963.

creative presentations. Many of the record albums made especially for use in schools (RCA *Adventures in Music* series, Bowmar Orchestral Library, Keyboard, Jr., etc.) come with accompanying pamphlets that contain a great deal of pertinent background information as well as valuable teaching suggestions for each piece of music. Record albums accompanying children's basic song series often contain not only the song material but also listening selections, with suggestions for their presentation. Themes and related reading matter written at the appropriate level of difficulty may be found in the children's books. There are many other sources of information, of course. (See the listings at the end of this chapter.) Securing further related material that is pertinent and meaningful to the children means that the teacher must spend extra time doing research, but it is well worth the reward of increased interest on the part of the class.

The teacher should plan to give his undivided attention while the music is being heard—not to use the playing time to grade papers, work on an overdue register, or, worse yet, hold a discussion with another teacher in the back of the room. If the teacher expects the children to give their complete attention during a listening activity, then they have the right to expect the same from him. If the music is not worthy of the undivided attention of everyone, then it should not be played at all.

Defining Objectives

Stating the objectives for any given lesson consists simply of indicating what it is hoped that lesson will accomplish. The teacher does not need to say how he intends to attain his goals or what devices he plans to use. Devices relating to the "how" and the "what" should be stated in terms of "procedures and related activities" or however the teacher chooses to describe them. The statements that follow are intended to relate to *objectives* only.

Teachers frequently divide objectives into two types, calling them "large" and "small," "general" and "specific," or "long-range" and "immediate," for example. We shall use the terms "general" and "specific" to refer to the two kinds of objectives.

When applied to music, the larger or more general objectives might be expressed in such terms as "to provide a richer and fuller life for every child," "to help a child develop discrimination and selectivity in what he hears," "to increase a child's listening repertoire," or "to increase a child's desire for further knowledge and understanding in music."

Specific or immediate objectives should pertain to a particular listening experience (or series of listening experiences) and should be clearly defined in terms of the musical elements, qualities, characteristics, etc., that the teacher wishes to bring under study in the specific listening experience, e.g., "to increase a child's awareness of musical form and design" or "to aid the child in understanding the term 'fugue' through illustrations in varied musical contexts." In effect, we are asking the child to discover what the music clearly states. In doing so, we are committed to providing focal points in the listening experiences as a means of helping him to achieve this desired outcome.

A composer can make a statement through the use of melody, harmony, rhythm, form, dynamics, tempo, or instrumentation or in many other ways. Whichever one or more of these other elements a child is asked to listen for is entirely dependent on the objectives that have been set up for that particular listening experience. It might be well to mention here that a given listening experience may not always be confined to one selection. For the purpose of illustrating a musical term or a common theme, it may be necessary to play several different selections. For example, if the teacher wishes to show *contrast* in the way in which two or more composers treat the same subject matter, obviously more than one selection will have to be played ("Morning Mood" from Grieg's *Peer Gynt Suite* contrasted with "Sunrise" from Grofé's *Grand Canyon Suite*, for example). The point to be made here is that merely hearing the difference in the overall sound of the two selections should not be defined as the main objective of the lesson. Rather, the main purpose might better be stated as "to help the child discover how different composers dealing with the same subject matter use the same musical elements in different ways to produce contrasting effects." Questions from the teacher such as, "Was the element of melody more prominent in one piece than the other?" or "How did each composer's choice of instruments contribute to the contrast in sound between the two selections?" would provide more specific direction to the child's listening and thinking.

Objectives might also be stated in terms of acquiring new knowledge based on previous information (or vice versa); e.g., having become familiar with the term "melody," the child could now be given the opportunity to view it in many different musical settings: theme, fugue, folk themes in larger works, popular tunes from larger works, national anthems in music, melodic variations on a given theme, modes, etc. Obviously, in the process of listening to many of these examples in connection with the term "melody," a child would be acquiring other musical learnings as well, since the objectives for each listening selection would be stated in terms of the total musical content of the piece. Further knowledge of the characteristics of various periods and styles of composers, as well as new terms such as "suite," "concerto," and "symphony" (if examples happened to be chosen from such works), could all be considered valid objectives also, along with increasing the child's knowledge of the concept of melody.

As a child's listening repertoire is broadened (and certainly we should always keep this general objective in mind) and as his knowledge is deepened, it is reasonable to expect that a vocabulary of terms will emerge; therefore, in this connection it would be well for the teacher to indicate somewhere in his objectives specifically what new terms might arise in the course of the given listening experience so that any needed explanations will not be overlooked.

Care should be exercised that *musical learnings* do not become confused with *motivational devices* or *related activities*. For example, when first being introduced to *Peer Gynt*, a child would, of necessity, have to hear the story because it is upon the story that the music is based; however, in defining *musical objectives*, familiarity with the story should not be the end result of the listening lesson. The story, of course, is part of the whole composition since it doubtlessly inspired the composer in the first place; however, the main purpose of the listening experience is not to have the children learn the story of Peer Gynt, but rather to help them discover how well the composer tells the story through the use of the many wonderful musical devices—mood, dynamics, instrumentation, etc—at his disposal. This is where so many listening lessons in the classroom fall short. They simply do not go far enough into the heart of the music itself, but rather are too much concerned with all the peripheral factors. Perhaps this happens because many teachers are not sure just what the *heart* of the music is. This uncertainty is reflected in rather vague objectives and in a consequent lack of direction in the lesson itself. Many classroom teachers may tend to avoid listening lessons altogether for this same reason.

All the foregoing is not to say that we must dissect and clinically examine every piece of music that is played in the classroom. Sometimes music is there just for quiet listening and dreaming to "melt the meanness" of the day, while resting. The point to be made is that when a teacher wishes to do some in-depth study of a piece of music with his class, he must first adequately prepare himself and then define his objectives carefully—determining them on the basis of the *content* of the music itself and the children's *level of development*. In addition, he must take care not to become trapped by the specifics while losing sight of the larger picture, nor should he remain so rigidly committed to the achievement of the stated objectives that he misses rich opportunities to savor beauty, suspense, and "teachable moments" along the way.

Procedures

GETTING CHILDREN TO LISTEN

Most teachers are aware of the fact that younger children often require more interesting motivating devices than do older children, but whatever the children's age, inducements to listen are always welcome and helpful.

Once he has chosen his listening selection and defined his objectives, a clever teacher can originate many unique ways of motivating the children to listen. He soon learns that in selecting appropriate motivation, the opening sentence is most important. The totally unimaginative beginning statement "Today I'm going to play . . ." simply won't do. Try drawing motivation from many varied sources. The following are but a few of the more obvious devices that can be used:

1. Something in the child's immediate or past experience that you can relate to the listening selection: "How many of you have ever

251

ridden on a train?" "How did you get to school this morning?" "What other ways do we have of getting from place to place?"

2. Something in another area of the curriculum that is under study at the moment and could be related to the listening selection. (This might be a comfortable starting point for the teacher who feels a bit timid about attempting his first listening lesson. (See "Vitalizing Other Subject Matter through Music," p. 314.)
3. An upcoming holiday or special day; a recent event; the season.
4. Poems, stories, legends, or folk tales upon which the music might have been based or which involve the same subject matter as the music.
5. Pictures, puppets, stuffed animals, or other objects related in some way to the listening. (A "surprise box" turned out to be a delightful introduction to the *Surprise Symphony*!)
6. Singing a familiar song, which will be heard later within the framework of the larger listening selection. (Many larger works contain folk themes and other familiar tunes.)
7. A costume or unusual instrument of folk origin.
8. Showing famous paintings or art objects related to the listening. (There are paintings whose titles include musical terms, as well as musical compositions that were inspired by famous paintings.)
9. Hearing a small portion of the piece itself as a "teaser." "Do you recognize this tune?"
10. Reference to, or a tape recording of, music used on a television or radio commercial that may relate in some way to the listening selection.
11. Filmstrips, sound films, and other visuals related to the listening. The use of the filmstrip is not recommended in lessons where the teacher intends to have the children draw pictures related to the music. They tend to draw what they have already seen, rather than to create their own images inspired wholly by the music.

Obviously, the choice of motivational devices is dependent upon the piece of music that is to be played.

QUESTIONS AND COMMENTS TO CHILDREN

In preparing questions dealing with musical listening experiences, care should be taken to phrase them in such a way that the child is forced to do some thinking of his own. Even before the record is played, it is important that the child be made to feel the need for careful, attentive listening if he expects to come up with a reasonable response. Well-structured questions by the teacher that require responses dependent upon closer attention to the music should help to ensure at least some interaction between the child and the music and, hopefully, could result in making the listening experience more meaningful to him.

Many teachers make the mistake of asking a question in such a way that their voice inflection immediately telegraphs the response the child is expected to make and leaves no room for thought on his part. "Did you *all* hear the *very loud* sound at the end of the music?" is a typical example of this type of question. A more desirable response, in musical terms, might be elicited if the question were worded, "What did you hear at the very end of the piece?"

When questioning younger children, the teacher should concentrate on the more obvious elements in the music, such as distinguishing between soft and loud, fast and slow, happy and sad, and high sounds and low sounds; deciding whether the music runs, walks, skips, or gallops; and identifying musical phrases and accent ("Can you find the ones?" "Does the music move in twos or threes?"). Since younger children are responsive to music that tells a story, they might be asked to listen for "when the bear comes in," for example. It is wise to let the children discover some of the action by themselves rather than risk taking away all the suspense by telling the *whole* story of the music right to the end. Say, for example, "Listen and see whether you can tell what the tailor did after the bear left."* (Went back to his sewing and whistling.) Then ask, "How do you know this?" (Because it's the same tune we heard at the beginning.)

In our haste to impart information to children, we often make a statement concerning some quality in the music and then add quickly, "Don't you think so?" Even if a child *didn't* think so, he probably wouldn't admit it.

Asking, "What did you like best about this piece?" is a much more positive way of getting the child to do some thinking and answering in musical terms than asking, "Didn't you *like* this piece?" (Voice inflection— "You were *supposed* to!") The author feels strongly that discretion should be used when asking children whether they like something—a song, a record, or anything else. In the first place, some children don't like anything the first time they're introduced to it. Secondly, there may be a few children who will *never* like something no matter how good it is, and it's disconcerting to see these heads shaking sideways when you'd prefer to see them shaking up and down. Still other children take longer to decide whether they like something or not. They do not choose to make immediate commitments. They need more time to savor the idea. Most teachers would probably agree that when a class as a whole really likes something, there's no need to ask. The "like" simply pops out all over.

Questions such as, "What did you think was the most outstanding musical element in this piece?" directs the child's thinking immediately to the *music*. If there is any doubt in a teacher's mind about a child's ability to discern a "musical element," it might be advisable to list a few such elements on the board and have the child choose the most appropriate one for the piece. This will help to rule out such diversionary possibilities as, "You had the record player turned up too loud!"

* McDowell, *Of a Tailor and a Bear*. RCA Victor Basic Library, *Listening*, vol. 2.

Responses relating to emotion may be difficult for some children to verbalize. A child may have difficulty answering a question such as, "How does this music make you feel?" because it is too personal, or he could conceivably make a response that was undesirable as far as classroom decorum is concerned. Here again, the teacher could put a list of descriptive words on the board, as a beginning, and then encourage the children to add words of their own. (Granted, the objective is the same—to have the children describe the mood of the piece—but the means of attaining it seem less intrusive.)

A class familiar with many musical elements as well as the characteristic sounds of the instruments of the orchestra would, of course, be expected to delve deeper into the music than simply describing the mood. They could be asked how the composer used instrumentation to create the effect in the piece. Later on, they might choose some descriptive word or create some scene or situation of their own and indicate what instruments as well as what musical devices they would use to portray it. Questions might be phrased as follows: "What instrument would you use if you were writing a song about children? About wars? About the sea?" "What instrument of the woodwind family do you feel best describes morning? Afternoon? Night?" "What instruments would you choose to depict a conversation between a giant and a small boy? A young man and an old woman? An elephant and a mouse?" "What instrument of the orchestra do you feel could best describe the quality of this color?" (Hold up either a brilliant or a pastel color.) In addition, several possible musical structures (ABA, fugue, rondo, etc., according to level of the class) might be listed on the board from which the children would be asked to choose the correct one for the selection heard. As a culminating activity following study of some of the basic forms, the teacher might like to encourage the children to create something of their own either within the traditional form or within new structures that they originate themselves.

One of the concepts that, hopefully, children will eventually grasp is that of the very different effects that can be produced when various elements of music are used in different ways. Asking, for example, "How does this composer use *melody* to portray this scene?" ensures the child's concentrating on the one musical element of *melody* in terms of its use in the given musical selection. In this attempt to answer the question, he discovers what a melody really is and what a wide range of musical possibilities it has. He finds that the notes of a melody can, for example, stay very close together or travel far apart; that a melody can be pitched high or low; that it can move quickly or slowly, depending on the character of the notes assigned to it; that it can flow smoothly in legato fashion or hop in birdlike staccato; and that its entire character and the effect it produces on the listener may be completely altered simply by changing its mode from major to minor, its dynamics from soft to loud, or its instrumentation from strings to brass. With this information and more, the child becomes more adequately equipped to suggest his own ways of using not only melody but also other elements of music to communicate whatever musical message he wishes to his listener.

254

Related Activities

Children need not be made to sit still and listen *every* time a given listening selection is played. There are many opportunities for creative expression in various areas that may logically emerge from listening experiences. The following are merely sample suggestions:

1. Choosing appropriate rhythm instruments to play with the listening selection. (The choice, of course, will be determined by the character of the piece, as the children define it.) Also, creating original scores for rhythm instruments and notating them on the board for the whole class to play. (See "Rhythm Instruments," p. 223.)

2. Improvising some body movement that fits the type of music heard. This will also be determined by the mood, tempo, rhythm, etc., of the piece. (Some children might be motivated by the sound of a particular orchestral instrument to move in a way that suggests its appearance.) The sounds of electronic music often elicit interesting responses from children.

3. Drawing designs or scenes inspired by the content and/or form of the music.

4. Creating stories or poems about the music.

5. Creating original words to particularly melodic themes heard in the music.

6. Doing creative dramatizations. (Listening selections particularly appropriate for this activity are listed at the end of this chapter.)

7. Illustrating various musical terms and qualities in the listening selection (fugue, theme and variations, form, crescendo, etc.) through the use of body movement. (See "Creating with Body Movement," p. 308.)

8. Illustrating various musical terms and qualities in the listening selection (as above) through the use of various art media and/or styles. (For example, the term "theme and variations" in music might be illustrated in art by having the children choose a subject and then vary it by using different art media or styles.)

9. Dancing the rhythm patterns in the music.

The activities suggested above, as well as others similar to them, should help to further the child's deeper involvement in the music because at the outset he knows he is expected to make a response; thus he is committed to more active listening in order that his response be one that is satisfying to him. It would be advisable to make provision for, as well as to encourage, many different forms of expression since not all children derive the same satisfaction from a given medium.

Participation in activities such as those described above often helps to facilitate the child's grasp of certain bodies of musical knowledge that the teacher may have defined in his objectives. Here again, as in motivation, the *activity* should not be confused with the *objective*. These activities are not the main objectives—any more than the learning of the story upon which a piece of music is based is—rather, they merely play an assigned part in helping to achieve the desired outcomes of a given listening experience. Obviously, these activities have their own intrinsic value, or they would not be suggested; however, their benefits are twofold, for they serve to further musical understandings as well. It might be advisable to mention also that their effectiveness is enhanced when they are used with discretion. For further suggestions, see "Rhythm Instruments," p. 223, "Creating with Body Movement," p. 308, and "Vitalizing Other Subject Matter through Music," p. 314.

Related Additional Listening Experiences

Once a teacher has defined a particular musical objective, he may discover that it will take not just one but a *series* of listening experiences in order to accomplish it in depth. For example, if he wishes to increase the children's knowledge of the fugue, he has a wide variety of musical illustrations from which to choose. Since he is committed to bringing before the children music of all types, he might choose to select fugue examples from many different sources, ranging from the past to the present. The more different fugues a child hears, hopefully, the better he will understand the meaning of the term "fugue." Meanwhile, his range of listening experiences is broadened considerably in the process.

The lists below contain but a few of the many listening selections that might be used to further illustrate a given musical term ("element," "characteristic," "quality," etc.). The headings of the lists of recordings are intended to act as a framework upon which the teacher may build a large listening repertoire for the enrichment of his class. In a sense, the terms provide a sort of built-in motivation of their own for further listening. The teacher might say, for example, "The other day we heard 'Pop Goes the Weasel' played in many ways and were introduced to the musical term 'variations.' Let's listen today to see whether we can discover what musical devices Charles Ives used to make his variations on another tune we all know well—'America.'"

There are many other possibilities, of course, but perhaps these should be sufficient to make the point here.

FUGUE *

> *Cat's Fugue* Scarlatti (KJ)
> *Fugue and Chorale on "Yankee Doodle"* Thomson (BOL, *Music in U.S.A.*)
> *Fugue in Bop Themes* Brubeck

* BOL—Bowmar Orchestral Library; AM—*Adventures in Music* Series, RCA Victor;
KJ—Keyboard, Jr., Publications.

Little Fugue in G Minor   Bach (AM, grade six, vol. 1, RCA)
Pumpkin-eater's Little Fugue   McBride (BOL, *Music in U.S.A*)

THEME AND VARIATIONS

Theme and Variations for Percussion Instruments   William Kraft
Theme and Variations from Surprise Symphony   Haydn
Under the Spreading Chestnut Tree   Weinberger
Variations on "America"   Ives
Variations on "I Got Rhythm"   George Gershwin
Variations on "Pop Goes the Weasel"   Caillet

DANCES IN LISTENING★

"Can Can"   Lecocq (BOL, *Dances*, Part II)
Concerto for Tap Dance and Orchestra   Gould
"Danzon" from *Fancy Free*   Bernstein
"Gavotte"   Kabalevsky (BOL, *Dances*, Part I)
"Gigue"   Bach (AM 1, RCA)
"Hoe-down" from *Rodeo*   Copland (AM 5, vol. 2, RCA)
"Mazurka in B♭," Opus 7, No. 1   Chopin (KJ)
"Minuet" from *Don Giovanni*   Mozart
"Polka" from *The Golden Age*   Shostakovich
Symphonic dances from *West Side Story*   Bernstein
"Tango," "Waltz," and "Ragtime" from *The Soldier's Tale*   Stravinsky
    (BOL, *Music of the Dance*)
"Tarantella"   Rossini-Respighi (BOL, *Dances*, Part II)
(Other types of dances in listening include the saraband, bourrée, horn-
    pipe, galop, allemande, polonaise, and rondo.)

FAMILIAR SONGS IN LARGER WORKS

Academic Festival Overture   Brahms ("Gaudeamus Igitur" and others)
Death Valley Suite   Grofé (Stephen Foster songs)
Symphony No. 1, Third Movement   Mahler ("Are You Sleeping,
    Brother John?")
Variations on "America"   Ives ("America")

MUSIC THAT TELLS A STORY★

Danse Macabre   Saint-Saëns (KJ)
Háry János   Kodály (KJ)
Of a Tailor and a Bear   MacDowell (RCA Basic Library, vol. 2)
Scheherazade   Rimsky-Korsakoff (KJ)
The Sorcerer's Apprentice   Dukas (KJ)
Till Eulenspiegel's Merry Pranks (KJ)

★ BOL—Bowmar Orchestral Library; AM—*Adventures in Music* Series, RCA Victor;
KJ—Keyboard, Jr., Publications.

MUSIC THAT PAINTS A PICTURE

Carnival of the Animals   Saint-Saëns
Grand Canyon Suite   Grofé
La Mer   Debussy
Pictures at an Exhibition   Moussorgsky
The Moldau   Smetana
Three Places in New England   Ives

MUSICAL STUDIES IN CONTRAST

(Could be expanded to include contrast in *treatment* of the *same subject* matter by two different composers.)

Eine kleine Nachtmusik (Mozart) and *A Night on Bald Mountain* (Moussorgsky)
"Flight of the Bumblebee" (Rimsky-Korsakov) and "The Swan" (Saint-Saëns)
Little Train of the Caipira (Villa-Lobos) and *Pacific 231* (Honegger)
"Pomp and Circumstance," (Elgar) and "Tales from the Vienna Woods" (J. Strauss)

CHILDREN'S LITERATURE IN LISTENING

Cinderella   Prokofiev
Cinderella   Coates
Hansel and Gretel   Humperdinck
Mother Goose Suite   Ravel
Once upon a Time Suite   Donaldson
Three Bears   Coates
Through the Looking Glass Suite   Taylor

Other musical frameworks around which a teacher might plan a series of listening experiences could conceivably include the following:

FOLK THEMES IN LARGER WORKS

Cowboy tunes from *Billy the Kid*   Copland
"Little Birch Tree" from *Symphony No. 4*, Fourth Movement   Tchaikovsky

NATIONALISM IN MUSIC

1812 Overture   Tchaikovsky
Finlandia   Sibelius

HUMOR IN MUSIC

The Glow Worm Turns (RCA *Family All Together* album)
"Scherzophrenia" from *Symphony No. 5½*   Don Gillis
Variations on "Mary Had a Little Lamb"   Edward Ballantine

OTHERS

Other less descriptive but still *musical* framework titles might include "Symphony," "Overture," "Concerto," "Suite," "Form in Music," "Non-Western Music," "Experimental Music" (electronic, computer, etc.), "Ballet in Listening," "Marches in Listening," "Melody" (as the principal characteristic of the selections chosen), and "Rhythm" (as the principal characteristic of the selections chosen).

There are still other frameworks—with nonmusical titles such as those listed below—upon which a teacher could, if he desired, build a series of listening experiences centering on a common theme.

TRANSPORTATION

Bydlo   Moussorgsky
En Bateau   Debussy
Little Train of the Caipira   Villa-Lobos
On Muleback   Charpentier
Pacific 231   Honegger
Wild Horseman   Schumann

THE CITY

An American in Paris   Gershwin
George Washington Bridge   W. Schuman
London Suite   Coates
Sunday in Brooklyn   Siegmeister

THE COUNTRY

Evening in the Village   Bartók
New England Triptych   W. Schuman
The Moldau   Smetana
Woodland Sketches   MacDowell

PORTRAITS

A Lincoln Portrait   Copland
Billy the Kid   Copland
Háry János   Kodály
Peter Grimes   Britten
Till Eulenspiegel's Merry Pranks   R. Strauss

ELEMENTS OF NATURE

"Snow Is Dancing" from *Children's Corner Suite*   Debussy
"Sunrise" and "Cloudburst" from *Grand Canyon Suite*   Grofé

CREATURES (LARGE AND SMALL)

"Dance of the Little Swans"   Tschaikovsky
"The Elephant" from *Carnival of the Animals*   Saint-Saëns
"Flight of the Bumblebee"   Rimsky-Korsakoff
"Mosquito Dance"   Liadov

In a lesson such as this (built around any of the foregoing nonmusical frameworks) where another area of the curriculum is involved, it might be pertinent to mention that a clear definition of objectives will be needed in order to determine the direction of the lesson. If it is the *music* lesson that is being planned for, the end results and learnings should be *musical* ones, and the objectives should be concerned mainly with further understandings that relate to music. On the other hand, if it is the *social studies* lesson that is being planned, the objectives must be stated in terms of social studies, and the music then becomes simply another means of reinforcement of the learnings defined for the social studies lesson. This is perfectly acceptable and reasonable. The point is that the objectives should be very clear so that they determine the direction and course of the lesson itself.

Teaching Instruments of the Orchestra

The instruments of the orchestra are easy to teach and fun for children to learn. Several records, filmstrips, and sound films that a teacher might find useful in introducing instruments to children are available. (See the listings at the end of this chapter.) Best of all, of course, are live instrumental demonstrations given right in the classroom by a parent, classmates, or children in other rooms who play an instrument. (Incidentally, preparing a demonstration lecture for classmates often proves to be a valuable experience for the players also.)

In some areas it is possible to secure instrumental groups (usually members of the local symphony orchestra) who specialize in daytime school performances of the lecture-demonstration-concert type. These are usually very informal, with each member of the group introducing his own instrument and encouraging questions from the children. When available, a large room where players may sit in the middle, with the children seated all around, is preferable to having the players on a stage far removed from the children. The advantage of these groups is that they provide the children with the opportunity to hear playing of a professional nature as well as to become acquainted with many of the more elaborate performing possibilities of each instrument. In addition, symphony orchestras, local bands, and other performing groups in some cities frequently give special concerts for children in the local concert hall. If a teacher intends to take his class to such a concert, he will certainly want to secure the program ahead of time in order to give his class some pertinent preparatory information—musical and otherwise—to enhance their listening experience. Some discussion of "concert etiquette" would also be most appropriate, since many children have never attended a live concert.

Instruments should never be taught all at once. In fact, in the lower grades, perhaps only four or five instruments per year will be presented to the children; however, it is expected that they will be learned *well* so that the children can recognize them by sound as well as by sight. The selection of the instruments to be introduced may be made from any of the groups below (or "choirs," as they are often called), and it is well to select from each group. By the end of the fourth grade, most children should be able to recognize all the instruments by sight and sound and to identify them according to the choir in which they belong.

Certainly some mention should be made to the children of the difference in instrumentation between a band and an orchestra (no strings in a band), and they should be encouraged to do some research on the origin of some of the instruments of the orchestra presently in use.

Children are often intrigued with ancient instruments as well as with primitive and folk instruments of various ethnic groups.

The list below is for the teacher's convenience. The random bits of information on a few of the instruments might prove interesting to some children. Further information on the instruments is available in the previously mentioned visual materials, as well as in the literature cited at the end of this chapter.

INSTRUMENTS OF THE ORCHESTRA

STRINGS

Harp (sometimes classed as a *percussion* rather than a *string* instrument)
Violin
Viola } These string instruments may be played with a bow or
Cello } plucked. Plucking is known as "pizzicato."
Bass viol

WOODWINDS

Piccolo
Flute
Double-reed woodwinds
   Oboe (name comes from French *hautbois*, meaning "high wood")
   English horn (originally called an "angled horn" because it was
     slightly curved)
   Bassoon
   Contrabassoon

261

Single-reed woodwinds
    Clarinet
    Bass clarinet
    Saxophone*

BRASS

Trumpet (one of the oldest instruments in the world)
French horn (descendant of old hunting horn—nearly 15 feet long when
    uncoiled)
Trombone (known as "sackbut" in the Middle Ages—derived from the
    Moorish word meaning "pump")
Tuba

PERCUSSION

Tympani (kettle drums)   Cymbals
Snare drum   Xylophone
Bass drum   Orchestra bells
Triangle   Chimes
Gong
Others for special effects: maracas, tone blocks, castanets, etc.

OTHER INSTRUMENTS (when included in orchestration)

Piano
Guitar

The tendency in much late-twentieth-century music seems to be toward music that is atonal, polytonal, and polyrhythmic. These tendencies are also reflected in modern orchestrations, which have become somewhat inventive, to say the least. Conventional instruments are being played in unconventional ways, while parts are being scored in large works for combs, bottles, noise-makers, and even exploding paper bags. These are merely small beginnings in what promises to be a "sound revolution."

Composers and arrangers are becoming more and more aware of the fact that when scoring for films and television programs dealing with space, for example, they simply cannot use the traditional instruments of the orchestra, but rather must reach out to find more unconventional sounds, such as those emitted by electronic devices. In the past, composers were limited by the play-ing range of the instrument as well as by the abilities of the players. In the music often referred to as "experimental", these limitations need no longer be considered. For example, using a sequence of numbers, any sound can be described mathematically. "Computer music" is composed by describing sounds mathematically and then feeding the sequence of numbers into a computer. No limitations in terms of human dexterity or the range of con-

* The saxophone, invented in 1840, was originally designed for use in bands and is still more commonly heard in military, concert, and dance bands than in symphony orchestras. Some composers, however, have scored for saxophone. Debussy's *Rhapsodie for Saxophone and Orchestra* and Ibert's *Concertino da Camera for Saxophone* are performed occasionally today.

ventional instruments are involved; therefore, it is now possible to program complicated rhythm patterns, chords, and notes that heretofore would have been impossible.

"Electronic music" is produced by distorting or modifying sounds through the process of re-recording them on electronic devices such as tape recorders. The sounds used may be the natural sounds in the environment (*musique concrète* uses these as a base) or those artificially created. Some composers of electronic music (Otto Luening and Vladimir Ussachevsky, for example) make use of both kinds in their experiments.

Some of the basic children's music texts include excellent explanatory and illustrative material (recordings) on this type of music, as well as other information related to music of the twentieth century.*

Children have a right to know about the newest techniques and devices that are being used in connection with the various media with which they come in contact daily. Hopefully, teachers will feel some responsibility for providing children with opportunities for further exploration in this field. A teacher never knows when there might be a budding film-music composer in his class!

At the conclusion of the listening experience or series of listening experiences, the teacher might attempt a little self-evaluation in the form of such questions as the following: (1) "Did I prepare myself through sufficient research on the recording?" (2) "Were the objectives stated in terms of the musical qualities?" (3) "Have I achieved the objectives—general and specific— that I originally set up?" (4) "What have the children learned about music?" (5) "How have I contributed to the learning?" (6) "Have these listening experiences contributed in any positive way to the lives of the children?"

In listening, as in other areas, much of the child's growth is dependent upon the teacher's implementation of a well-planned curriculum. A child will never be capable of a significant amount of intellectual enjoyment of music if his listening selections are not carefully chosen and skillfully presented at each level of his development. We simply cannot feed him *Peter and the Wolf* forever.

Suggested Listening Selections for Creative Dramatization**

"Anxious Leaf," "Chicken Little," "Three Billy Goats," and "The Snowmaiden" from *Once Upon a Time Suite* Donaldson (BOL, *Nature and Make Believe*)

* *Exploring Music.* Holt, Rinehart and Winston, Inc., New York, 1966; *Making Music Your Own.* Silver Burdett Company, Morristown, N.J., 1963; *Discovering Music Together.* Follett Publishing Company, Chicago, 1966.
** BOL—Bowmar Orchestral Library; L 3—*Listening*, vol. III, RCA Basic Record Library in Elementary Schools; AM—*Adventures in Music* Series, RCA Victor; KJ—Keyboard, Jr., Publications.

263

Carnival of the Animals　Saint-Saëns (KJ)★
"Children's Dance"　Hanson (AM 3, vol. 1, RCA)★
Cinderella　Coates (BOL,★ *Fairy Tales in Music*)
"Circus Music" from *Red Pony*　Copland (AM 3, RCA)★
Danse Macabre　Saint-Saëns (KJ)★
"Fairy Tale," Second Movement of *Children's Symphony*　Zador
　(BOL,★ *Miniatures in Music*)
Hansel and Gretel　Humperdinck (BOL,★ *Stories in Ballet and Opera*)
"March of the Dwarfs"　Grieg (L 3, RCA)★
"March of the Gnomes"　Rebikoff (L 3, RCA)★
Mother Goose Suite　Ravel (BOL,★ *Fairy Tales in Music*)
Peter and the Wolf　Prokofiev
Punch and Judy　McBride (KJ)★
"Sleeping Time"　Pinto (*Listening*, vol. I, RCA)
The Sorcerer's Apprentice　Dukas (KJ)★
"Viennese Musical Clock"　Kodály (KJ)★

Vocabulary

It is hopefully assumed that a child will become familiar with many of the following terms as an outgrowth of his *listening* experiences:

melody	variations	solo
rhythm	major and minor	duet
harmony	staccato	trio
form	legato	quartet
instrument	lento	chorus
conductor	andante	soprano, alto, tenor, bass
composer	allegro	mixed chorus
orchestra	vivace	
band	presto	
accelerando	symphony	cantata
ritard	overture	oratorio
decrescendo	concerto	opera
crescendo	tone poem	operetta
diminuendo	suite	musical comedy
	fugue	romantic
	chorale	impressionist
	ballet	classical
		baroque
		contemporary
		jazz
		folk song
		experimental music
		non-Western music

★ BOL—Bowmar Orchestral Library; L 3 *Listening*, vol. III, RCA Basic Record Library in Elementary Schools; AM—*Adventures in Music* Series, RCA Victor; KJ—Keyboard, Jr., Publications.

Materials for Listening

READINGS

GENERAL

Austin, William W.: *Music in the 20th Century*. W. W. Norton & Company, Inc., New York, 1966.

Bernstein, Leonard: *The Joy of Music*. Simon and Schuster, Inc., New York, 1959.

Chase, Gilbert: *America's Music: From the Pilgrims to the Present*. McGraw-Hill Book Company, New York, 1955.

Copland, Aaron: *What to Listen for in Music*, rev. ed. McGraw-Hill Book Company, New York, 1957.

Dallin, Leon: *Listener's Guide to Musical Understanding*. Wm. C. Brown Co., Dubuque, Iowa, 1959.

Fleming, William, and Abraham Veinus: *Understanding Music*. Holt, Rinehart and Winston, Inc., New York, 1958.

Gillespie, John: *The Musical Experience*. Wadsworth Publishing Co., Belmont, Calif., 1968.

Grout, Donald J.: *A History of Western Music*. W. W. Norton & Company, Inc., New York, 1964.

Machlis, Joseph: *The Enjoyment of Music*. W. W. Norton & Company, Inc., New York, 1963.

McKinney, Howard: *Music and Man*. American Book Company, New York, 1953.

Miller, Hugh M.: *Introduction to Music*. College Outline Series, Barnes & Noble, Inc., New York, 1958.

Nettl, Bruno: *Folk and Traditional Music of the Western Continents*. Prentice-Hall, Inc., Englewood Cliffs, N.J., 1965.

Portnoy, Julius: *Music in the Life of Man*. Holt, Rinehart and Winston, Inc., New York, 1963.

Ulrich, Homer: *Music: A Design for Listening*. Harcourt, Brace & World, Inc., New York, 1962.

SPECIALIZED

Bowra, C. M.: *Primitive Song*. The World Publishing Company, Cleveland, 1962.

Dolan, Robert E.: *Music in Modern Media*. G. Schirmer, Inc., New York, 1967.

Hiller, Lejaren A., Jr., and Leonard M. Isaacson: *Experimental Music: Composition with an Electronic Computer*. McGraw-Hill Book Company, New York, 1959.

Strasser, Bruce, and Max Mathews: *Music from Mathematics*. Bell Telephone Laboratories, 1961. (Related recording available also.)

FOR YOUNG READERS

Baldwin, Lillian: *Music for Young Listeners*. Silver Burdett Company, Morristown N.J., 1951, vols. 1, 2, and 3.

Barbour, Harriett, and Warren Freeman: *A Story of Music*. Summy-Birchard Company, Evanston, Ill., 1938.

Britten, Benjamin, and Imogen Holst: *The Wonderful World of Music*. Garden City Books, New York.

Buchanan, Fannie, and Charles Luckenbill: *How Man Made Music*. Follett Publishing Company, Chicago.

Cotton, Marian, and Adelaide Bradburn: *Music throughout the World*. Summy-Birchard Company, Evanston, Ill.

Hughes, Langston: *First Book of Jazz*. Franklin Watts, New York, 1955.

Keyboard Publications, New Haven, Conn. (See Appendix for titles.)

Kinscella, Hazel G.: *Stories in Music Appreciation*. University of Nebraska Press, Lincoln, Neb., 1951.

Laprade, Ernest: *Alice in Orchestralia*. Doubleday & Company, Inc., Garden City, New York, 1948.

Norman, Gertrude: *First Book of Music*. Franklin Watts, New York, 1954.

See also selected chapters in the professional literature (see "Professional Reading," p. 7) and selected pages in the teacher's editions of the children's basic music texts.

RECORDS

Just as there are certain songs that belong in a child's repertoire because they are considered "heritage" songs, so also are there certain listening selections with which, hopefully, he will become familiar and perhaps grow to love during the course of his school experience. Although the following list is far from complete, it is offered here as suggestive of this type of selection.

The appropriate grade levels have been left unspecified on purpose because some of the pieces may conceivably be used in all grades. Obviously, the same sounds would emit from the record, but the objectives and depth of study of the selection would vary according to the grade level. It is left to the individual teacher to decide whether to use the selections in whole or in part in any particular grade.

Academic Festival Overture Brahms
"Barcarolle" Offenbach
Carmen ("Habanera" and "Toreador Song") Bizet
Carnival of the Animals Saint-Saëns
Children's Corner Suite Debussy
"Claire de Lune" Debussy
Clock Symphony Haydn
Concerto in A Minor Grieg
Concerto No. 2 Rachmaninoff
Concerto No. 1 in B♭ Minor Tchaikovsky
"Country Gardens" Grainger
Danse Macabre Saint-Saëns
1812 Overture Tchaikovsky
Eine kleine Nachtmusik Mozart
En Bateau Debussy
"Entrance of the Little Fauns" Pierné

"Fantasie Impromptu"   Chopin
"Farandole" from *L' Arlésienne*   Bizet
Finlandia   Sibelius
The Fire Bird   Stravinsky
"Flight of the Bumblebee"   Rimsky-Korsakov
"Funeral March of a Marionette"   Gounod
"Hallelujah Chorus"   Handel
Hansel and Gretel   Humperdinck
"Happy Farmer"   Schumann
Háry János   Kodály
In a Clock Store   Orth
In the Steppes of Central Asia   Borodin
Invitation to the Dance   Von Weber
"Jesu, Joy of Man's Desiring"   Bach
La Mer   Debussy
"Largo al Factorum" from *The Barber of Seville*   Rossini
Les Préludes   Liszt
Light Cavalry Overture   Von Suppé
Little Fugue in G Minor   Bach
Lohengrin ("Prelude" to Act III and "Wedding March")   Wagner
"Londonderry Air"   Anon
"Lullaby"   Brahms
"Marche Slav"   Tchaikovsky
"March of the Dwarfs"   Grieg
"March of the Little Lead Soldiers"   Pierné
"March Militaire"   Schubert
Die Meistersinger ("Prelude" and excerpts)   Wagner
A Midsummer Night's Dream (excerpts)   Mendelssohn
"Minuet"   Paderewski
"Minuet in G"   Beethoven
The Moldau   Smetana
Mother Goose Suite   Ravel
A Night on Bald Mountain   Moussorgsky
"Norwegian Dance No. 2"   Grieg
Nutcracker Suite   Tchaikovsky
Of a Tailor and a Bear   MacDowell
"Overture": *Fingal's Cave*   Mendelssohn
"Overture": *William Tell*   Rossini
Peer Gynt Suite   Grieg
Peter and the Wolf   Prokofiev
Petite Suite   Bizet
Pictures at an Exhibition   Moussorgsky
"Pomp and Circumstance"   Elgar
"Prelude in C Sharp Minor"   Rachmaninoff
Prelude to the Afternoon of a Faun   Debussy
"Ride of the Valkyries"   Wagner
Russian Easter Overture   Rimsky-Korsakov
Scheherezade   Rimsky-Korsakov
"Skater's Waltz"   Waldteufel
"Sleeping Beauty Waltz"   Tchaikovsky

"Song of India"   Rimsky-Korsakov
The Sorcerer's Apprentice   Dukas
Symphony No. 3   Beethoven
Symphony No. 5   Beethoven
Symphony No. 6 ("Pastoral")   Beethoven
Symphony No. 9   Beethoven
Symphony No. 5 (second movement)   Dvorak
Symphony No. 94 ("Surprise")   Haydn
Symphony No. 40   Mozart
Symphony No. 4   Tchaikovsky
Symphony No. 5   Tchaikovsky
Symphony No. 6   Tchaikovsky
Till Eulenspiegel's Merry Pranks   R. Strauss
Toy Symphony   Haydn
"Triumphal March" from *Aida*   Verdi
Unfinished Symphony   Schubert
Variations on "Pop Goes the Weasel"   Caillet
Variations on "Ah, vous dirai-je Maman" ("Twinkle, Twinkle, Little Star") Mozart
"Waltz" from *Faust*   Gounod
The Wand of Youth   Elgar
"War March of the Priests"   Mendelssohn
Water Music   Handel
Wild Horseman   Schumann

Although, for the most part, the foregoing list contains only the more traditional selections, this does not mean that the children's listening experience should be limited to these alone, by any means. As was stated earlier in this chapter, children should have a wide variety of listening experiences, drawn from many sources and periods, including the present. In this connection, the following suggestions are offered as representative of this type of listening selection. They might also prove helpful to the teacher who wishes to further pursue certain specialized areas or who wishes merely to enlarge the children's listening repertoire in general.

Adventures in a Perambulator   Carpenter
Afro-American Symphony   William Grant Still
Amahl and the Night Visitors   Gian-Carlo Menotti
An American in Paris   Gershwin
American Salute   Gould
Appalachian Spring   Copland
"The Banshee"   Cowell
"Bear Dance"   Bartók
Billy the Kid   Copland
"The Blue Danube"   J. Strauss
Boléro   Ravel
Children's Symphony   Harl McDonald
Cinderella   Prokofiev
Classical Symphony   Prokofiev
Death Valley Suite   Grofé
Fantasia on "Greensleeves"   Vaughan Williams
"Galop" from *The Comedians*   Kabalevsky

Grand Canyon Suite   Grofé
Little Train of the Caipira   Villa-Lobos
"March" from *Love for Three Oranges*   Prokofiev
Merry Mount Suite (selections)   Hanson
Mississippi Suite   Grofé
Pacific 231   Honegger
Petrouchka   Stravinsky
"Polka" from *The Golden Age*   Shostokovich
Porgy and Bess (selections)   Gershwin
"Prelude No. 2"   Gershwin
Red Pony (selections)   Copland
Rhapsody in Blue   Gershwin
Rodeo   Copland
"Russian Sailor's Dance" from *Red Poppy*   Glière
"Three Bears"   Coates
Three Places in New England   Ives
West Side Story (selections)   Bernstein

CONTEMPORARY SOUNDS

Gymnopedie   Erik Satie
Ionization   Varese
Iron Foundry   Mossolov
Kleine Kammermusik, Opus 24, No. 2, Fifth Movement   Hindemith★
Six Pieces for Orchestra, Opus 6, First Piece   Anton Webern★
"Toccata for Percussion"   Chavez

JAZZ AND BLUES	SOURCE
American Jazz	*Exploring Music*
("When the Saints Go Marchin' In,"	Book 6, album. Holt, Rine-
"Take the A Train")	hart and Winston, Inc.
Armstrong Favorites (Louis Armstrong)	Columbia
Benny Goodman: Carnegie Hall Jazz Concert	Columbia
Bessie Smith Story, vol. 1	Columbia
Bix Beiderbecke Story	Columbia
Brandenburg Gate: Revisited (Brubeck)	Columbia
Classics in Jazz series (four-record set)	Capitol
The Solid South	
The Golden Era	
Then Came Swing	
This Modern Age	
Dialogues for Jazz Combo and Orchestra, Fourth Movement (blues)	Columbia
Guide to Jazz	RCA Victor
W. C. Handy Blues	Folkways
Jazz Legato Leroy Anderson	RCA Victor
Jazz Pizzicato Leroy Anderson	RCA Victor

★ See *Exploring Music*, Book 6, record album. Holt, Rinehart and Winston, Inc., New York, 1966.

Jazz: The South (work and church songs, hollers, vol. 1)	Folkways
Music of New Orleans (birth of jazz) vol. 4	Folkways
Story of Jazz (Langston Hughes)	Folkways
Transformation Gunther Schuller	Atlantic
Understanding Jazz	Keyboard Publications
What is Jazz? (music and commentary by Leonard Bernstein)	Columbia

THE JAZZ IDIOM IN LARGER WORKS

Concerto for Clarinet and Orchestra Copland	Columbia
Concerto for Piano in G Ravel	Columbia
Concerto in F Gershwin	RCA Victor
La Création du Monde Milhaud	Columbia
L'Histoire du Soldat Stravinsky	Bowmar Orchestral Library
Ragtime for 11 Instruments Stravinsky	Columbia
Rhapsody in Blue Gershwin	RCA Victor

ELECTRONIC MUSIC

Composition for Synthesizer Milton Babbitt★

Compositions on a Well Tempered Computer (From *Music from Mathematics*, album and book. Bell Telephone Laboratories.)

Contrast No. 5 Dick Raaijmakers (*Discovering Music Together*, Book 8, record album. Follett Publishing Company.)

Five Improvisations on Magnetic Tape, Nos. 1 and 2 (Keyboard Publications.)

★*Leilya and the Poet* Halim El-Dabh

Sonic Contours Ussachevsky (*Exploring Music*, Book 1, record album. Holt, Rinehart and Winston, Inc.)

★*Stereo Electronic Music No. 1* Bulent Arel

RECORDS FOR TEACHING INSTRUMENTS (of the orchestra and otherwise)

Instruments of the Orchestra Capitol Records	
Instruments of the Orchestra Keyboard Publications	
Instruments of the Orchestra RCA Victor	
Meet the Instruments Bowmar Records (with filmstrips)	
Pan the Piper Columbia Records	
Peter and the Wolf Columbia Records (and others)	
Rusty in Orchestraville Capitol Records	
Sparkey's Magic Piano Capitol Records	
Tubby the Tuba Columbia Records	
Young Person's Guide to the Orchestra Columbia Records (and others)	

★ From *Exploring Music*, Book 6, record album. Holt, Rinehart and Winston, Inc., New York. Further information in the teacher's edition of the same book.

YOUNG PEOPLES RECORD CLUB and CHILDREN'S RECORD GUILD
(publications)

King's Trumpet
Licorice Stick
Rondo for Bassoon
Said the Piano to the Harpsichord
Wonderful Violin

FOLK INSTRUMENTS

Folk Instruments of the World   Follett Publishing Company (pictures also)
Man's Early Musical Instruments   Folkways

Photographs of instruments of the orchestra for classroom use may be obtained from (addresses in Appendix E):
Bowmar Records
Keyboard Publications
J. W. Pepper & Sons

TEACHING RECORDS

Child's Introduction to Gilbert and Sullivan   Golden Records
Child's Introduction to Jazz   Golden Records
Child's Introduction to Opera   Golden Records
First Listening Experiences   Classroom Materials, Inc., Great Neck, N.Y.
Vox Library of Composers (biographies and music)   Vox
Young Peoples Record Clubs
 The Clock That Went Backwards (styles in music)
 Copland and His Music
 Round and Round   (Fugue)
 Sleeping Beauty (story and Tchaikovsky's music)
 Stravinsky for Young People

MUSIC OF THE WORLD

Music of the World's Peoples, vols. 1–5   Folkways
Primitive Music of the World   Folkways

You might like to know that *Pops Christmas Party* (RCA Victor) contains many of the hard-to-find secular songs that children enjoy singing during the holiday time, played by the Boston Pops orchestra. It's a nice addition to the record library.

FILMSTRIPS AND FILMS

FILMSTRIPS (with records)

1. Jam Handy Corporation, Detroit, Mich.
   Great Composers and Their Music: Bach, Beethoven, Handel, Haydn, Mozart, Schubert

Music Stories: Peter and the Wolf; Hansel and Gretel; The Nutcracker Suite; Peer Gynt; Fire Bird; The Sorcerer's Apprentice

Opera and Ballet Suites: The Magic Flute; Lohengrin; Aida; The Barber of Seville; Die Meistersinger; Coppelia

Stories of Music Classics: William Tell; Sleeping Beauty; Swan Lake; The Bartered Bride; A Midsummer Night's Dream; Scheherezade

2. Society for Visual Education, Inc., 1345 Diversey Parkway, Chicago

   Musical Books for Young People (six filmstrips with records)

   The Story of Handel's Messiah (filmstrip with record)

   The Story of the Nutcracker (filmstrip with record)

3. Bowmar Records, Inc., 622 Rodier Drive, Glendale, Cal., 91201

   Biographies of Great Composers (filmstrip with record of each of the following: Haydn, Mozart, Beethoven, Schubert, Verdi, Puccini)

   Meet the Instruments (filmstrip with record of instruments of the orchestra)

4. Keyboard, Jr., Publications

   Pathways to Music (filmstrips, records, and teachers' guides)

SOUND FILMS

1. Association Films, Inc., Broad at Elm, Ridgefield, N.J.

   Pacific 231

   Peter and the Wolf

   Toot, Whistle, Plunk and Boom (instruments of the orchestra)

2. NET Film Service, Indiana University, Bloomington, Ind.

   Percussion: The Pulse of Music (percussion instruments)

3. Churchill Films, 662 North Robertson Blvd., Los Angeles, Cal.

   New Sounds in Music

   Percussion Sounds

   What Is Music?

4. Bailey Film Associates, 11559 Santa Monica Blvd., Los Angeles, Cal.

   Discovering the Music of Africa

   Discovering the Music of Japan

   Discovering the Music of the Middle Ages

   Discovering the Music of the Middle East

8

EXPERIENCES IN MOVEMENT

One of the many ways in which children can express themselves in the classroom is through the use of body movement. Since all children love to move (in one way or another), a teacher is blessed with "built-in" motivation in this area; thus his only real task lies in helping the children discover the many exciting possibilities of using their entire bodies rather than just a few selected parts.

Free body movement should be started at the very early primary level and continued throughout the grades. This continuity will, hopefully, prevent the development of the inhibitions and the reluctance to participate that often characterize some upper-grade children whose creative body-movement experiences terminated in kindergarten.

In order to gain the maximum benefit from body-movement activity and to pursue its many aspects, it is most advantageous to have a large-enough floor space in which to move freely. An activity room, a gymnasium, or individual classrooms in which the furniture is movable can usually provide the needed space. Lacking these, a teacher simply exercises a little ingenuity and finds a way to "make do" in his own classroom either by selecting activities that can be performed in a small space and/or by having fewer children moving at one time within the space available.

As is the case in many other areas, there are several schools of thought regarding the use of body movement in the classroom. Some music educators feel that it doesn't belong in the music program at all. Others insist that there should be no structured movement with young children—there should be nothing but "free expression" and a "do what the music tells you to do" type of activity because this total "freedom" allows a child to make a more "creative" response. Advocates of this philosophy further contend that *any* prescribed suggestion to a child interferes with the possibility of his producing an original response. (This hardly seems reasonable, except, perhaps, in those rare instances where a classroom teacher is so totally prescriptive that there is no acceptable response other than the one that *he* feels is appropriate.)

The procedures suggested in this chapter are based on the philosophy that some structured movement should be provided for children before they are asked to engage in unstructured movement. To "create" means to "bring into being." "Creativity" is often defined as the ability to put together old ideas in new combinations—to use old things in new ways. Studies indicate that successful creations depend to a great extent on the individual's store of knowledge in the field. Should we ask a child to *create* movement of some sort when he has had little or no background of movement experience? Where are the "old things" for him to put together in "new ways"?

The amount of structured movement needed before engaging in free expression will vary among individual children, of course. Some will need little or no help from the teacher, and others will need more, but this is as it should be. Certainly *all* children should be exposed to (and, hopefully, become familiar with) some of the movement vocabulary (terms such as "level," "range," etc.) so that experiences related to these terms may be more easily expited. With older children, the vocabulary would be expanded to include dance terms of a more intricate nature.

The vital factor here is that whatever a given child's creations are, they should give him a feeling of satisfaction and an increased sense of self-worth. The better equipped he is, the more worthy the result.

To this end, then, it is suggested that a child first be exposed to a wide variety of singing games and action songs, a selected few of which are included here. More may be found elsewhere in this book (see Song Index, p. 369), as well as in the basic music texts and on records. (See "Singing Materials," p. 59.)

Too-ra-ray

Traditional Words   American Folk Song

Moth-er, won't you teach me? Too-dum a lid-dle-dum, Too-dum a lid-dle-dum,

Too-dum a-long! Moth-er, won't you teach me? Too-dum a lid-dle-dum,

Long sum-mer day! Kick up and shine, Too-ra-ray! Kick up and shine,

Too-ra-ray! Kick up and shine, Too-ra-ray! Long sum-mer day!

1. Billy, will you skip around etc.?
2. Billy, will you jump around, etc? (hop, walk, bounce)

CREDIT: *By permission from American Book Company. From* Meeting Music, Music for Young Americans *series. Copyright 1966.*

275

Step and Clap

Lightly

Anne Beyer and Elsie Smith

1. Step, step, clap, clap! Step, step, clap, clap! Turn your-self a-round and then you clap, clap, clap!

2. Bend and clap, clap
   Bend and clap, clap, etc.
3. Hands up! Clap, clap,
   Hands up! Clap, clap, etc.

4. Stoop down, clap, clap,
   Stoop down, clap, clap,
   Turn yourself around,
   And then you clap, clap, clap
5. Repeat Stanza 1 to end of song.

CREDIT: *By permission from American Book Company. From* Sharing Music, Music for Young Americans *series. Copyright 1966.*

Under the Spreading Chestnut Tree

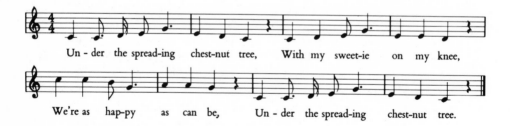

Un - der the spread-ing chest-nut tree, With my sweet-ie on my knee,

We're as hap-py as can be, Un - der the spread-ing chest-nut tree.

Sing through the first time with no actions.

Sing through repeated number of times, omitting an action word and substituting the action each time. (Be sure to sing the words in between!)

ACTIONS:
"*Under*"—*bend over.*
"*Spreading*"—*spread arms apart.*
"*Chest*"—*touch chest.*
"*Nut*"—*touch head.*
"*Tree*"—*arms over head, palms up, elbows bent as though holding something.*

276

Hokey Pokey

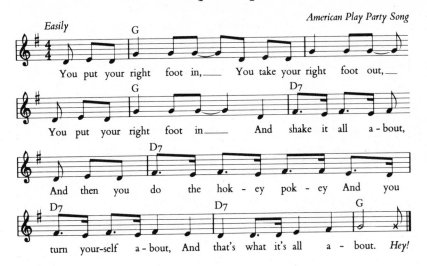

CREDIT: *From Growing with Music, Book 3, by H. R. Wilson et al.,* © *1966 by Prentice-Hall, Inc., Englewood Cliffs, N.J. Reprinted with permission.*

Later in the year a child may be introduced to simple folk dances ("Danish Dance of Greeting" and "I See You," for example,) which he will enjoy learning and which may be taught as early as kindergarten. (Directions and music for these are available from several companies. See "Materials for Movement," p. 299.)

Locomotor and Nonlocomotor Movement

Since all nonhandicapped children are walking or running or using some other form of foot transportation most of the time, it is only fitting that these "locomotor" movements, as they are termed, be among the first to be introduced in the classroom. They may be accompanied either by the beat of the teacher's tom-tom or by music. Through the execution of these movements a child may become aware of slow and fast tempo, even and uneven rhythm patterns, heavy and light beats, and other musical elements.

The "nonlocomotor" (sometimes referred to as "axial") movements involve movement but not necessarily transportation, as it were. Rather, the body remains in one place and, in effect, moves on its "axis." Bending, swaying, and stretching, are examples of nonlocomotor movement. By their very nature, these movements, when executed, evoke a different response in a child from the one he feels when he is galloping, skipping, running, or even walking; thus, he soon becomes aware that movement has quality, just as music does.

277

Both locomotor and nonlocomotor movements may be varied in character through the use of such devices as a change in the *level* (high, medium, or low) of the body, through an increase or decrease in the *size* of the movement, and in many other ways, depending upon the desired outcome. For example,

WALKING

Like a giant (slow and heavy)
Like a tiny fairy (light and quick)
Like we're late for school
Like a sneaky goblin
Like a giraffe (high at the top!)
Like a turtle (?)
Like we're going to church (in our best clothes!)
In different directions (forward, backward, etc.)
Making our initials
Making circles, squares, and triangles
Making designs
Happy; sad

Rhythm for walking should be *steady* and *even*. Suggested rhythm and meter.

$\frac{4}{4}$ or $\frac{2}{4}$ ♩ ♩ ♩ ♩

RUNNING

On tiptoe
Up the stairs
Against the wind
In place
With the wind behind us

Rhythm for running should be *even* and *faster* than walking rhythm. Suggested rhythm and meter:

$\frac{4}{4}$ or $\frac{2}{4}$ ♪ ♪ ♪ ♪ ♪ ♪

> = accent when beating.

SKIPPING

Light and happy
Heavy and tired

Many children do not know how to skip well and will need help from the teacher. A skip is actually a traveling step-hop. Rhythm for skipping should be *uneven*. Suggested rhythms and meters:

$\frac{6}{8}$ ♩ ♪ ♩ ♪

$\frac{2}{4}$ ♩. ♪ ♩. ♪

> = accent

HOPPING OR JUMPING

Like a kangaroo
Like a rabbit
Like a frog
Like a grasshopper
Like a bird
As we do when we play hopscotch
Over a big stream
Over a little brook

Rhythm for hopping and jumping should be *even*. Suggested meter and rhythm:

$\frac{4}{4}$ or $\frac{2}{4}$ ♪ 𝄾 ♪ 𝄾 ♪ 𝄾 ♪ 𝄾

> = accent

MARCHING

On tiptoe
Like a toy soldier
Like a real soldier
Like a puppet

(In upper grades, try a good old grand march!) Rhythm for marching should be *steady* and *even*. Suggested meter and rhythm:

$\frac{2}{4}$ or $\frac{4}{4}$ ♩ ♩ ♩ ♩

Marches are sometimes written in $\frac{6}{8}$ time, but the tempo is usually so fast that the beat is in two rather than six.

Other locomotor movements: leaping, galloping, sliding.

SWAYING

Like a tree in the wind (the teacher may vary the character of the sway by such clues as, "A soft breeze is brushing by this tree," "The wind is getting stronger," "It's a hurricane!")
In a swing
Like wheat in a field
Like a pendulum (use different parts of the body—fingers, hands, head, trunk, etc.)

Rhythm for swaying should be *even*. Suggested meters and rhythms:

> = accent

STRETCHING

Like a cat
To touch a star
To catch a drifting balloon

Other nonlocomotor (axial) movements: bending, turning, rocking, twisting.

SUGGESTED ACTIVITIES USING LOCOMOTOR AND NON-LOCOMOTOR MOVEMENT

1. Have the children form a circle. Beat on the tom-tom in various rhythms such as walking, running, and skipping. The class listens to the drum, tries to identify the movement indicated by the beat, and then executes the movement. You should change the rhythm often without pausing between changes. This requires the children to listen carefully so that they may respond immediately to the change.
2. Have the children originate their own combinations of locomotor and nonlocomotor movements and execute them, e.g.,

3. Have the children execute the movements at different levels and tempos and in varied directions.

4. Have the children move in the manner of different kinds of animals, creatures, people, and things. (See "Communicating an Idea through Body Movement," p. 288.)

5. Have the children originate simple "action stories" or scenes involving the use of locomotor and nonlocomotor movements and execute them. You might like to make up one yourself just to get things started. Keep it simple! Here is an example: "One day a little boy went walking in the woods with his father. All at once the little boy said, 'I think I hear something over by that tree. Let's sneak up and see what it is.' So they crept quietly up and looked behind the tree. 'It's a bear!' shouted the little boy. 'Run!' cried his father, and they both ran faster than they ever had before, right out of the woods."

6. Have the class interpret familiar stories through simple movements. For example, Cinderella might show her dejection through a slow *walk* with head bowed. The Fairy Godmother would enter with *running* steps, the horses would be identified by a *galloping* rhythm (let individual children or groups portray these characters, including the horses), while the *swaying* rhythm could be used for the ball. You may accompany with appropriate rhythms on the tom-tom.

7. Have the children interpret nursery rhymes (such as "Hey Diddle, Diddle," for example) through simple movements.

SUGGESTED ACTIVITIES USING RHYTHM INSTRUMENTS WITH LOCOMOTOR AND NONLOCOMOTOR MOVEMENT

Ask the children to:

1. Start walking while the drum beats the rhythm. Tell them to run when they hear the sound of the bells, skip when they hear the tambourine, etc.

2. Start walking while the drum beats the rhythm. Tell them to walk on tiptoe when the triangle sounds and to stoop way down when the cymbals clash.

3. Start walking while the drum beats the rhythm. Tell them to change the direction of their walk when they hear the sound of the triangle.

4. Skip in time to the drumbeat. Tell them to freeze like a statue at whatever level they wish (high, medium, or low) when they hear the sound of the cymbals.

5. Let children improvise a movement, and then have them select the rhythm instrument and the way of playing it that will sound well as an accompaniment to the movement. Allow time for refining both the movement and the instrumental accompaniment. The rhythm pattern selected for the instrument should be appropriate for the movement. Then have them originate another movement. Have the class repeat the process, choosing different instruments.

Divide the class into groups, assigning some for movement and some for accompaniment. With two movements, there would be four groups. Have the first groups play and move, then the next two groups play and move, and then the first two groups repeat their original movement with instruments. This activity could be used to illustrate various types of form in music, if desired, by using contrasting movement and instruments for the A and B parts, etc.

Clapping

Much can be done with simple clapping, and certainly it is one of the easiest activities to execute. Clapping with the fingertips or with cupped hands produces interesting variations. Percussive sounds are also possible when the clapping is done on different parts of the body using flat hands, the fingertips, or cupped hands. In fact, the body makes a fine percussion instrument. Some children can perform an activity known as "hamboning," in which various parts of the body are struck with the heel or the flat of the hand rhythmically and at a fast tempo. The effect produced is most interesting because of the intricate rhythm patterns that emerge.

The following suggestions are based primarily on hand clapping; however, they may be adapted to use with drums or other percussion instruments, if desired.

1. Have the class clap in time to any given music, one clap on each beat. As a variation, have the children clap in time to the music but *stop* when the music stops. Using either the piano or a record, stop the music at unexpected points. After the first few times when many children are "caught" still clapping after the music has stopped, the class will sense the need for closer listening.
2. Have the children clap their own names—one clap for each syllable.
3. Have the children clap the name of the town or state in which they live.
4. Clap a familiar song rhythm for the children to identify. (Be sure to clap all the syllables of the words; otherwise identification can be impossible.)
5. Clap four-beat rhythms such as:

$\frac{4}{4}$ a. ♪ ♪ ♩ ♪ ♪ ♩

b. ♩ ♪. ♪ ♪ ♪ ♩

Have the class imitate.
Have individual children clap rhythms for the class to imitate.
Clap longer and more difficult rhythms, such as:

282 $\frac{4}{4}$ ♪. ♪ ♪. ♪ ♪. ♪ ♩ ♫ ♫ ♩ ♩

6. Clap the first line of a familiar song. Then the children clap the second, you clap the third, the children clap the fourth, etc.

7. Try some "drum talk" either with the drums or through clapping. (Children can make their own small drums out of oatmeal or cornmeal boxes or other similar containers.)

   A child beats a sentence on the drum.

   You or another child answers on the drum.

   Occasionally, when possible, translate some of the sentences into notation on the board:

   How are you? ♩ ♩ ♩

   Where did you come from? ♩ ♫ ♩ ♩

   Translate into body movement if desired.

8. Have the class create rhythm patterns of their own for executing through clapping or on percussion instruments once the patterns have been established. Some of these may fit songs the class already knows and could be used for accompaniment. (See "Rhythm Instruments," p. 223.)

9. Putting sentences to a rhythm pattern will help the children maintain the established pattern when several different rhythm patterns are going on within the class simultaneously:

   Come and see us: ♩ ♩ ♩ ♩

   We like the teacher : ♪ ♩ ♪ ♩ ♩

   It is snowing very hard: ♪ ♪ ♪ ♪ ♪ ♪ ♩

   One for you, one for me: ♪ ♪ ♩ ♪ ♪ ♩

   In the above activity, there may be any combination of rhythms. Since they are done "by ear," as it were, it is not necessary to have studied them as a skill or to be able to use them well in note singing. The sole requirement here is that the basic meter be the same $\left(\frac{2}{4}, \frac{3}{4}, \frac{4}{4}, \frac{6}{8}, \text{etc.}\right)$ and that the same number of measures be used, for each different sentence, if they are to be clapped or chanted simultaneously.

10. Divide the children into two groups—one *question* group and one *answer* group. Put four rhythms on the board such as the following (use notation in upper grades and long and short lines in lower grades:)

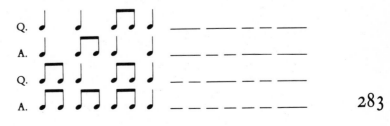

Have the question group clap the first line, the answer group clap the second line, etc. Translate into body movements such as walk-walk-run-run-walk or any others the children may suggest. Take care that the running notes are executed exactly *twice* as fast as the walking notes so that the children will get a better feel of the relationship between quarter notes and eighth notes. Use percussion instruments such as shakers and drums, if desired. (It often helps to keep the beat if the children say aloud, "long-long-short-short-long, "quarter-quarter-eighth-eighth-quarter," or whatever the rhythm happens to be.)

"Bingo" is a fine song to sing for fun and for practice in clapping rhythms.

Bingo

There was a farm-er had a dog and Bing-o was his name - o.

B - I - N-G-O, B - I - N-G-O, B - I - N-G-O and Bing-o was his name.

Repeat entire song, clapping on the letter "B" instead of singing.
Repeat entire song, clapping on the letters "B" and "I" instead of singing.
Continue repeating song, clapping another letter each time until all letters have been clapped.
Do not sing on the letters being clapped—just clap them in rhythm.

Gesture and Pantomime

Gesture and pantomime are the very basic forms of movement that a teacher may use to introduce a child to movement that is "interpretive" in nature. They are a good beginning because they may be based on functions the child performs almost daily. The differences between simple gestures such as laughing, shaking hands, and waving hello and good-bye can in themselves become a basis for artistic expression when children begin to discover possibilities for varying such gestures in character through the use of changes in tempo, range, intensity, etc.

Children can practice pantomime by going through the motions of such simple activities as:

Climbing a rope
Sliding down a pole
Throwing a lasso

284

Raking leaves
Swimming
Shoveling snow
Jumping rope (in various styles)

Try these on a rainy day if no inside play space is available. They may be done standing by the desks. Some are even rhythmical enough to be done with musical accompaniment. After the children have had a fair amount of experience in the various activities, enlarge the scope of each activity by adding a little action through clues such as, "Rake the leaves into a pile, put them into a basket, carry the full basket into the woods, and empty it. Bring the basket back empty and start raking again."

Children also enjoy pantomiming stories, scenes, and situations they have improvised themselves. They should be encouraged to refine their pantomime actions with each succeeding experience so that some growth in this ability may be shown.

With a little imagination and a lot of body movement, children can be:

1. Ways of traveling:
   a. Boats (rowboats, canoes, tugboats, etc.)
   b. Trains
   c. Bicycles (tandem, too!)
   d. Automobiles
   e. Horses
   f. Scooters
   g. Airplanes
   h. Dogsleds
   i. Camels
   (Let these suggestions come from the children.)
2. Countries
   a. Holland—windmills
   b. China—jinrikishas
   c. Italy—Venetian gondoliers
   (Let the children suggest others.)
3. People at work
   a. Fireman, doctor, farmer, factory worker, Santa Claus, etc.
   b. People in occupations representative of the United States
   c. People in occupations representative of other countries
4. Animals and creatures
5. Things
   a. Engines (with pistons)
   b. Wheels
   c. Rubber bands
   d. Window shades
   e. Elevators
   f. Haystacks
   g. Windshield wipers
   h. Instruments of the orchestra
   i. Punctuation marks
   (Let the children suggest others.)

THROUGH SIGHT

COLOR

Hold up a piece of paper or a card colored completely black. Ask, "Who would like to show us in movement how this color makes you feel?" Hold up a brightly colored (yellow or orange) sheet. Ask, "Does this color make you feel different? What movement do you think you'd like to use to express how you feel?" Then play highly contrasting pieces of music and ask the class, "Which of these two pieces of music that I played best describes the movement that (child's name) did when he was showing us how the black paper made him feel?"

An interesting variation on the above consists in having various colored sheets of construction paper represent certain movements; e.g., green might mean to sway and turn, yellow might stand for skipping, and red might represent standing with the arms outstretched. Let the children suggest the movements. Have individual children arrange the sheets so that different patterns are created. Obviously, there are many possibilities. In like manner, songs may be illustrated and interpreted line by line through the use of colors and movement. If desired, stick figures illustrating the chosen movements may be drawn on the appropriately colored papers.

PICTURES, ETC.

Show pictures, paintings, scenes, designs, or objects of various shapes. Ask the children to describe them in movement or move the way the object made them feel.

THROUGH SOUND

ENVIRONMENTAL SOUND

Have the children close their eyes and listen to various sounds—one at a time only. As you complete the playing of each sound, ask the class (or individual children) to move the way the sound made them feel. Sounds such as a clock ticking, a woodblock tapping a steady beat, a triangle ringing (hit in a circle inside), a typewriter, taped sounds of an automobile starting up, waves on the shore, a storm, a washing machine, and many others may be used.

WORDS, PHRASES, AND IMPROMPTU STORIES

You can encourage the children to suggest variations on ideas for activities by saying, for example, "Let's think of words that begin with 'D.'" Of course, other letters may be used. The children may all perform the activities together, or individual children may act out an activity and let the others in the class guess which word it is, knowing only that it begins with "D" (or whatever letter you have suggested). This same procedure may be followed in acting out different toys or animals for the class to identify. Toys such as mechanical dolls, wooden soldiers, and tops lend themselves well to this type of activity.

Movement may also be inspired by selected phrases such as:

"Draw a rainbow in the sky. Higher! Longer!"
"Reach for the moon!"
"Melt like a snowman."

You (or the children) can create longer impromptu situations and stories such as: "You are a terribly frightened rabbit being chased by a fox. Suddenly you see a place to hide, but it's very small. Will you fit?"

FAVORITE STORIES

Children like to interpret favorite stories. Choose those containing several characters and assign the characters to various children. As the story is told, each character moves at the appropriate time. (A delightful story for use with younger children is "Chicken Licken,"*) Add a special sound of a rhythm instrument for each character, too.

POETRY

Read a poem containing particularly descriptive words. Ask the class or individual children to move in the ways they feel best describes the words as they are read. Read the poem aloud in your best interpretive manner to give proper feeling to the words and spirit, without waiting in between lines or words for physical responses from the children. With extensive experience in body movement, this activity may be done in all grades using poetry suitable for the grade level. Rhythm instruments may also be added to heighten dramatic effects.

MUSIC

Have the class listen to various types of music—marches, lullabies, waltzes, and short portions of larger works such as overtures, symphonies, etc. Ask the children to improvise movement that they feel is appropriate for the selection heard. (This may not always be what *you* consider appropriate!)

THROUGH TOUCH

Have the children close their eyes and feel certain objects that you have provided (one object at a time) in their hands. Ask individual children to move the way the object made them feel. (Try using such objects as soft scarves, balls, pencils, and sandpaper.) Play two contrasting pieces of music and ask the children which piece best describes the way one of the objects made them feel.

* *First Grade Book.* Ginn and Company, Boston.

Communicating an Idea through Body Movement

If the way we move can be affected by the way we feel at the moment, then it should follow that moving in certain ways can communicate various ideas, emotions, and feelings to others. This should be the essence of interpretive movement—communicating an idea, whatever it may be, to someone else. Dance, like the other arts, is a form of communication.

Using a simple example of levels, the two positions shown in Fig. 8–1 communicate two contrasting ideas—when the body is turned inward, downward, or both, it creates a feeling of defeat or pain; when it is turned outward and upward, a more positive, optimistic feeling of joy is communicated.

Dramatic interpretation of words in movement is frequently a pleasurable challenge to children. This type of activity helps to develop a child's feeling for expressive or interpretive movement as it is used to communicate an emotion or meaning.

FIGURE 8–1 *Two figures of a boy—one with head drooped, one with head and arms up.*

Ask the question, "If we suddenly lost the power of speech, how could we express the following words using only our bodies?"

Glory
Peace
Trouble
Joy
Shame
Triumph
Defeat
Praise
Prayer
Welcome
Never
Please

Interpreting words also provides many opportunites for creating stories in movement. How much more meaningful words become to a child when he is forced to stop and think about them carefully in order to determine how he may best communicate their meaning without using his voice—only his body. (Try saying "please" without making a sound!) He soon learns that now he must rely solely on his facial expression, the carriage of his body, and the use of his arms and hands. The words themselves begin to take on new importance to him as he finds that he must examine more closely their emotional content, if any, in relation to the way in which he must move in order to communicate accurately their true meaning.

When they have been provided with a suitable background of movement experiences, children can express poems, legends, folk tales, and fairy tales more beautifully in movement.

Exploring Musical Terms through Movement

The meanings of musical terms may also be more easily grasped when they are explored through the medium of body movement. The following are but a few examples.

TEMPO

Children may be made much more aware of tempo (fast or slow) when they respond rhythmically to it. When fast music is played, ask, "What are some of the things that go fast?" Answers might include planes and trains, for example. Then suggest to individual children that they *be* one of the fast things in response to the music. Try the same procedure using slow music and asking about things that move slowly.

The feeling for tempo as well as form can often be established through the playing of a short musical selection in which there are contrasting fast and slow sections. Divide the class into two groups—one to respond to the fast music and the other to respond to the slow music. (The responses should be of the children's own creation.) When the music appropriate for each group is heard, that group responds accordingly. Rhythm instruments may also be added—one type to play with the slow music, and another with the fast.

ACCENT AND METER

Feeling for accent and meter may be enhanced by having the children execute body movements in time to various meters. Movements on all the beats might be the same, such as clapping for four beats, snapping the fingers for four beats, marching for four beats, and nodding the head for four beats, with each clap, snap, or nod getting one beat, or the children may suggest a movement or action on the *accented* beat, followed by a *different* movement on the *unaccented* beats. The class may even choose to have three like movements on the first three beats, with something different for the fourth beat (when counting in fours). Very simple suggestions could conceivably result in combinations such as:

```
(4s) stamp    clap    clap    clap
     walk      walk    walk    lunge (swinging one arm forward and up)
(3s) sway      sway    clap
(2s) step      bend
```

FORM

Well-known rounds provide many opportunities for rhythmic interpretation by the children and should be executed in "round" form, just as they are sung. Have the children suggest their own movements for these. Try to encourage total body movement rather than just small hand actions. The intent is not to turn the round into an action song, but simply to interpret this musical form in movement. Begin with simple rounds such as "Are You Sleeping, Brother John?" (p. 75), in which the movements would be fairly concrete. As the children progress and develop their movement vocabulary, let them create more abstract movement in round form to the beautiful "Dona Nobis Pacem" (p. 72).

ABA form, rondo form, etc., may all be interpreted through the use of repetition and contrast in movement in the same manner that these devices are used in music.

In interpreting the canon, fugue, etc., the *entrance* of each voice, as well as any contrapuntal *imitation*, may be represented by a dancer performing the movement he considers appropriate for the music he hears.

Additional musical terms such as "theme and variations," "crescendo," "diminuendo," "legato," "staccato," etc., offer even greater challenges to children to originate movement patterns that will communicate the meaning of each term; e.g., the meaning of the term "crescendo" might be shown by increasing the *size* of a given movement and using more space in executing it.

RHYTHM PATTERNS

Even and uneven rhythm patterns are very adaptable to execution in body movement. Further suggestions may be found in Chapter 7, Listening Experiences (p. 255), and Chapter 9, Creating Experiences (p. 308).

Listening Selections for Body Movement

The following listening selections are samples of the type of piece that has proved very suitable for use with various body-movement activities. (Further information on the music is given on the record jackets or in the accompanying pamphlets in the albums.)★

SLOW

"Pavanne of the Sleeping Beauty" from *Mother Goose Suite* (BOL, *Fairy Tales in Music*, no. 57)
"Sarabande" from *Suite for Strings*　Corelli (BOL, *Concert Matinee*, no. 63)

FAST

"Badinerie" from *Suite for Strings*　Corelli (BOL, *Concert Matinee*, no. 63)
"Intermezzo"　Kabalevsky (BOL, *Pictures and Patterns*, no. 53)
"Tarantella"　Rossini-Respighi (AM 3, vol. 2)

SOFT-AND-LOUD CONTRAST

"The Ball"　Bizet (AM 1)
"Bydlo"　Moussorgsky (AM 2)
"Can Can"　Rossini-Respighi (AM 2)

ABA FORM

"Dance of the Little Swans"　Tchaikovsky (AM 1)
"March of the Dwarfs"　Grieg (BOL, *Nature and Make Believe*, no. 52)
"Norwegian Dance No. 2"　Grieg (BOL, *Concert Matinee*, no. 63)

RONDO FORM
"Viennese Musical Clock"　Kodály (Keyboard Jr. and AM 2)
"Waltz on the Ice"　Prokofiev (AM 3, vol. 2)

★ BOL—Bowmar Orchestral Library; L2—*Listening*, vol. 2, RCA Basic Record Library for Elementary Schools; AM—*Adventures in Music* series, RCA Victor.

LEGATO

"Waltz in A♭" Brahms (L2, RCA)

STACCATO

Light Cavalry Overture Von Suppé (L2, RCA)

OTHER

"Children's Dance" Hanson (AM, 3 vol. 1)
"Fairies"; "Giants" Elgar (AM 3, vol. 1)
"German Waltz" (BOL, *Pictures and Patterns*, no. 53)
"Gigue" Bach (AM 1)
"Gigue" Gretry (AM 1)
"March" Kabalevsky (AM 3, vol. 1)
"March of the Toys" Herbert (AM 2)
"Petite Ballerina" Shostakovich (AM 2)
"Ride of the Valkyries" Wagner (BOL, *Masters of Music*, no. 62)
"Walking Song" Thomson (AM 1)

(See also "Creative Dramatization," p. 263, for further suggestions.)

Sacred and Secular Texts in Dance

Dance is still used as a form of worship among many peoples. Consider the possibilities in this area of interpreting religious music or text such as the psalms, as is frequently done in many churches. The Twenty-third Psalm, "O Come All Ye Faithful," and the song "The Lord's Prayer," for example, lend themselves well to this. For variation, a choral speaking group could be used instead of music.

Religious music is not the only kind of music that can be interpreted through dance, by any means. Give the children an opportunity to try their talents at creating movement for such folk favorites as "Down in the Valley" (p. 199) or "On Top of Old Smoky" (p. 81). "The Twelve Days of Christmas" offers a wonderful challenge in terms of devising twelve different movements appropriate to the objects named in the song, as well as using selected rhythm instruments for added effects.

It should be pointed out here that the purpose of interpretive movement is not merely to pantomime an activity; it is much broader in scope as well as more subtle in character.

Whenever possible, a teacher should familiarize himself with some of the basic exercises and movements used in modern dance so that he can introduce them to his class. (See "Materials for Movement," p. 299.) With even a limited foundation, the children can build and enlarge on these, using their own ideas, and improve their "movement vocabulary," as it were. This should result in more interesting and more highly creative compositions by the class. As a child matures, so should his movement experience grow in depth, enabling him to progress from a simple, concrete imitation of an activity to a more complex abstraction of an idea.

Adapting Movement to the Season

Movement, like songs, can be adapted to fit the season. This requires nothing more than a little imagination on the part of the teacher and the children. The suggestions below are offered merely as *samples* of the type of activities that might be appropriate for the Thanksgiving and Christmas seasons.

SUGGESTED ACTIVITIES FOR THANKSGIVING AND CHRISTMAS

(The division by grade levels is merely by way of suggestion. Teachers should feel free to use any activity or modification of it at either level if they deem it suitable for their particular class.)

KINDERGARTEN TO GRADE THREE

1. Being trees swaying and bending in the wind.
2. Running against the wind.
3. Running with the wind behind you.
4. Being cornstalks and pumpkins in a field.
5. Being scarecrows. (*Listen and Do* record is excellent for this.*)
6. Being snowflakes falling.
7. Beating Indian rhythms using drums made by the children. Have the children make up their own patterns for all to beat.
   Walking out rhythm patterns.
   Beating out their own names.
   Using drum talk.
8. Moving to the rhythm of the teacher's drumbeat.
9. Dramatizing "Mr. Duck and Mr. Turkey."**
10. Marching around the Christmas tree.
11. Pantomiming toys in motion for the others to guess (jack-in-the-box, top, toy soldier, etc.).
12. Dramatizing original stories by the class, using familiar rhythms and interpretive movements.

* American Book Company, Audio-Education Division, New York.
** *Music in Our Town.* Music for Living series, Silver Burdett Company, Morristown, N.J.

13. Using bells and woodblocks to accompany "Over the River and through the Wood."
14. Using bells and triangles for "Jingle Bells"—the bells beat a steady rhythm of eighth notes; the triangles beat two beats to each measure.
15. Creating a dance or activity to "Jingle Bells";

    a. Clap, clap, clap (hands low).   "Jingle Bells . . ."
    b. Clap, clap, clap (hands high).   "Jingle Bells . . ."
    c. Turn in a circle.   "Jingle all the way . . ."
    d. Run in place holding reins.   "Oh what fun it is to ride . . . sleigh"

    Repeat *a*, *b*, and *c*.
    Pull back on reins and retard speed.   "In a one-horse open sleigh."
16. Improvising movement to favorite holiday songs and listening selections.

GRADES FOUR TO SIX

1. Building a log cabin in movement.
2. Pantomiming movements of workers in the field at harvest time.
3. Dramatizing the first Thanksgiving. (Draw out the ideas from the class about how the Pilgrims would move in contrast to the Indians, etc.)
4. Doing Indian dances and beating out characteristic Indian rhythms.
5. Having the children originate movements on the basis of such suggestions as:
    "Ride in a sleigh."
    "Fall like a leaf."
    "Pray for guidance."
    "Cut down a Christmas tree."
    "Sway like a tree in a small breeze."
    "Sway like a tree in a hurricane wind."
    "Decorate a tall tree."
6. Trying movements depicting Christmas customs in other countries, e.g., breaking the piñata (Mexico).
7. Dramatizing an original story by the class about Thanksgiving or Christmas, e.g., "An Old-fashioned Christmas": Run to sleigh, get in, ride, pull up reins, get out, tie up reins, run to wood, select tree, chop down, etc.
8. Drawing out original ideas from the class for appropriate body movements and/or gestures for particularly descriptive words found in carols or Thanksgiving music, e.g., "glory," "peace." Try executing "The Twelve Days of Christmas" and/or "O Come All Ye Faithful" in interpretive movement.
9. Interpreting favorite holiday stories, poems, and songs through body movement.
10. Improvising movement to holiday listening selections.

294

Folk Dances

The following American folk dances are included here because they may be executed with singing accompaniment in the event that the teacher has no dance records or record player handy when he feels the need for a little "hoe-down."

Oh, Susanna

MUSIC:	"Oh, Susanna"
FORMATION:	Single circle, ladies on gents' right.
WORDS:	I come from Alabama with my banjo on my knee
ACTION:	All ladies walk four steps toward the center of the circle and four steps back to place. (Walking back should be done without turning around.)
WORDS:	I'm going to Louisiana, my true love for to see.
ACTION:	All gents walk four steps forward and four steps backward.
WORDS:	It rained all night the day I left, The weather it was dry, The sun so hot I froze to death, Susanna, don't you cry.
ACTION:	Grand right and left as follows: Partners face each other and join right hands. They move forward, passing right shoulders with each other then drop right hands and extend the left hand to the oncoming person, pass left shoulders, drop left hand, extend right hand to the oncoming person, etc. Direction should always be forward—do not turn around when taking hands. The ladies move clockwise around the circle, and the gents counterclockwise, weaving in and out.
WORDS:	Oh, Susanna, oh don't you cry for me
ACTION:	On the word "cry," each gent takes the nearest lady for his new partner, and they swing all the way around once until they sing the word "me."
WORDS:	For I come from Alabama with my banjo on my knee.
ACTION:	Partners cross hands, skating fashion, and promenade (walk) around the circle counterclockwise. The gents are on the inside, and the ladies on the outside. Continue promenading with partner until the word "knee" is sung. Repeat entire song and action as often as desired.

Hinky Dinky Parlez-Vous

MUSIC:	"Hinky Dinky Parlez-Vous" using words below, which describe actions.

295

FORMATION:	Square of four couples, ladies on gents' right.
SINGING WORDS AND ACTION:	1. Head two ladies go forward and back, parlez-vous Forward again and do-si-so, parlez-vous. Do-si-so with your corners all and do the same with your own little doll, hinky dinky parlez-vous.★
	2. Side two ladies go forward and back, etc.
	3. Head two gents go forward and back, etc.
	4. Side two gents go forward and back, etc.

Patty-Cake Polka

MUSIC:	"Little Brown Jug" (or suitable substitute)
FORMATION:	Double circle, ladies facing in, gents facing out. Closed position (lady and gent facing each other). Lady's step is counterpart of gent's. Partners hold both hands.
ACTION:	Start with left foot (lady's left—gent's right). Place left heel out to side, and then bring foot back and place toe behind left foot.
	Repeat heel and toe.
	Four slides to left.
	Opposite direction—heel and toe, heel and toe, four slides.
	Patty-cake right hands 1–2–3. Patty-cake left hands 1–2–3.
	Patty-cake both hands 1–2–3. Slap knees 1–2–3.
	Hook right arms, walk once around.
	Ladies stay in same place, gents move to right to new partner.
	Repeat as many times as desired.

Skip to My Lou

MUSIC:	"Skip to My Lou"
FORMATION:	Single circle, ladies on gents' right.
ACTION:	1. Ladies to the center.
	2. Gents to the center.
	3. Swing your partner.
	4. Promenade all.
	5. Lost my partner (ladies continue in direction of promenade).
	6. Found another (gents find new partner and promenade—new partner means the nearest lady when this verse starts).

★ For more advanced groups, "Allemande left with your corners all, grand right and left around the hall" may be substituted at this point.

Each number above refers to a verse and should be sung as such while the actions are being done. For example:

1. Ladies to the center, skip to my Lou
   Ladies to the center, skip to my Lou
   Ladies to the center, skip to my Lou
   Skip to my Lou, my darling.

Pop Goes the Weasel

MUSIC: "Pop Goes the Weasel"

FORMATION: Double circle with any even number of couples. Ladies on gents' right. Each couple faces another couple, with all participants in groups of four around the circle.

WORDS: All around the cobbler's bench, the monkey chased the weasel

ACTION: Each group of four joins hands and circles to the left clockwise, for eight steps.

WORDS: The monkey thought 'twas all in fun, pop goes the weasel!

ACTION: With hands still joined, reverse directions and circle right (counterclockwise) for eight steps, ending in original starting position.

WORDS: Penny for a spool of thread

ACTION: All take four short steps center, at the same time raising joined hands high.

WORDS: Penny for a needle

ACTION: Four short steps backward, lowering joined hands.

WORDS: That's the way the money goes, pop goes the weasel!

ACTION: All couples facing clockwise raise hands high. Other couples clap on "pop." New couples join hands in a new set and repeat as many times as desired.

Listed below are a few of the more familiar folk dances of the United States and other countries. Directions and accompanying music may be found in the RCA *World of Folk Dances* albums or similar records.

BAVARIA
Bavarian Landler

BELGIUM
Chimes of Dunkirk

CZECHOSLOVAKIA
The Wheat
Turn around Me

DENMARK

Ace of Diamonds
Crested Hen
Danish Dance of Greeting
French Reel
Moskrosser
Seven Jumps
Shoemaker's Dance
Sisken

ENGLAND

Chestnut Tree
Gathering Peascods
Greensleeves
Maypole Dance
Ribbon Dance
Round and Round the Village
Sellenger's Round

ESTONIA

Kiigidi Kaagidi

FRANCE

Bridge of Avignon
Chimes of Dunkirk
Corsican Dance
Gay Musician
Minuet
Varsovienne

GERMANY

Bummel Schottische (Germany-
    America)
Come Let Us Be Joyful
Hansel and Gretel
Kinderpolka
Seven Steps

GREECE

Kolas
Mirsirlou (Greece-America)
Tsamiko

HUNGARY

Cshebogar
Czardas-Vengerka

INTERNATIONAL

All Purpose Polka
Buggy Schotissche
Sailor's Hornpipe

IRELAND

Irish Lilt
Irish Washerwoman
Joy for Two
Rakes of Mallow (Ireland-
    America)

ISRAEL

Cherkassiya
Hora
Shiboleth Basadeh

ITALY

Sicilian Tarantella

LATVIA

Sudmalinas

LITHUANIA

Klumpakojis
Noriu Miego

MEXICO

El Jarabe Tapatio
La Cucaracha
La Raspa
Mexican Mixer

NETHERLANDS

Dutch Couples

NORWAY

Norwegian Mountain March
Tra-La-La Ja Saa

PHILIPPINES

Carinosa
Tinikling

POLAND

Krakowiak

SCANDINAVIA

Lott'Ist Tod

SCOTLAND

Dashing White Sergeant
Gie Gordons
Highland Fling
Highland Schottische

SERBIA

Djurdjevka
Milanovo Kolo

SPAIN

Fado Blanquita

SWEDEN

Bleiking
Carrousel
Gustaf's Skoal
Hopp Mor Annika
How Do You Do My Partner

I See You
Klappdans
Nigarepolska
Tantoli
Tivoli Hambo

SWITZERLAND

May Dance

UNITED STATES

Bingo (Scotland)
Blackberry Quadrille
Bummel Schottische
Cotton Eyed Joe
Glow Worm
Jump Jim Jo
O, Susanna
Polly Wolly Doodle
Pop Goes the Weasel
Soldier's Joy
Spanish Circle Waltz
Ten Pretty Girls
Virginia Reel

Materials for Movement

READINGS

Andrews, Gladys: *Creative Rhythmic Movement for Children.* Prentice-Hall, Inc., Englewood Cliffs, N.J., 1954.

Barrow, Billie: *A Method for Teaching Creative Dance.* Southern Connecticut State College, New Haven, Conn., 1960.

Coit, Lottie, and Ruth Bampton: *Follow the Music.* Summy-Birchard Company, Evanston, Ill., 1948.

Cooperative Recreation Service Publications:

Beliajus, V. F.: *Merrily Dance* (Lithuanian dances).

Bidstrup, Marguerite: *19 Folk Dances from Denmark.*

Dunsing, Gretel, and Paul Dunsing: *Dance Lightly.*

Farwell, Jane: *Folk Dances for Fun.*

Golden Bridge (German folk recreation).

Handy Folk Dance Book.

Handy Play Party Book.

Handy Square Dance Book.

Rohrbough, Lynn (ed.): *Treasures from Abroad.*

Stefanski-Budzikowski, Natalie: *Having Fun the Polish Way.*

Doll, Edna, and Mary Jarman Nelson: *Rhythms Today!* Silver Burdett Company, Morristown, N.J., 1964. (Correlated record also.)

Fisk, Margaret: *The Art of the Rhythmic Choir.* Harper & Row, Publishers, Incorporated, New York, 1950.

Gilbert, Pia, and Aileene Lockhart: *Music for the Modern Dance.* Wm. C. Brown Co., Dubuque, Iowa, 1961.

Humphreys, Louise, and Jerrold Ross: *Interpreting Music through Movement.* Prentice-Hall, Inc., Englewood Cliffs, N.J., 1964.

LaSalle, Dorothy: *Rhythms and Dances for Elementary Schools*, rev. ed. A. S. Barnes & Co., Inc., New York, 1951.

Monsour, Sally, Marilyn Cohen, and Patricia Lindell: *Rhythm in Music and Dance for Children.* Wadsworth Publishing Co., Belmont, Calif., 1966.

Murray, Ruth Lovell: *Dance in Elementary Education*, 2d ed. Harper & Row, Publishers, Incorporated, New York, 1963.

Saffran, Rosanna B.: *First Book of Creative Rhythms.* Holt, Rinehart and Winston, Inc., New York, 1963.

Tobitt, Janet: *Promenade All.* Box 97, Pleasantville, N.Y.

See also selected chapters in the professional literature. (See "Professional Reading," p. 7.)

RECORDS

SINGING GAMES AND ACTION SONGS

Activity Songs. Rhythms Productions, 1107 El Centro Avenue, Los Angeles, Calif.

Basic Singing Games. RCA Victor Record Library for Elementary Schools.

Singing Games. Bowmar Records, North Hollywood, Calif., vols. 1–3.

Sing'n Do Songs. Bowmar Records.

DANCE AND CREATIVE MOVEMENT

Basic Rhythm and Music for Movement and Space. Kay Ortmans Productions, Ltd., 1644 West Broadway, Vancouver, B.C.

Come and See the Peppermint Tree. Educational Record Sales, 157 Chambers Street, New York.

Dance Along. Folkways.

Dance a Story. Paul and Anne Barlin, Ginn and Company, Boston, vol. 1 (*Little Duck*), vol. 2 (*Noah's Ark*), vol. 3 (*Magic Mountain*), vol. 4 (*Balloons*).

Improvisation and Dance. Classroom Materials, Inc., Great Neck, N.Y., vols. 1–3.

Listen and Do series. American Book Company, Audio Education series, New York, vol. 1 (*Friendly Train* and *Ginger and Josh*), vol. 2 (*Handsome Scarecrow* and *The Little Clown*), vol. 3 (*Panda Balloon* and *Jacko, the Dancing Monkey*), vol. 4 (*Work and Sing* and *Play and Sing*).

Listen, Move and Dance. Capitol Records, vols. 1 and 2.

Music for Dance Rhythms. Folkways.

FUNDAMENTAL RHYTHMS AND RHYTHMIC RESPONSE

Adventures in Rhythm. Ella Jenkins, Folkways.
Primary Music: Rhythm. American Book Company, Audio Education series, New York.
Rhythms for Children. Ella Jenkins, Folkways.
Rhythms of Childhood. Ella Jenkins, Folkways.
This Is Rhythm. Ella Jenkins, Folkways.

FOLK AND SQUARE DANCING

RCA Victor *Folk Dance* series (*The World of Folk Dances*)
   All Purpose Folk Dances
   Festival Folk Dances
   First Folk Dances
   Folk Dances for All Ages
   Folk Dances for Fun
   Happy Folk Dances
   Special Folk Dances
   Square Dances, vols. 1 and 2

Bowmar Educational Records
   Canadian Folk Dances
   Folk Dances from around the World
   Folk Dances of Hawaii
   Folk Dances of Latin America
   Mexican Folk Dances

PARTICIPATION RECORDS

Young Peoples Record Club and Children's Record Guild
   Do This, Do That
   Let's Play Together
   The Little Puppet
   My Playmate, the Wind
   Sunday in the Park
   A Visit to My Little Friend

OTHER (These may include combinations of dance, rhythmic response, etc.)

Children's Rhythms in Symphony. Bowmar Records.
Phoebe James Creative Rhythms. Educational Record Sales, 157 Chambers Street, New York. (Series of twenty-three records.)
The Rhythm Program. RCA Victor Library for Elementary Schools. (Consists of six volumes.)
Rhythms Today! Silver Burdett Company, Morristown, N.J. (Record correlated with book of same title.)
Ruth Evans Childhood Rhythm Records. 326 Forest Park Avenue, Springfield, Mass.

FILMS

African Rhythms. Association Films, Inc., Broad at Elm, Ridgefield, N.J.

Building Children's Personalities with Creative Dancing. University of California, Educational Film Sales Department, University Extension, Los Angeles, Calif. (For teacher viewing.)

Music for Children. Carl Orff: National Film Board of Canada, Contemporary Films, 267 West Twenty-fifth Street, New York. (Thirteen minutes, black and white.)

Rhythm: Instruments and Movements. Encyclopedia Britannica Films, Willmette, Ill.

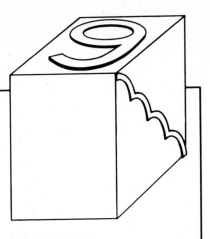

CREATING
EXPERIENCES

Idea came knocking
At the door of my mind
I welcomed him with music
And together we make a poem
   Matsuko Toyama, age eleven

From *Let Them Write Poetry*, by
Nina Willis Walter. Copyright ©
1962 by Holt, Rinehart and Winston,
Inc. Reprinted by permission of Holt,
Rinehart and Winston, Inc.

Children derive a great deal of pleasure from creating something they can feel is uniquely their own. It is assumed, of course, that abundant opportunities for children to create will be provided within all areas of the classroom musical experience. Several possibilities for adventure have already been mentioned in previous chapters; however, it seems appropriate to set aside a separate chapter here to take a closer look at the creative activities discussed earlier as well as to suggest some additional ones.

It has been found that creating successfully in any field depends to a great extent upon the individual's fund of information in that field; thus we may presume that the more meaningful musical experiences (as well as knowledges) with which a child has been provided, the better equipped he is to produce substantial creations of his own.

303

Composing Words to Familiar Tunes

Music offers many avenues for creation because of its broad range of activities. In singing, for example, a child might burst forth with new words to an old tune when he is inspired by such inevitables as a change of season or weather, an upcoming holiday, a recent field trip, a special occasion such as a birthday, a push for better health habits, an urge to engage in some body movement, or simply the need to remember something. The following are samples of a few such efforts on the part of kindergarten and first grade children:

TUNE: "The Farmer in the Dell"

1. Today's a sunny day, etc.
2. This is the month of June, etc.
3. Oh, spring is coming soon, etc.
4. The Christmas tree is tall, etc.
5. Today we saw the zoo, etc.

TUNE: "Here We Go round the Mulberry Bush"

1. Santa is going to visit me, etc.
2. Here we go walking like a duck, etc., all around the room.

TUNE: "Skip to My Lou"

1. Stand on your toes and touch the sky, etc.

TUNE: "Mary Had a Little Lamb"

1. Have we brushed our teeth today, etc. (additional verses for other duties).

At Halloween time, "Ten Little Indians" become "Ten Little Witches," while during the Easter season they turn into "Ten Little Bunnies."

In upper grades, the urges are the same, but the efforts are slightly more sophisticated. A group of sixth grade children felt the need to fill their own "Twelve Day of Christmas" with culinary delights to which they could relate more easily than to French hens and colly birds:

On the first day of Christmas my true love gave to me
A dee-lish-us tur-ur-ur-key.

It's written just the way they sang it. The remaining eleven days were spent with two sweet potatoes, three golden eggs, four cans of cranberries, five helpings of stuffing, six glasses of cider, seven bags of walnuts, eight candy canes, nine skinny carrots, ten scoops of ice cream, eleven pods of stringbeans, and twelve purple grapes! Needless to say, the original rhythm patterns in the song had to undergo a few slight modifications to make things fit, but when you're creating such an exotic menu just before lunch, a few rhythmic deviations hardly seem to matter.

Another sixth grade, which was studying the UN in depth and engaging in frequent discussions about brotherhood, composed their songs individually and then performed them for the class. One child wrote words to the tune of "Shortnin' Bread":

> I am an assistant at FAO, I show people how to make crops grow.
> I am a worker at UPU, I help people get their letters through.

Children also like to try putting words to less familiar tunes, such as some particularly melodic theme heard during a listening experience. The practice of putting words to themes from larger works is frowned upon by music educators; however, more often than not, the "frowning" is found to be the result of personal prejudice. Perhaps these educators have been subjected to travesties, rather than creations from the heart such as the following, written by a fourth grade class★ to the lovely theme heard in *Little Train of the Caipira* (Villa-Lobos):

> Look, here comes the train,
> It's coming down the track
> Watch out, everyone! Look out and step right back,
> Where, where will it take me?
> Where, where will it go?
> Down, down through the meadows where the wild red berries grow.

Composing Tunes to Familiar Poems

Children at all grade levels can compose tunes to familiar poems. Tunes do tend to come a little harder than words, but actually it's only the initial line that needs the extra effort. Once that's established, it's whoever gets his hand up first, followed by a careful selection of the best offerings by the class. It is up to the class, of course, to decide which of the suggested tunes are the best, and the more experience they gain in this activity, the more discriminating they become.

Frequently, the teacher must find his own special "code" for taking down the tunes suggested by the individual children so that the class can sing them. Sometimes, when asked to repeat his tune, the moment of inspiration has passed and the child has forgotten what he sang. Using lines or curves to indicate the general direction of the melody might prove helpful to the teacher who finds it difficult to transcribe tunes directly to a staff in notation. Long and short lines might be used to indicate the general rhythmic pattern of long and short notes.

★ Under the direction of Lynda Kyle, music specialist, New Britain, Conn., public schools. 305

The meter signature is easily arrived at by simply reading the poem from the board and noting where the accents seem to fall. A poem can be divided into metrical groupings, which will eventually become measures in music, by marking a slanted line *before* each accented word. Reading the poem again to the children to give them the feel of the flow and accent (as indicated by the slanted lines) in combination with the long and short lines noted within each measure will enable them to determine the kind of notes that should be written for each syllable of the poem. If the children have not as yet been introduced to note values, the teacher may find this system helpful for himself in transferring the song to the staff so that it can be saved for future use.

Composing Words and Music

Primary as well as upper-grade children are capable of composing both words and music to create an entirely new song. For the teacher, this may prove to be the most involved activity related to creating song material (as far as notating is concerned) as well as the most interesting.

The procedure for notating what the children sing is the same as that suggested above—use lines or curves to indicate the general melodic direction and long and short lines to indicate the general rhythmic pattern. In addition, of course, the children's original *words* must also be written down. Some children will contribute words *and* melody all at once; others will offer only words and leave the melody to someone else. All contributions should be cheerfully accepted and notated somewhere on the board so that the class may evaluate and select the final product. When children have had sufficient background in basic rhythmic and melodic skills, they should be able to work out the rhythm and melody of a song by themselves. Some fifth and sixth grade children have been known to compose their own operas, writing an original libretto as well as original music.

Other musical areas also lend themselves well to creating experiences. On the following pages, a few of these areas are mentioned and suggestions are given for creating experiences in each.

Creating with Harmony (Upper Grades)

Making up simple chants, descants, and ostinati to accompany familiar tunes
Composing melodies to fit in given harmony structures
Selecting appropriate chord harmony for a given melody
Composing a harmony part for a given melody
(For further suggestions related to creating with harmony, see Chapter 3, Harmonizing Experiences, p. 64.)

Creating with Rhythm Instruments

Creating accompaniments to poetry and stories with rhythm instruments.

Using rhythm instruments to describe a scene or tell a story with no narration.

Creating original orchestrations for use with rhythm instruments.

Creating original percussion accompaniments.

Discovering new ways to play familiar instruments (strum piano strings, etc.).

Composing tunes on bells. (See "Twelve-tone Row," p. 310.)

(For further suggestions related to creating with instruments, see "Rhythm Instruments," p. 223.)

Creating with Listening

Composing original themes (very short and simple) and then creating *variations* on the theme through changes in tempo, mode, meter, etc., and/or through the use of different musical media (instruments, voice, etc.). In-depth exposure to a variety of selected listening experiences will enable older children to do this.

Making up original compositions using various *forms*, such as rondo or ABA form.

Originating *new* forms.

Making up original rhythmic compositions (rhythm patterns only—no melody) using various forms. In ABA form, for example, one rhythm pattern could represent the A section, while a contrasting rhythm pattern could represent the B section. Use selected rhythm instruments for each section to execute the patterns.

Dramatizing listening selections heard.

Painting, drawing, or using some other art medium to visually represent the music heard. The creation might depict a scene, a character in a story, or something of a more abstract nature, depending upon the music.

Choosing appropriate (in terms of mood, tempo, character of selection, etc.) rhythm instruments to accompany listening selections.

Selecting appropriate orchestral instruments for portraying suggested situations, objects, scenes, etc.

Originating two- or three-line stories or situations and then telling them musically, through a simple performance on a classroom instrument (such as piano or song bells). For example: "A boy went walking very slowly up a steep hill. When he got to the top, he remembered that he had left his lunch at the bottom of the hill, so he turned around and ran back down as quickly as he could." This example is over-simplified, but the object is to make the story descriptive in such a way that children can tell it musically simply through the use of **307** direction (up or down), dynamics (loud or soft), and tempo (fast or slow). A few extra "sound effects" that would challenge a child's imagination, in terms of reproducing them on a classroom instrument, might also be added to liven things up.

(For further suggestions related to creating with listening, see Chapter 7, Listening Experiences, p. 242.)

Creating with Body Movement

Creating movement to tell a familiar story, legend, fairy tale, or folk tale.
Composing original "ballets."
Creating original dances to familiar tunes.
Improvising movement to listening selections heard.
Improvising a theme in movement and creating variations on the theme.
Improvising movement to illustrate other musical terms such as:

Round	Presto, largo, and other tempo
Canon	terms
Fugue	Crescendo
AB form, ABA form, rondo	Diminuendo
form	Duple meter
Repeat	Triple meter
Polyrhythms	

(For further suggestions related to creating with body movement, see Chapter 8, Experiences in Movement, p. 273.)

Creating with Electronic Music

Increasing interest in the use of electronic music has inspired a number of teachers to encourage their children to experiment in small ways in this area.

A simple beginning might be to record various sounds on the tape recorder and play them back at different speeds. The sounds used may be natural sounds in the environment or those contrived by the children. Some children's music texts include suggestions in this area.*

(For further information on electronic music, see Chapter 7, Listening Experiences, p. 263.)

* See *Exploring Music*, Holt, Rinehart and Winston, Inc., New York, 1966, Book 6, "Compose Your Own Electronic Music."

Creating *original* scales through varying the traditional arrangement of whole and half steps.

Creating original songs based on scales other than the major, such as those discussed below.

PENTATONIC SCALE

This is a five-tone scale known throughout the world. It contains no half steps between the tones. The syllables are *do, re, mi, sol, la*, arranged in the following intervals:

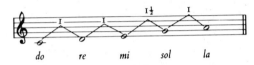

The pentatonic scale may be constructed from any given tone. An easy way to play this scale is to use all black keys:

Children will enjoy composing their own tunes using only the five tones of the pentatonic scale. They should be allowed ample opportunity to experiment with it on the song bells, resonator bells, and piano when available, as well as with their voices, using the syllables suggested above arranged in different order.

The following songs are based on the pentatonic scale and may be played using all black keys. Have the children try picking out a few of the tunes. Starting tones are given:

Mary Had a Little Lamb	Start B♭
Old MacDonald Had a Farm	Start G♭
The Farmer in the Dell	Start D♭
Swing Low, Sweet Chariot	Start B♭
Auld Lang Syne	Start D♭

MINOR SCALES

Minor scales may appear in any one of three forms:

The "natural" minor (sometimes called "normal" or "pure"):

The "harmonic" minor (the *seventh* tone is a half step higher):

la ti do re mi fa si la la si fa mi re do ti la

The "melodic" minor (the *sixth* and *seventh* tones are a half step higher *ascending only*):

la ti do re mi fi si la la sol fa mi re do ti la

(Further information on minor scales may be found in Appendix A.)

WHOLE-TONE SCALE

The whole-tone scale consists of six notes spaced a *whole* step apart:

BLUES SCALE

"Blues" songs are usually considered to have originated in the United States. The tunes are characterized by the lowered third and seventh tones of the scale. (Sometimes the fifth is also lowered.) Although a given blues melody contains these lowered tones, they need not necessarily be present in the harmonizing accompaniment as well. The slight dissonance that is created as a result contributes to the unique sound of the blues.

TWELVE-TONE ROW

The twelve-tone row (or set) was first used by the contemporary composer Arnold Schoenberg. The tones that comprise it are known as the "chromatic scale"; however, no mention is made of a scale when referring to the tone row, for there is no home tone. The tones are usually stated in a given order and are seldom repeated. Children may wish to select their own "subject" or "statement" and then explore possibilities in "inversion" and "retrograde" (see Glossary, p. 345).

Interesting results are possible using resonator bells for each of the twelve tones shown above. Arrange them in ascending order and then rearrange them at random and play in the rearranged order. Notate the order on the board.★ (Bells are marked with letter names.) Try writing the "composition" in inversion or retrograde. Some children's music texts make mention of the twelve-tone row. (See list at the end of this chapter.)

Creating with Sound

Let the class experiment with ways of making interesting and varied sounds from all kinds of materials; then suggest that they compose a piece using the sounds. (Have them find ways to notate the piece so that it may be kept for future use.) When the "orchestration" is complete, ask them to choose a conductor (or ask for volunteers), and then play their composition.

Let the class discover ways in which the body may be used as a percussion instrument, and then create a composition using only those sounds. (See Chapter 8, Experiences in Movement, p. 273.)

The tape recorder should be used frequently to preserve as many creations as possible, not only for the children's pleasure in listening to their own work, but also for evaluative purposes. Use of the tape recorder also enables parents and the teachers and children in other classes to hear these original compositions.

If a teacher has set up a music center in his classroom, certainly as many original creations as possible should be displayed there. An original song could be notated on a chart and hung on the wall, with the children's suggested orchestration for the rhythm instruments indicated below it.

The success of any creative activity is almost wholly dependent upon the atmosphere the teacher has created in his room. If all the children have been made to feel that their contributions, be they ever so humble, are always welcome, then the climate is right for creative effort, and such effort will be forthcoming. On the other hand, if the environment is characterized by tension and shattered dignities, it will serve as a deterrent to any kind of original thinking.

★ For variation on this activity, see *Making Music Your Own*, Book 6. Silver Burdett Company, Morristown, N.J. (teacher's edition).

The foregoing material is meant to illustrate in a small way how the creating process can permeate all classroom music experiences. Hopefully, many teachers will choose to experiment even further in this area. (Additional related activities may also be found in Chapter 10, Further Adventures, p. 314.)

For Further Exploration

DISCOVERING MUSIC TOGETHER (FOLLETT)

Book 6
 The Pentatonic Scale
 Harmony in Minor

EXPLORING MUSIC (HOLT)

Book 1 Teacher's Edition
 Improvising Accompaniments
 Mimetic Play and Creative Dramatics
 Dance Improvisations
 Adding New Verses
Book 2 Teacher's Edition
 Play Your Own Music
 Compose a Musical Story
Book 5 Teacher's Edition
 Improvisation in Rhythm
 Exploring Music through Improvisation and Children's Compositions.
Book 6 Teacher's Edition
 Improvise Your Own Calypso
 Compose Your Own Electronic Music

GROWING WITH MUSIC (PRENTICE-HALL)

Book 3 Teacher's Edition
 Writing Music
Book 4 Teacher's Edition
 Creating Music

MAKING MUSIC YOUR OWN (SILVER BURDETT)

Book 6 Teacher's Edition
 New Arrangements of Tones
 Creating a Song

MUSIC FOR YOUNG AMERICANS (AMERICAN BOOK)

Meeting Music   Teacher's Edition
   Improvisation at the Piano
Sharing Music   Teacher's Edition
   Improvisation at the Piano
Studying Music   Teacher's Edition
   The Tone Row

See also selected chapters in the professional literature. (See "Professional Reading," p. 7.)

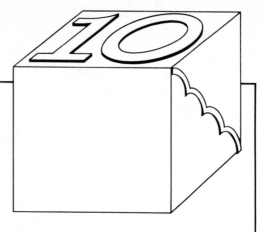

FURTHER
ADVENTURES

*"Life is either a daring adventure
or nothing."*
    Helen Keller

Vitalizing Other Subject Matter through Music

One of the many reasons to be thankful for the existence of music in any school curriculum is that it may be used so effectively in breathing life into other subject-matter areas. There is, in fact, an interaction here, for frequently a strong background in other subject matter can help to enrich a musical experience.

Folk music, which is described as "that type of music that originates among the common people of a country and thus embodies their characteristic qualities and feelings,"* would lose its meaning if it were studied in isolation

* Howard McKinney, *Music and Man.* American Book Company, New York, 1953.

from its setting, since living is the very reason for its being. Some tribes have songs for all aspects of living—births, deaths, bountiful harvests, victories in battle, etc. Environmental factors and mode of living may even determine the kind of instruments people use as well as the kind of music they produce. In an area where there are many trees, for example, some tribes would probably be more inclined to use instruments that can be made easily from wood—drums, xylophones, flutes, etc.—simply because the material is available. Where no suitable materials exist, the voice would more likely predominate.

The *way* in which instruments are used might also be determined by the location of the people using them and by their particular way of life. In some primitive areas, not only are deep-toned drums made for singing and dancing, but they also serve as a means of communication between one village and another.

The foregoing obviously concerns the area of social studies; however, music may be integrated into other areas of the curriculum as well, providing a teacher with many springboards for further pursuits. The more relationships a child is exposed to, the more meaningful the learning becomes to him. Certainly, we should not attempt to isolate music from the rest of the curriculum, any more than we should try to fragment the activities that constitute the total music experience in the classroom. A child's involvement in one almost inevitably means his involvement in another in some way.

A few musical activities relating to other areas of the curriculum are suggested below. Of course some areas relate more closely than others, thus affording an opportunity for a greater number and variety of combined activities.

SOCIAL STUDIES

Singing songs based on actual historical events (e.g., "Yankee Doodle" and "Springfield Mountain")

Singing songs with foreign texts, as well as foreign songs with English texts

Discovering the history of the United States as it is revealed through the medium of the song

Discovering the folk music that emerged from the cultural contribution of the various ethnic groups migrating to the United States

Singing songs by American composers from the early days (e.g., Billings and Hopkinson) to the present

Performing street cries and calls and songs for selling wares from the United States and other countries

Creating original words to familiar tunes (or original tunes) relating to topics under study

Composing original songs dealing with current topics

Learning rhythms representative of other nations and playing them on native instruments

Tracing the origin of folk themes used by a composer in a long musical
work

Exploring the environmental factors that may have influenced music
throughout the ages; relating musical works of the time to periods in
history

Studying folk instruments of the world by sight and sound

Listening to musical works that portray historical events (e.g., *1812
Overture*)

Listening to musical works portraying nationalism (events, heroes,
patriotic themes, etc.)

Listening to musical works describing methods of transportation

Relating the surroundings in musical terms:

Tempo: "Is the tempo of your neighbourhood slow or fast in the
morning?"

Pitch: "Does the siren sound lower or higher than the foghorn?"

Rhythm: "What sounds in our surroundings seem to have rhythm?"

Motivating body movement by the texture (either by sight or by touch)
of a product imported from another country

Motivating body movement by the mention of a product or industry
representative of a section of the country:

Being a field of wheat in the Middle West

Being a factory in the East

Moving to traffic sounds and other sounds of the city

Moving to sounds of the country

Discovering how the rhythm of a work song evolved from the movement of the work itself

Depicting occupations of various countries in body movement

Depicting emotion in body movement

Creating original dances to folk music of other countries; noting
uncommon meter signatures (such as $\frac{7}{8}$, sometimes found in music
from Greece)

Executing dances of the United States and other countries

Executing court dances of the seventeenth, eighteenth, and nineteenth
centuries

ART

Illustrating terms common to music and art ("harmony," "form,"
"color," "design," etc.) through representative examples in each of
the media

Listening to musical compositions inspired by artists' works (e.g., *Seven
Studies on Themes of Paul Klee*, by Gunther Schuller, and *Isle of the
Dead*, by Rachmaninoff)

Painting to contrasting musical selections in major and minor keys

Drawing (or executing in some other art medium) a means of travel, an
animal, or another suitable subject appropriate to a musical selection
in presto tempo; in largo tempo

Motivating abstract art creations through listening

Motivating a mural through the use of a musical suite

Illustrating stories told in music (or, as a variation, listening to an unfamiliar piece of music, making up a story to suit it, and then illustrating the story)

Illustrating scenes in music (e.g., "Festival of Baghdad" from Rimsky-Korsakoff's *Scheherazade*)

Making puppets for dramatization of stories in music

Drawing costumes of various countries under study

Choosing and using various colors inspired by contrasting moods in listening selections

Designing and building scenery for a musical production by the class

Choosing a picture (from a series displayed in the room) that best fits a given listening selection (also, after a broad background of listening experiences, choosing a listening selection that best fits a given picture)

Improvising body movement motivated by viewing a painting, color, or design

Creating designs inspired by music in contrasting meters, e.g., duple and triple

Creating designs inspired by music of different types, e.g., a march and a waltz

Illustrating musical terms through art: (1) showing ABA form, for example, by using one color for the A section and a contrasting color for the B section or showing the contrast by the means of the media, style, or subject matter used (subject matter conceivably varying from some aspect of nature—flowers, trees, etc.—to geometric shapes); (2) showing variations on a theme, for example, by executing the same subject in different media or styles

LANGUAGE ARTS

Using body movement and percussion instruments to accompany poetry

Composing original poetry and music and/or original poetry to familiar tunes

Composing an opera, operetta, or play with music

Comparing forms of songs with forms of poetry

Creating dramatizations inspired by listening selections

Stimulating creative writing through appropriate listening experiences

Spelling words and making punctuation marks in body movement

Improving reading skills through reading words of songs

Relating choral speaking to music in terms of voice production and interpretation

Making words from letter names of lines and spaces

Selecting listening experiences based on children's literature

SCIENCE

Using the science of sound as a basis for a science unit (to include acoustics, vibrations, air columns, etc.) and relating it to the construction of musical instruments

Playing simple tunes on water glasses filled with varying amounts of
water to produce different tones

Blowing over the tops of bottles filled with varying amounts of water to
produce tunes, scales, and chords

Studying electronic music and creating some when possible

Using sounds of nature such as the wind, surf, etc., as motivation for
body movement

Collecting various types of bells and comparing tones

Comparing the sounds produced by an old cylinder or disk-type record
player with those produced by modern recording equipment

Reproducing some sounds heard in the neighborhood

Composing original pieces using sounds only

Discovering ways of producing various kinds of sounds with available
materials

Discovering differences in sound between hollow and solid objects

Motivating body movement through suggesting how different types of
weather make people feel

Discovering the moving parts of the body

Discovering different ways of using the body as a percussion instrument
to produce different sounds

Composing songs about new discoveries in science

PHYSICAL EDUCATION

Exploring the meaning of musical terms (e.g., "crescendo," "diminuendo," "fugue") through dance

Exploring terms common to music and dance

Finding movements to describe the sound of selected rhythm instruments

Finding ways to produce different kinds of notes through movement

Moving in a rhythm pattern—even, uneven, etc.: relating walking,
skipping, and other fundamental rhythms to note values and rhythmic
patterns in music

Using rhythm instruments to accompany body movement; choosing
the best instrument for the movement

Performing singing games and dances

Creating a dance to familiar music

Expressing musical forms in body movement (e.g., ABA, rondo, fugue)

Using contrasting styles in music as motivation for original body movement

Creating music to accompany an original dance

MATHEMATICS

Singing counting songs

Interpreting shapes through body movement (cone, square, etc.)

Relating note values and meter signatures to numbers

Dividing lines of rhythm patterns into appropriate number of measures
according to a given meter signature

Sample Seasonal Suggestions for Singing and Related Listening Experiences

The following songs and listening selections are included here simply to illustrate how a season, holiday, or other special event might serve as a springboard for the planning of music in the classroom. Although only two areas are included here, obviously other musical experiences may also be adapted for seasonal use.

Words and music for songs marked with an asterisk★ may be found elsewhere in this text. (See Song Index, p. 369.) The sources of other songs are indicated either by the name of the music publisher (addresses given in Appendix E) or by the following code, which refers to titles of the standard children's music texts:

TIM: *This Is Music.* Allyn and Bacon, Inc., Boston, 1962.
MMYO: *Making Music Your Own.* Silver Burdett Company, Morristown, N.J., 1965.
GWM: *Growing with Music.* Prentice-Hall, Inc., Englewood Cliffs, N.J., 1963.
EM: *Exploring Music.* Holt, Rinehart and Winston, Inc., New York, 1966.
MFL: *Music for Living.* Silver Burdett Company, Morristown, N.J., 1956.
MYA: *Music for Young Americans.* American Book Company, New York, 1966.

Many of the sacred songs may be found in any church hymnal. For additional sources as well as additional songs, see the list of song collections given at the end of Chapter 2, Singing Experiences, p. 60.)

SEPTEMBER–OCTOBER (School opening, Fall, Columbus Day, Halloween)

SINGING .

Heigh, Ho, Come to the Fair
O Dear! What Can the Matter Be?
Songs of Columbus
Songs of Halloween
Getting to Know You (from *The King and I*)
Happy Wanderer   (TIM, Books 2 and 3)
Football songs

LISTENING

"A Hunt in the Black Forest"   Voelcker
"Overture" from *William Tell*   Rossini

"The Little Hunters" Kullak
"March of the Dwarfs" Grieg
"Andante" from *Symphony No. 94* ("Surprise") Haydn
"The Witch" Tchaikovsky
"Witch's Ride" from *Hansel and Gretel* Humperdinck
Danse Macabre Saint-Saëns
The Sorcerer's Apprentice Dukas
"Witch's Dance" MacDowell
"In the Hall of the Mountain King" from *Peer Gynt Suite* Grieg
A Night on Bald Mountain Moussorgsky
"Halloween" Ives

NOVEMBER (Veterans Day, Thanksgiving)

VETERANS DAY

SINGING

1. Service songs

   Marine's Hymn
   Air Corps Song
   Coast Guard Song (Semper Paratus)
   Anchors Aweigh
   Caisson Song (MYA, *Studying Music*)

2. War songs

   a. Songs of the American Revolution
      Johnny Has Gone for a Soldier (MMYO, Book 5)
      Riflemen of Bennington (MMYO, Book 5)
      Yankee Doodle
   b. Songs of the Civil War
      Tenting Tonight
      When Johnny Comes Marching Home Again
      John Brown's Body
   c. Songs of World War I
      You're a Grand Old Flag★
      Yankee Doodle Boy★
      Keep the Home Fires Burning
      It's a Long Way to Tipperary
      Oh, How I Hate to Get Up in the Morning
      My Buddy
   d. Songs of World War II
      I've Got Sixpence (MFL, *Music around the World*)
      This Is the Army, Mr. Jones
   e. Patriotic songs
      America
      America, the Beautiful
      There Are Many Flags in Many Lands (EM, Book 3)
      This Land Is Your Land (MMYO, Book 5)

Columbia, the Gem of the Ocean
This Is My Country   (Shawnee Press)
The Star-spangled Banner
God Bless America   (EM, Book 5)

f. Others
Stout Hearted Men   (Harms Music)
I Love a Parade   (Harms Music)
Gee, but I Want to Go Home
Reveille
Taps

LISTENING

"American Salute" (variations on "When Johnny Comes Marching Home")   Gould
"Marche Militaire"   Schubert
Selected other marches as desired
1812 *Overture*   Tchaikovsky

THANKSGIVING

SINGING

Pow Wow★
Swing the Shining Sickle   (MFL, *Music Near and Far*)
We Plow the Fields and Scatter
For Health and Strength   (MMYO, Book 4, and TIM, Book 3)
Now Thank We All Our God   (MYA, *Making Music*)
Come Ye Thankful People
We Gather Together (Harvest Hymn)   (MMYO, Book 5)
Chester   (MMYO, Book 5)
America, the Beautiful
Over the River and through the Wood★
Mr. Duck and Mr. Turkey   (MFL, *Music in Our Town*)
For the Beauty of the Earth   (MMYO, Book 4 and MYA, *Understanding Music*)
Faith of Our Fathers
Oh God, beneath Thy Guiding Hand
Dona Nobis Pacem★
Old Hundred   (MFL, *Music in Our Country*)
Pop Goes the Weasel
Ten Little Indians
In Good Old Colony Times   (MFL, *Music in Our Country*)

LISTENING

"Hens and Cocks" from *Carnival of the Animals*   Saint-Saëns
"Turkey in the Straw"
Selections from *Indian Suites*   MacDowell
"Little Indian Drum"   (Young Peoples Record Club)

Selections from *This Is My Country* album or *America, the Beautiful* album
   (RCA Victor)
Variations on Pop Goes the Weasel   Caillet
"Dagger Dance" from *Natoma*   Victor Herbert
"Wheat Dance" from *Estancia*   Ginastera
"Hoe-down" from *Rodeo*   Copland
"Pumpkin Eater's Little Fugue"   McBride
"Chester" from *New England Triptych*   William Schuman
Selections from *Music of American Indians*   (RCA Victor Album)
Selections from *North American Indian Songs*   (Bowmar album)

DECEMBER (Traditional holidays)

SINGING

Traditional carols and holiday songs
I Wonder as I Wander   (EM, Book 6)
Dona Nobis Pacem★
Boar's Head Carol   (MFL, *Music around the World*)
Children Go★
Mary Had a Baby★
Rise Up Shepherd and Follow   (MFL, *Music around the World*)
Behold that Star
My Dreydel   (MFL, *Music in Our Town*)
Hannukah   (EM, Book 2)
Joyous Chanukah   (MMYO, Book 5)
Bring a Torch, Jeanette Isabella (French words also)   (MYA, *Studying Music*)
Echo Carol
March of the Three Kings   (MFL, *Music around the World*, EM, Book 5)
O Tannenbaum (O Christmas Tree)
Las Posados (Mexican)
Piñata (Mexican)   (MMYO, Book 3)
Silent Night (German words)
Adeste Fidelis (Latin words)   (EM, Book 6)
Il est Né (French words)   (EM, Book 6)
Christmas Is Coming★
Pat-a-pan   (MMYO, Book 4 and EM, Book 6)
Fum Fum Fum   (MMYO, Book 6)
The Twelve Days of Christmas   (MYA, *Understanding Music*)
Masters in this Hall   (GWM, Book 6)
What Child Is This? (tune of Greensleeves)
Go Tell It on the Mountain   (MMYO, Book 5)
Friendly Beasts   (EM, Book 2)
Winds through the Olive Trees   (EM, Book 2)
Pray God Bless (round)
Jesu, Joy of Man's Desiring   (EM, Book 6)
Coventry Carol   (MMYO, Book 4)
Winter Wonderland (children's words)★
Here We Come A-wassailing   (MMYO, Book 6; EM, Books 5 and 6)

Silver Bells   (*Fred Waring Songbook*, Shawnee Press)
Up on the House Top   (EM, Book 1)
Jolly Old St. Nicholas   (EM, Book 1)
Santa Claus Is Coming to Town
Rudolph, the Red-nosed Reindeer   (St. Nicholas Music Co.)

LISTENING

"Dance of the Chinese Dolls"   Rebikoff
"March of the Gnomes"   Rebikoff
Nutcracker Suite   Tchaikovsky
"March of the Toys"   Victor Herbert
"Jack in the Box" from *Mikrokosmos Suite No. 2*   Bartok
"Waltzing Doll"   Poldini
"Impromptu, The Top"   Bizet
"In a Clock Store"   Orth
Children's Symphony, Second Movement   McDonald
"March of the Three Kings" (Farandole)   Bizet
"Allegro in G"   Mendelssohn
"Viennese Musical Clock"   Kodály
"Sleigh Ride"   Leroy Anderson
Selections from *Christmas Hymns and Carols*   (RCA Victor Album,
    Robert Shaw Chorale)
"Jesu, Joy of Man's Desiring"   Bach
"Hallelujah Chorus" and other selections from *The Messiah*   Handel

(For related body movement, see "Suggested Activities for Thanksgiving and Christmas," p. 293.)

JANUARY–FEBRUARY (Lincoln's birthday, Washington's birthday, winter)

SINGING

Battle Hymn of the Republic
Yankee Doodle
Songs of Washington and Lincoln
Songs of patriotism (see "November" list)
Songs of winter

LISTENING

"The Sleigh"   Mozart
Winter Fun   (Young Peoples Record Club)
"Skater's Waltz"   Waldteufel
"Skater's Waltz"   Meyerbeer
"Chorale and Fugue on Yankee Doodle"   Thomson
"Waltz on the Ice"   Prokofiev
A Lincoln Portrait   Copland

"Mardi Gras" from *Mississippi Suite*   Grofé
"Snow Is Dancing" from *Children's Corner Suite*   Debussy
"Departure"   Prokofiev
"Skating"   Kullak
Selected minuets, gavottes, and other dance forms of the period
Said the Piano to the Harpsichord   (Young Peoples Record Club)

MARCH–APRIL (St. Patrick's Day, early spring)

SINGING

Molly Malone (Cockles and Mussels)   (EM, Book 6)
Minstrel Boy   (EM, Book 6)
When Irish Eyes Are Smiling
My Wild Irish Rose
Too-ra-loo-ra-loo-ra   (GWM, Book 6)
The Wearing of the Green
Piping Tim of Galway
McNamara's Band   (Jerry Vogel Music Co.)
Oh, What a Beautiful Morning (from Oklahoma)
Oklahoma
Zip-a-dee-doo-dah
Six Little Ducks
Surrey with the Fringe on Top
This Is My Father's World
Take Me out to the Ball Game
April Showers   (Harms Music)
Little Peter Rabbit★
Mister Rabbit
Easter Parade   (Irving Berlin Music Co.)
Peter Cottontail   (GWM, Book 3)
White Coral Bells★
I Love the Mountains★

LISTENING

"Irish Washerwoman" (folk song)
"Rakes of Mallow" from *Irish Suite*   Leroy Anderson
"To Spring"   Grieg
"Spring Song"   Mendelssohn
"Forest Murmurs"   Wagner
"Amaryllis"   Ghys
Russian Easter Overture   Rimsky-Korsakoff
"Hurdy Gurdy"   Carpenter
Of Bre'r Rabbit   MacDowell
"Ballet of the Unhatched Chicks" from *Pictures at an Exhibition*   Moussorgsky
Appalachian Spring   Copland
Folk Songs of the Old World   (Ireland section, Columbia Records, Roger Wagner Chorale)

MAY–JUNE (Late spring, Flag Day, Memorial Day, weddings, graduations, summer)

SINGING

Bicycle Built for Two (Daisy)
Old Mill Stream
Moonlight Bay
In the Good Old Summertime
Songs for Memorial Day (see "Patriotic" and/or "Veterans Day" songs)
    and Flag Day
See songs for early spring (above under "March–April")

LISTENING

"Boating on the Lake"   Kullak
"Scherzo" and "Nocturne" from *A Midsummer Night's Dream*   Mendelssohn
"Butterfly Étude"   Chopin
"Flight of the Bumblebee"   Rimsky-Korsakoff
"The Bee"   Schubert
"To a Waterlily"   MacDowell
Mother Goose Suite   Ravel
"Three Bears"   Coates
Cinderella   Prokofiev
Cinderella   Coates
"Huckleberry Finn" from *Mississippi Suite*   Grofé
"On the Trail" from *Grand Canyon Suite*   Grofé
"Circus Polka"   Stravinsky
"Under the Big Top"   Donaldson
Circus Music from *Red Pony Suite*   Copland
"Happy Farmer"   Schumann
"Morning Mood" from *Peer Gynt Suite*   Grieg
Prélude to the Afternoon of a Faun   Debussy
"Play of the Waves" from *La Mer*   Debussy
The Moldau   Smetana
"Clair de Lune"   Debussy
"Wedding Day at Troldhaugen"   Grieg
"Wedding March" from *Lohengrin*   Wagner
"Wedding March" from *A Midsummer Night's Dream*   Mendelssohn
Academic Festival Overture   Brahms
"Pomp and Circumstance"   Elgar

Programs for Performance

Every teacher, at one time or another, is asked to put on an assembly program in his school. In fact, if he is a sixth grade teacher, he may be asked to prepare his class for an evening with the PTA or a similar group. It is well for children occasionally to polish up a performance so that it is good enough for public presentation. This type of activity can provide as much learning for the class as pleasure for the audience, provided the teacher exercises a little ingenuity and creative leadership. The following suggestions are offered to teachers who feel the need for more ideas in this area:

1. *Keep it simple!* A simple thing done well is far more desirable than an ambitious undertaking less well executed.

2. Try to evolve a theme around which the entire program may be built. The whole production will transcend the ordinary if it is tied together in some way—for example, by something as simple as a conversation at one corner of the stage between two children, a child turning the pages of a large book, a dream being told, or a sequence of historical events seen through the eyes of an inanimate object such as a drum, a flag, or a tree.

3. Let the program be an outgrowth, as far as possible, of the musical experiences that the children have had in the classroom during the year. Much can be done with well-known folk songs, using simple costumes, Autoharps (if available), and pantomime. "Soldier, Soldier, Won't You Marry Me?" is a good example of songs of this type. "Arkansas Traveler" (*Music Everywhere*, Summy-Birchard Company) lends itself to interesting dramatization; the two characters take the dialogue parts, either singing or speaking in rhythm, while the chorus sings the narrative section. "Bicycle Built for Two" offers unlimited possibilities for acting out the words in pantomime while a chorus sings the song. (Hats are the only costuming needed to create the proper atmosphere for the period.)

4. Variety in any program is desirable but especially in school performances because with variety, every child in the class has the opportunity to participate in some way. Children who sing out of tune can play drums, maracas, claves, etc., for rhythm accompaniment to some songs. Those who are particularly good in movement might do a square dance or folk dance or create other rhythmic movement to interpret the words of a song. The possibilities here are numerous.

5. Try some entrances from the back of the auditorium for variety. These are expecially effective in Christmas programs, where simply robed choirs might be used in procession.

6. If no stage is available for your presentation, try it "in the round"; the action can take place in the middle of the gymnasium or auditorium (or any other room), with the audience seated around the production areas.

7. Many fine programs are marred by lack of discipline during the "getting on and off" periods. Teaching the children to enter and leave the stage properly will probably take up a lot of the rehearsal time, but it's well worth it! Oddly enough, a performance that is good in this respect is often remembered long after the content of the program is forgotten.

8. Insist that the children do the best job they can. They may be surprised to find how great their capabilities are! (And *you* will be too.) Stretch them a little by insisting on their very best.

9. Enlist the help of parents and friends for costumes, scenery, etc., if needed. Bear in mind that every public performance by a school group comes under the heading of good "public relations." This may be the only time many parents ever visit the school and the only time they will ever have the opportunity to see their children perform. Try to make it an occasion they'll remember.

The following songs have been extremely well received as program numbers. Words and music are included elsewhere in this text so that you may try a few of them in your next program.

When You and I Were Young Maggie Blues
Little Boy Song and Little Girl Song
Let Us Sing Together
Alleluia (Mozart)
Let There Be Peace on Earth
Morning Song
Medley of Yankee Doodle Boy and You're a Grand Old Flag (add other George M. Cohan songs, if desired)
Cert'nly Lord
There Was an Old Woman
Michael Finnigin
Tancuj
There's Work to Be Done and No Need to Hurry as partner songs (sing individually first, then combine)
Dona Nobis Pacem (use with dance group doing interpretive movement in round form)
Peace of the River (two parts)
Standin' in the Need of Prayer (two parts)
Tell Me Why (two parts)
Little Ships (two parts)
Witchcraft (verse and chorus as partner songs)
Hawaiian Rainbows (with hand movements and ukulele accompaniment)

Try one or more of the following activities on your next program:

Bottle band (playing melodies, then simple chords for accompaniment to singing)
Harmonica band
Ukulele group
Drumming group (use wooden pads or the floor)
Kitchen Band (see "Novelty Instruments," p. 180)
Interpretive movement originated by the children to a favorite secular or sacred piece of music
Choral speaking with rhythm-instrument accompaniment
Selections with rhythm instruments (see "Rhythm Instruments," p. 223)
"Community sing" with audience joining the children in old favorites (Don't forget to supply the words!)

Musical Bulletin Boards

SUGGESTED TITLE	CONTENT
1. *Our Orchestra*	Children's illustrations of instruments of the orchestra
2. *Listening We Like*	Children's illustrations and/or titles of selected listening experiences
3. *The Whole World Plays*	Folk instruments of the world illustrated
4. *The Whole World Sings*	Songs of the United States and other nations
5. *Ancient Instruments*	Illustrations of various ancient instruments
6. *We're Thankful for Music*	Musical items of choice
7. *Musical Christmas Tree*	Selected Christmas listening, songs, etc.
8. *Toys in Music*	Titles and/or illustrations of selected listening pieces related to toys
9. *Sing a Scale*	Seasonal subject matter (e.g., a series of ascending snowmen, flowers, or pumpkins, with the name of a scale tone written on each)
10. *Clocks in Music*	Songs and/or listening selections related to clocks
11. *A Look at Listening*	Visual illustrations by the children of musical terms such as ABA form, rondo form, fugue, legato, etc.

Other possibilities for bulletin boards might conceivably include *Transportation in Music, Literature in Music, Nature in Music, Animals in Music,* etc.

The foregoing are but a few samples of various musical areas from which subject matter could be drawn. Certainly the titles could be improved upon, and many teachers will have much more imaginative ideas for the content.

Musical Games

1. Unscramble the following words and find an instrument:

oniap	piano
tuelf	flute
phar	harp
groan	organ
cloopic	piccolo
creton	cornet
sprensciou	percussion

trealing	triangle
speaxhoon	saxophone
livoni	violin
telicran	clarinet
snoboas	bassoon

2. Play a match game:

1. Violin	*A.* Brass
2. Piccolo	*B.* "Anitra's Dance"
3. French horn	*C.* *Surprise Symphony*
4. Haydn	*D.* Highest string instrument
5. Legato	*E.* Smallest woodwind
6. *Peer Gynt Suite*	*F.* Tchaikovsky
7. Russian	*G.* Smoothly connected

3. Play another match game:

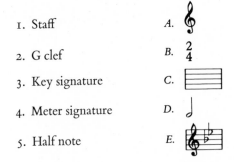

1. Staff	*A.*
2. G clef	*B.*
3. Key signature	*C.*
4. Meter signature	*D.*
5. Half note	*E.*

4. Make up a musical crossword puzzle. Try using pictures instead of definitions.

APPENDIX:
REVIEW OF
FUNDAMENTALS

Staff

fourth space	fifth line
	fourth line
third space	
	third line
second space	
	second line
first space	
	first line

A staff has five lines and four spaces. The first line is on the bottom, and the fifth line on top; the first space is on the bottom, and the fourth space on top; etc.

Clefs

Every staff has a *clef* sign at the beginning.
Below is a *treble clef*, sometimes called a *G clef*:

Below is a *bass clef*, sometimes called an *F clef*:

Music played from the treble clef, or G sounds higher than music played from the bass, or F clef. Some instruments play from the treble clef, and others play from the bass clef, depending on the range (highness or lowness) of the instrument. Children's songs are usually written on the treble clef.

Bar Lines

Throughout a staff may also be found a series of equally spaced vertical lines. These are called *bar lines* and serve to divide any given staff into *measures*. A *double bar* is usually found at the *end* of any given piece of music to indicate the completion of the selection:

Lines and Spaces

Every line and space of the staff has a letter name:

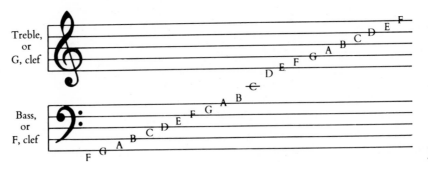

Note that the lines and spaces of the bass clef have different letter names from those of the treble clef.

Note also that in both the bass and the treble clefs, the letter names of the lines and spaces proceed in alphabetical order to G and then begin all over again with A. No letter beyond G is used in music.

Leger Lines

It is possible to add lines and/or spaces above and below the staff through the use of *leger lines*. These must be lettered in proper alphabetical order accordingly:

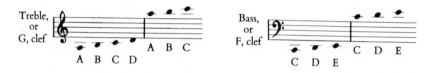

Note that each preceding line and space must be accounted for when leger lines are used.

Key Signatures

Next to the clef sign on the staff may be found one or more symbols like these:

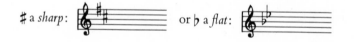

This group of sharps or flats is called a *key signature*. A key signature contains *either* sharps or flats, or it may contain neither. It cannot contain both.

Placement of sharps and flats on the staff is done in an established order. It cannot be altered. The first sharp, for example, is *always* placed on the *F line:*

Note that in the treble clef, the F falls on the fifth line, while in the bass clef, F is on the fourth line.

In writing a key signature of two sharps, the first sharp must be placed on the F line, and the second sharp on the C space:

In writing a key signature of three sharps, the first sharp must be put in its established place on the F line, the second sharp in its established place on the C space, and the third sharp on the G space:

There may be as many as seven sharps in a key signature, placed as follows:

In placing flats on a staff, the first flat has its prescribed place on the B line:

In a key signature of two flats, the first flat must be placed on the B line and the second on the E space:

There may be as many as seven flats in a key signature, placed as follows:

Finding do

A *key signature* enables us to determine in what *key* the music is written and/or where *do* may be found. *Do* may be anywhere on the staff, depending on the key signature.

In any given key signature, it is very easy to determine where *do* is through the use of the following simple rules:

1. When there are sharps in the key signature, call the last sharp to the right (the one farthest away from the clef sign) *ti* and count up one place to *do*. If *ti* falls on a space, *do* will be on the line above it.

333

2. When *ti* falls on a line, *do* will be on the space above it:

3. When there are flats in the key signature, call the last flat to the right (the one farthest away from the clef sign) *fa* and count *down* to *do*, using the notes in the *descending* scale:

4. It is also possible to count *up* to find *do* in a flat key signature, provided the notes of the *ascending* scale are used:

Thus, saying that a song is in the key of D, the key of E, or any other key means merely that *do* is located on the line or space bearing that particular letter name. For example, in a key signature of two sharps, using the aforementioned rule for finding *do* with sharps, we call the last sharp to the right *ti* and count up one place to find *do* on the fourth line. The name of the fourth line on the staff is D; therefore, the name of the key having a signature of two sharps is D.

In a key signature of four sharps, using the same rule, we find that *do* falls on the fourth space, which is E; thus the name of the key having a signature of four sharps is E.

In the case of six or seven sharps, note that the place in which *do* falls has a sharp on it in the key signature. When this occurs, the key must not be called by merely its letter name—the word "sharp" must follow it (or the sharp symbol—♯).

Key of F sharp, or F♯

Key of C sharp, or C♯

334

In naming keys with flats in the signature, using the rule for finding *do* with flats, we call the last flat to the right *fa* and count down to find *do*. In the example below, *fa* is on the third line—*do* is on the first space, the name of the first space is F, and thus it is the key of F:

Key of F

When there are two flats, *do* is located on the third line, on which a flat has already been placed as part of the established order of placing flats on the staff. As with sharps, when this occurs, the key must be called by its letter name followed by the word "flat" or the symbol for flat—♭—as follows:

Key of B♭

In summary, then, the sharp keys (those with sharps in the key signature) are as follows:

Key of G Key of D Key of A Key of E

Key of B Key of F♯ Key of C♯

The flat keys (those with flats in the key signature) are as follows:

Key of F Key of B♭ Key of E♭ Key of A♭

Key of D♭ Key of G♭ Key of C♭

When there are no sharps or flats in the key signature, *do* is always found on the third space (or first line below the staff). This is known as the *key of C*:

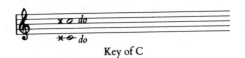

Key of C

On the bass clef, the method of finding *do* through the use of the last sharp or the last flat is the same as on the treble clef:

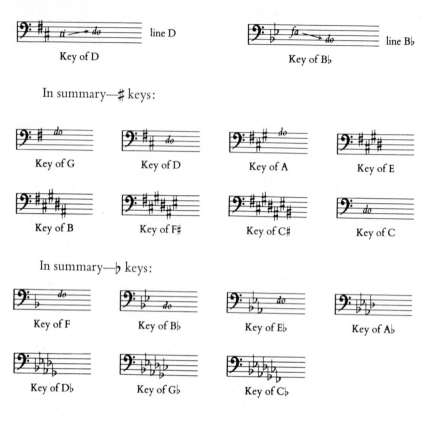

In summary—♯ keys:

In summary—♭ keys:

Major Scales

Every key has its own scale. A major scale contains the following notes or "syllables," as they are sometimes called:

do re mi fa sol la ti do

When a major scale is written on the staff, it looks like this ascending:

And like this descending:

It may begin anywhere on the staff, depending on the key signature:

do re mi fa sol la ti do   do re mi fa sol la ti do

The relationship of the tones must always remain the same and the pattern for this relationship has been arbitrarily established as follows: Using the C scale (playing C as the first note and proceeding through the musical alphabet until C reappears—C, D, E, F, G, A, B, C,) as a model, we note that between E and F and between B and C there is a distance of only a half step (no black key in between), whereas between all other tones there is a distance of a whole step (black keys in between).

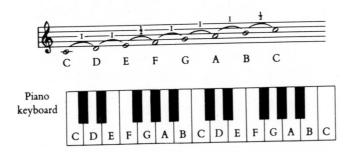

Piano keyboard

Thus the rule for building any major scale is based on the pattern of half steps between the third and fourth (*mi* and *fa*) tones of the scale and between the seventh and eighth (*ti* and *do*) tones of the scale. All the rest must be *whole* steps. As noted above, when starting on C, the half steps and whole steps fall in their correct places; however, when starting on any note other than C, it becomes necessary to alter certain tones in order to maintain the established pattern of whole steps and half steps so that the scale will sound as it should. These alterations are possible through the use of sharps or flats.

For example, in the piano keyboard shown, if one decided to play the scale of D, starting on D as the first note and proceeding through the musical alphabet until D reappears—D, E, etc—one would notice, if only white keys were played, that the sound of the scale was simply not right. This would be due to the fact that the pattern of maintaining *half steps* between the third and fourth and between the seventh and eighth tones of the scale and of maintaining *whole steps* between all others was not being followed. Let us examine the scale of D and see what alterations would be necessary in order to maintain our established pattern. Marks between the third and fourth and between the seventh and eighth tones indicate that half steps are required here:

D   E   F   G   A   B   C   D

337

All others must be whole steps. On closer inspection, it is apparent that between F and G (third and fourth tones), according to our piano keyboard, there is a whole step. Our rule dictates a half step here. How do we make a needed half step out of a given whole step? Merely by shortening the distance between the two tones—either make the third tone a half step higher by placing a sharp in front of it or make the fourth tone a half step lower by placing a flat in front of it. In this particular case, the *sharp* is called for—in front of the F—because if a *flat* were used in front of the G, it would disturb the relationship (a whole step is required) between the G and the A that follows. Looking at the seventh and eighth tones, we find the same problem—a half step is needed, and a whole step is given; thus we must place a sharp in front of the C. Our scale of D, then, would look something like this when written correctly:

When we play it on the piano, we must remember to play the *black* key directly above F (to the right) and the *black* key directly above C (to the right) in place of the white key F and the white key C when we come to them in the scale.

In a longer piece of music, the sharps are not placed in front of these two notes *every* time they should occur; rather, they are placed at the *beginning* of the staff to the right of the clef sign, where they become known as the *key signature*. They affect *every* F and *every* C that occurs in that piece of music:

Minor Scales

Just as families are related, so scales may be related also. Every *major* scale has what is known as its *relative minor* scale. The relationship between the two scales is based on a *common key signature*; however, the starting tone of a major scale is always *do*, whereas the starting tone of a minor scale is always *la*.

To find the relative minor scale of any given major scale, simply count down to *la* from the *do* of the major scale:

338

Counting down from *do* (which is G in this example) to *la*, we find that *la* falls on E; therefore, E would be the starting tone of the *relative minor* scale of G and would be called the *e minor* scale. (Minor-scale names are usually written in lowercase letters.) Note that the key signature for the *e minor* scale above is the same as that for the G major scale.

In another example:

In the scale of F major, *do* is on F, and the key signature is one flat. Counting down from *do*, which is on F, to *la*, we find that *la* falls on D; therefore, D would be the starting tone of the *relative minor* scale of F and would be called the *d minor* scale.

Obviously, with a different starting tone in a minor scale, the arrangement of whole and half steps required for a major scale is bound to be different in a minor scale.

Note that in the above minor scales, the half steps occur between the second and third tones and between the fifth and sixth tones of the scale because this is where *ti-do* and *mi-fa* fall, respectively. Minor scales with this arrangement, such as those shown above, are known as *natural* minor scales (sometimes called *pure* minor or *normal* minor). There are, in addition, two other types of minor scales—the *harmonic minor scale* and the *melodic minor scale*.

In the harmonic minor scale, the half steps occur between the second and third and between the fifth and sixth tones, as they did in the natural minor; however, there is also an *additional* half step that occurs between the seventh and eighth tones of this scale. This additional half step is what distinguishes the harmonic minor from the natural minor and is made possible through the use of some kind of appropriate chromatic sign (see "Chromatics," p. 163) that will indicate that the seventh tone of the scale is to be sounded a half step higher. Note also that the addition of the chromatic sign increases the distance between the sixth and seventh tones of the scale to one and a half steps.

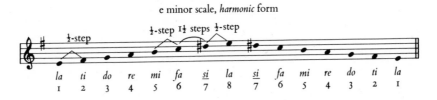

Note that *sol* must be called *si* since the sharp indicates that it is to be sung a half tone higher. The natural minor and the harmonic minor scales maintain the same order in their ascending and in their descending forms. This

339

is not true, however, of the melodic minor scale—a third kind of minor scale, in which the whole and half steps are arranged in an order different from that of the other two types of minor scales.

e minor scale, *melodic* form

| la | ti | do | re | mi | fi | si | la | sol | fa | mi | re | do | ti | la |
| 1 | 2 | 3 | 4 | 5 | 6 | 7 | 8 | 7 | 6 | 5 | 4 | 3 | 2 | 1 |

In addition to *sol* being sung a half step higher (*si*), note that *fa* is also to be sung a half step higher and thus will be called *fi*. As mentioned previously, the descending form of the melodic minor scale differs from its ascending form. It will be noted in the above example that the descending form is actually the natural minor scale descending.

In summary, then:

Natural minor scale	*la ti do re mi fa sol la*
Harmonic minor scale	*la ti do re mi fa si la*
Melodic minor scale	*la ti do re mi fi si la sol fa mi re do ti la*

A song is considered to be in a minor mode if it ends on *la*; however, minor songs do not always *begin* on *la*. If the tone *si* occurs within a song written in the minor mode, the song is said to be written in the *harmonic* minor. If the two tones *fi* and *si* occur, the song is said to be written in the *melodic* minor. When neither *si* nor *fi* occurs, the song is in the *natural* minor.

Meter (Time) Signatures

Next to the key signature on any given piece of music may be found what appears to be a fraction (although it is written without the dividing fraction line):

It is a combination of two numbers—one on top of the other. This is known as a *meter* or *time signature*. Just as a key signature denotes what key the music is written in, so a meter signature denotes what kind of time the music is written in. The upper figure of any given meter signature indicates the number of beats that we may expect to find in each measure of the music; the lower figure indicates what kind of note will receive one beat.

For example, in the meter signature $\frac{2}{4}$, the upper figure indicates that there are *two* beats in every measure. In the meter signature $\frac{4}{4}$, the upper figure indicates that there are *four* beats in every measure.

A note is a symbol in music denoting a certain time value as prescribed by the lower figure of the given meter signature. The following are examples of notes commonly found in children's music:

Quarter note ♩

Half note ♩

Whole note ○

Dotted half note ♩.

Eighth note ♪

Sixteenth note ♬

Dotted quarter note ♩.

Dotted eighth note ♪.

Less common are thirty-second notes (♬) and sixty-fourth notes (♬) which are more likely to found in instrumental music than in children's vocal music.

Each note has a corresponding rest:

Quarter rest 𝄽

Half rest ▬

Whole rest ▬

Eighth rest 𝄾

Sixteenth rest 𝄿

Notes may also be dotted. A dot is worth *half* the value of the note and increases the value of the note by that amount. For example, if a note receives four beats, a dot added to it will receive half of four beats—or two beats—increasing the total value of the note to six beats. If a note receives one beat, a dot added to it will receive a half beat, increasing the total value of the note to one and a half beats.

We have already established the fact that in the meter signature $\frac{2}{4}$ the upper figure indicates that there will be two beats in every measure. The lower figure indicates that the *quarter* note will receive one beat. Using the quarter note as the unit of beat, it naturally follows that:

A half note (♩) will receive two beats.

A whole note (○) will receive four beats.

An eighth note (♪) will receive a half beat.

A sixteenth note (♬) will receive a quarter beat.

A dotted half note (♩.) will receive three beats.

341

This will always hold true as long as the lower figure of any given meter signature is 4:

$$\frac{2}{4} \quad \frac{3}{4} \quad \frac{4}{4} \quad \frac{6}{4}$$

Lower figures may vary, however. Meter signatures with 8 or 2 as the lower figure are not uncommon:

$$\frac{6}{8} \quad \frac{9}{8} \quad \frac{12}{8} \quad \frac{3}{2} \quad \frac{4}{2}$$

When the *lower* figure is 8, the unit of beat becomes an eighth note (♪), and the other notes change their values accordingly. For example, if an eighth note receives one beat, then:

A quarter note (♩) receives two beats.

A half note (♩) receives four beats.

A sixteenth note (♬) receives a half beat.

A dotted half note (♩.) receives six beats, etc.

When the lower figure is 2, the unit of beat becomes a half note (♩), and the other notes change their values accordingly. For example, if a half note receives one beat, then:

A quarter note (♩) receives a half beat.

A whole note (𝅝) receives two beats.

An eighth note (♪) receives a quarter beat.

A dotted half note (♩.) receives one and a half beats, etc.

It is to be noted here that regardless of the lower figure of the meter signature, the relationship between the notes remains the same. For example, a quarter note is always held twice as long as an eighth note, a half note is always held twice as long as a quarter note, and a whole note is always held twice as long as a half note. Keeping this fact in mind will prove most helpful in learning to read new rhythms, regardless of what meter signatures are indicated.

In summary, then, when the meter signature $\frac{3}{4}$ appears in any given piece of music, it means that there are *three* beats in every measure (upper figure) and that every *quarter* note (lower figure) gets one beat.

When the meter signature $\frac{6}{8}$ appears, it means that there are *six* beats in every measure (upper figure) and that every *eighth* note (lower figure) gets one beat.

When the meter signature $\frac{3}{2}$ appears, it means that there are *three* beats in every measure (upper figure) and that every *half* note (lower figure) gets one beat.

The upper figure of the time signature also determines how many beats a whole rest (━▬━) receives since a whole rest occupies the whole measure.

A meter signature also determines in which direction a conductor may move his hand when conducting an orchestra or chorus. The following patterns are the most commonly used and are considered basic conducting patterns:

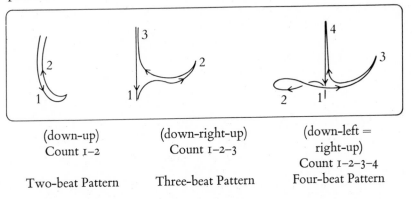

(down–up)	(down-right-up)	(down-left = right-up)
Count 1–2	Count 1–2–3	Count 1–2–3–4
Two-beat Pattern	Three-beat Pattern	Four-beat Pattern

Note that on the count of *"one,"* the direction is always *down*, meaning that the *first beat* of every measure will always be indicated by a *downward* motion of the hand.

Slow $\frac{6}{8}$ time calls for the following conducting pattern:

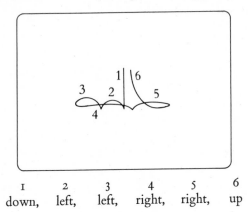

1	2	3	4	5	6
down,	left,	left,	right,	right,	up

When the music is written in fast $\frac{6}{8}$ time, the *two-beat* pattern above may be used.

Simple and Compound Meters

$\frac{6}{8}, \frac{9}{8},$ and $\frac{12}{8}$ meters are often referred to as *compound* meters since they may be evenly divided into smaller units. To determine whether music is written in **343** simple or compound time, simply divide the number "3" into the *upper* figure of the meter signature. If it will go more than once, evenly, the music is said to be written in *compound* meter; if 3 will *not* go into the upper figure of the meter signature more than once evenly, the music is written in *simple* meter. Therefore, upper figures of 6, 9, 12, etc., indicate compound meter, whereas upper figures of 3, 4, 2, 5, etc., indicate simple meters. The lower figure of the meter signature is *not* a factor in determining whether the music is written in simple or compound meter.

For further information regarding musical terms, symbols, definitions, etc., see Glossary, p. 345.

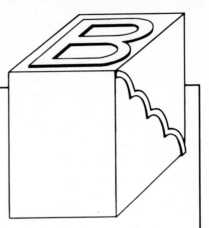

APPENDIX: GLOSSARY

Absolute music   Nondescriptive music.

Allemande   A fairly lively dance in $\frac{4}{4}$ time; also the first movement of dance suites of the seventeenth and eighteenth centuries.

Alto   The lowest treble voice. May also refer to a part within a certain range played by an instrument or sung.

Atonal   Lacking a fixed reference point such as a home tone or key.

Augmentation   An imitative device by which the second melody moves in notes of longer duration than those in the first melody, but in the same proportion to one another.

Band   A group of performers or a certain specified group of instruments. A band does not include string instruments, as a rule.

Bar lines   Vertical lines drawn at measured distances on the staff for the purpose of dividing it into measures.

Baroque   Refers to the period from about 1600 to 1750, characterized by grandeur and heavy elaboration of design in music.

Bass   The lowest male voice. May also refer to a part within a certain range played by an instrument or sung.

Binary form   Two-part form; the structure of a musical composition consisting of two main sections.

Bourrée   A fast dance of the baroque period of French and Spanish origin, usually in $\frac{2}{4}$ or $\frac{4}{4}$ meter; also a movement in early suites.

Cadenza   A brilliant passage for a solo instrument, designed to display the virtuosity of the performer.

Canon   A musical form in which a given melody is imitated by two or more voices beginning at different times.

Cantata   A short lyric form dealing with either secular or sacred subject matter.

Chant   A repeated group of notes sung against (and usually below) the main tune of a song.

Chanteys   British and American sailor songs.

Chord   Three or more tones combined and sounded simultaneously.

Chorus   A number of persons singing together. May also refer to a composition written for combined voices.

Chromatic   Refers to tones foreign to a given key or scale; also pertains to all tones of the chromatic scale.

Chromatic scale   A twelve-tone scale within any given octave that includes the diatonic scale tones (*do-re-mi-fa-sol-la-ti*) plus the five intermediate half steps (*di-ri-fi-si-li*).

Classical   Refers to that period from approximately 1750 to 1800, characterized musically by objectivity of the composer, emotional restraint, and simple harmonies.

Coda   Literally "tail." An added ending on a musical composition.

Composer   One who writes music.

Computer music   Music composed by describing sounds mathematically and then feeding the sequence of numbers into a computer.

Concerto   A symphonic composition written for a solo instrument (or group of instruments) and orchestra; usually consists of three contrasting movements, with a cadenza often occurring near the close of the first movement.

Conductor   One who directs a musical group (chorus, orchestra, band, etc.).

Consonance   A simultaneous sounding of tones that produces a feeling of rest, i.e., a feeling that there is no need for further resolution.

Contemporary   Refers to the period from about 1900 to the present, characterized by the use of old sounds in new ways, as well as the introduction of new sounds.

Da capo   From the beginning. A direction to repeat the entire composition from the beginning to the place where the word *fine* appears or to the end.

Dal segno   A direction to repeat from the sign to the word *fine*.

Descant   A melody that is sung or played against the main melody of a song.

Diatonic   Pertaining to a standard major or minor eight-tone scale.

Dissonance   A simultaneous sounding of tones that produces a feeling of tension or unrest and/or a feeling that further resolution is needed.

Duet   A musical performance by two voices or instruments.

Duple meter   Meter in which there are two beats or some multiple of two to the measure.

Dynamics   Varying intensities of sound throughout a given musical composition.

Electronic music   Music produced by distorting or modifying various sounds through the process of electronic devices.

Fine   The end of a piece.

Folk song   A song, usually of unknown origin, arising as an outgrowth of a people.

Form   The basic structure of a musical composition, which results from the arrangement of repetition and contrast in the material.

Fugue   Literally "flight." A contrapuntal form involving two or more voices in which a subject (theme) is introduced and developed through a series of imitations.

Galop   A vigorous nineteenth-century round dance in $\frac{2}{4}$ time.

Gavotte   A French peasant dance of the baroque period, modified for use by court nobility; usually in $\frac{4}{4}$ time with steps beginning on the third beat. Also a movement of an early suite.

Gigue   "Jig." A lively dance in compound time. Also a movement of a baroque suite.

Glissando   A sweeping motion up or down a keyboard in which all tones are sounded in rapid succession.

Harmony   The sound resulting from the simultaneous sounding of two or more tones consonant with each other.

Hold   Indicated by the sign ⌢ over the note, meaning to hold longer than the given rhythm of the note would ordinarily require. Also known as a *fermata*.

Hornpipe   An English sailor dance of the baroque period, accompanied by an instrument known as a "hornpipe," from which the dance derives its name. It was done first in three-beat meter and then in four-beat meter.

Imitation   The reproducing of a given melody by several voices at different times.

Instrument   An implement with which musical sounds are produced.

Interval   The distance between two tones.

Inversion   (1) In contrapuntal forms, the movement of a second voice in the same melody pattern as the first, but in the opposite direction. (2) In harmony, the presence of any tone other than the root as the bass note of a chord.

347

Jazz   A twentieth-century musical style characterized by duple meter, syncopation, and improvisation. Considered to be typically American.

Mazurka   A Polish national dance in triple meter with a strongly accented second or third beat.

Measure   A space on the staff enclosed between two bar lines.

Melody   An arrangement of single tones in a meaningful sequence.

Minuet   A stately French dance of the baroque period in $\frac{3}{4}$ time. Also included in larger symphonic works in modified forms. From the French word *menu*, meaning "small."

Mixed chorus   A group of male and female singers.

Musical comedy   A musical show with songs, dances, etc., unified by a plot, which is usually light in character.

Musique concrète   Electronic music based on natural sounds.

Opera   A musical drama consisting of recitatives, arias, choruses, orchestral music, etc., using scenery and costumes.

Operetta   A light musical drama with action, costumes, and scenery. Dialogue is usually spoken.

Oratorio   A large dramatic production using narrator, soloists, chorus, and orchestra but no costumes, staging, or scenery. Also contains an overture, arias and recitatives, plus small vocal ensembles. The text is always biblical.

Orchestra   A group of instrumental performers or a certain specified group of instruments.

Ostinato   A repeated melodic fragment.

Overture   An instrumental selection which is usually performed before the curtain goes up on a musical play and which contains tunes that will be heard later in the production.

Phrase   A small section of a compostion comprising a musical thought. Comparable to a sentence in language.

Pitch   The highness or lowness of a tone, determined by the frequency of vibration of sound waves. The larger the number of vibrations, the higher the resulting pitch.

Polka   A lively nineteenth-century Bohemian couple dance in duple meter.

Polonaise   A moderately slow eighteenth- and nineteenth-century Polish dance in triple meter. Also a movement of a baroque suite.

Polyphonic music   Music in which two or more melodies sound simultaneously.

Polyphony   Literally "many voices." The combining of a number of individual harmonizing melodies.

Polyrhythms   Two or more contrasting rhythms sounding simultaneously.

Polytonal music   Music in which two or more keys are used simultaneously in a given composition.

Program music   Music of a descriptive nature that tells a story, sets a scene, paints a picture, sets a mood, or describes an event.

Quartet   A musical group of four voices or instruments. Also refers to a composition written for four parts.

Retrograde   A form of contrapuntal imitation in which the melody is played backward.

Romantic   Refers to the nineteenth century musical period characterized by subjectivity on the part of the composer, emotionalism in music, longer musical forms, and richer harmonies.

Rondo   An instrumental form consisting of three different themes in which the recurring main theme (A) alternates with the other two secondary themes (B and C). The rondo was originally a dance form, which came out of round singing.

Root   The tone of the scale upon which a chord is built.

Root position   The position of a chord in which the root appears as the lowest tone.

Round   A form of imitative singing in which each voice enters at measured intervals and sings its part as often as desired.

Sarabande   A slow Spanish court dance in triple meter. Also a slow movement of a baroque suite.

Scale   From the Italian word *scala*, meaning "ladder." A graduated series of tones arranged in a specified order.

Scherzo   Literally "joke." A sprightly movement in larger symphonic works, light and humorous in nature. Usually in triple meter.

Sequence   A succession of melodic figures repeated on various degrees of the scale.

Slur   A curved line drawn over two or more notes of different pitches, indicating that they are to be executed in a smoothly connected manner, without a break:

Solo   A musical performance by one voice or instrument.

Soprano   The highest treble voice. Also refers a part within a certain range played by an instrument or sung.

Staff   Five equally spaced horizontal lines upon which music is written.

Subject   The principal theme on which a musical composition is based.

Suite   An instrumental form that may consist of a group of dances, a group of descriptive pieces, or a group of pieces from a ballet or opera. It is often unified through a story or idea.

Symphony   A large musical work in sonata form for full orchestra.

Syncopation   The rhythmic result produced when a regularly accented beat is displaced on to an unaccented beat.

Tarantelle, tarantella   A fast dance, usually in $\frac{6}{8}$ time. The name is derived from the word "tarantula." It was believed that doing a wild dance would cure the bite of the tarantula spider.

Tempo   The rate of speed at which a musical composition is performed.

Tenor   The highest male voice. Also a part within a certain range played by an instrument or sung.

Ternary form   A three-part structure of a musical composition consisting of three sections, the middle section of which contrasts with the first and last sections.

Theme   A short musical passage that states an idea. It often provides the basis for variations, development, etc., in a musical composition.

Tie   A curved line connecting two or more notes of the same pitch. When played or sung, the first note in the series is sounded and held for the duration of the combined beats of all the others throughout the length of the tie: ♩ ♩.

Timbre   The quality of a musical tone that distinguishes voices and instruments.

Tonal music   Music in a definite key, in which one pitch is used as a reference or home tone.

Tonality   The feeling of the presence of, and a tendency to be drawn toward, a certain home tone or key in a musical composition—a feeling produced by the musical scheme of the composition.

Tone   (1) A musical sound. (2) The quality of a musical sound. (3) The larger interval between adjacent sounds of a scale—a whole tone (step) as opposed to a semitone (half step).

Tone poem   An orchestral piece in one movement, usually descriptive in nature.

Tonic   The keynote of a given key.

Transpose   To transfer a musical composition from one key into another.

Trio   A musical group of three voices or instruments. Also a composition written for three parts.

Triple meter   Meter in which there are three beats or some multiple of three to the measure.

Triplet   Three notes performed in the time of two of the same value.

Twelve-tone row   All twelve tones contained in any given octave, as in a chromatic scale.

Variations   Different treatments of a given theme or melody through changes in rhythm, mood, tempo, meter, etc.

Waltz   From the German word *walzen*, meaning "to roll about." Original waltzes were much heavier and less graceful in character than those we know today.

Whole-tone scale   A scale of six tones in which all intervals are whole steps.

Dynamics Terms

Crescendo   gradually growing louder
Diminuendo   gradually growing softer
Forte (f)   loud
Fortissimo (ff)   very loud
Mezzo forte (mf)   moderately loud
Mezzo piano (mp)   moderately soft
Pianissimo (pp)   very soft
Piano (p)   soft
Sforzando (sf)   explosively

Expression Terms

Legato   smoothly connected
Maestoso   majestically
Sostenuto   sustained
Spirito   spiritedly
Staccato   disconnectedly
Vivace   vivaciously

Tempo Terms

Accelerando   gradually growing faster
Allegretto   rather fast
Allegro   fast
Andante   slow
Andantino   rather slow
Largo   very slow
Lento   slow
Moderato   at a moderate pace
Presto   very fast
Ritardando   gradually growing slower

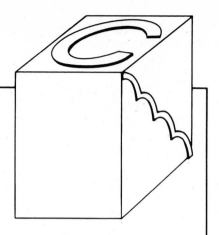

APPENDIX:

CLASSROOM MUSIC
EQUIPMENT

Many of the following items have been mentioned previously in connection with their use in various areas in music. They are listed together here for quick reference.

To do your very *best* job and achieve optimum results, you need:

Record player
Recordings and suitable storage facilities
Autoharp
Song bells and/or resonator bells
Rhythm instruments and suitable storage facilities
Set of songbooks for the class with accompanying record album of the
    songs

Teacher's edition of the children's texts
Other resource material
Access to:
    Tape recorder
    Overhead projector and transparencies
    Sound film, slide, and filmstrip projectors and related materials for
       use with these
Staff liner
Pitch pipe
Faith

It's nice to have:

Piano
Flannel board and/or magnetic music board or similar timesaving
    visual device

You'll be doing your children a favor (as well as yourself) if you try to arrange to have a music center somewhere in the classroom equipped with a record player and/or a tape recorder that can handle multiple sets of earphones. As mentioned before, such a center might include, for example, compositions by the children, original orchestrations written out, and a display of handmade instruments, as well as a few things to make music on.

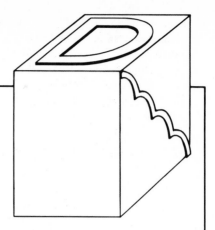

APPENDIX:
RECORD CATALOGS

Following are the complete catalog listings of RCA Victor *Adventures in Music* series, Bowmar Orchestral Library, and Keyboard Publications records.

Alphabetical Listing of Selections in Adventures in Music *Series, RCA Victor*

Anderson: Irish Suite—THE GIRL I LEFT BEHIND ME **GR. 5, Vol. 2**

Bach:

  Cantata No. 147—JESU, JOY OF MAN'S DESIRING **GR. 5, Vol. 1**

  LITTLE FUGUE IN G MINOR (Arr. by L. Cailliet) **GR. 6, Vol. 1**

  Suite No. 2—BADINERIE **GR. 3, Vol. 1**

  Suite No. 3—GIGUE **GR. 1**

355

Guarnieri: BRAZILIAN DANCE
GR. 6, Vol. 2

Handel:
Royal Fireworks Music—BOUR-REE, MENUETTO No. 2
GR. 3, Vol. 2
Water Music—HORNPIPE   GR. 2

Hanson: Merry Mount Suite—CHIL-DREN'S DANCE   GR. 3, Vol. 1

Herbert:
Babes in Toyland—MARCH OF THE TOYS   GR. 2
Natoma—DAGGER DANCE
GR. 3, Vol. 1

Humperdinck: Hansel and Gretel—PRE-LUDE   GR. 5, Vol. 2

Holst: The Perfect Fool—SPIRITS OF THE EARTH   GR. 6, Vol. 2

Ibert:
Divertissement—PARADE   GR. 1
Histories No. 2—THE LITTLE WHITE DONKEY   GR. 2

Kabalevsky:
The Comedians—MARCH, COMEDIANS GALOP
GR. 3, Vol. 1
The Comedians—PANTOMIME
GR. 1

Khachaturian: Masquerade Suite—WALTZ   GR. 4, Vol. 2

Kodaly:
Hary Janos Suite—ENTRANCE OF THE EMPEROR AND HIS COURT   GR. 4, Vol. 2
Hary Janos Suite—VIENNESE MUSICAL CLOCK   GR. 2

Lecuona: Suite Andalucia — ANDA-LUCIA   GR. 4, Vol. 1

Lully: Ballet Suite—MARCH
GR. 3, Vol. 2

MacDowell: Second (Indian) Suite—IN WARTIME   GR. 5, Vol. 1

Massenet: Le Cid—ARAGONAISE
GR. 1

McDonald:
Children's Symphony (1st Move-ment)—LONDON BRIDGE, BAA, BAA, BLACK SHEEP
GR. 3, Vol. 2

Children's Symphony (3rd Move-ment)—FARMER IN THE DELL, JINGLE BELLS   GR. 2

Menotti: Amahl and the Night Visitors —SHEPHERDS' DANCE
GR. 4, Vol. 2

Meyerbeer: Les Patineurs—WALTZ
GR. 2

Milhaud:
Saudades do Brazil—COPACA-BANA   GR. 4. Vol. 2
Saudades do Brazil—LARANJEIRAS
GR. 2

Moussorgsky:
Pictures at an Exhibition—BALLET OF THE UNHATCHED CHICKS (Orchestrated by Ravel)   GR. 1
Pictures at an Exhibition—BYDLO (Orchestrated by Ravel)   GR. 2

Mozart:
Divertimento No. 17—MENU-ETTO No. 1   GR. 5, Vol. 2
Eine kleine Nachtmusik—ROMANZE   GR. 4, Vol. 1

Offenbach: The Tales of Hoffmann—BARCAROLLE   GR. 3, Vol. 1

Prokofieff:
Children's Suite—WALTZ ON THE ICE   GR. 3, Vol. 2
Summer Day Suite—MARCH GR. 1
Winter Holiday—DEPARTURE
GR. 2

Ravel:
Mother Goose Suite—THE CON-VERSATIONS OF BEAUTY AND THE BEAST   GR. 5, Vol. 1
Mother Goose Suite—LAIDERON-NETTE EMPRESS OF THE PAGODAS   GR. 4, Vol. 2

Respighi:
Brazilian Impressions—DANZA
GR. 5, Vol. 2
Pines of Rome—PINES OF THE VILLA BORGHESE GR. 4, Vol. 1

Rimsky-Korsakoff: Le Coq d'Or Suite—BRIDAL PROCESSION
GR. 4, Vol. 1

Rossini: William Tell Overture—FINALE   GR. 3, Vol. 1

Rossini-Britten: Soirees Musicales—
MARCH   **GR. 1**

Rossini-Respighi:
The Fantastic Toyshop—CAN-
CAN   **GR. 2**
The Fantastic Toyshop—TARAN-
TELLA   **GR. 3, Vol. 2**

Saint-Saens: Carnival of the Animals—
THE SWAN   **GR. 3, Vol. 2**

Scarlatti-Tommasini: The Good-Hum-
ored Ladies—NON PRESTO MA
A TEMPO DI BALLO
                GR. 4, Vol. 2

Schubert: Symphony No. 5—FIRST
MOVEMENT   **GR. 5, Vol. 1**

Schumann: Scenes from Childhood—
TRAUMEREI   **GR. 4, Vol. 2**

Shostakovich:
Ballet Suite No. 1—PETITE BAL-
LERINA   **GR. 2**
Ballet Suite No. 1—PIZZICATO
POLKA   **GR. 1**

Sibelius: Karelia Suite—ALLA MAR-
CIA   **GR. 5, Vol. 1**

Smetana: The Bartered Bride—DANCE
OF THE COMEDIANS
                GR. 6, Vol. 2

Sousa:
SEMPER FIDELIS   **GR. 3, Vol. 2**
STARS AND STRIPES FOREVER
                GR. 4, Vol. 2

Strauss: R. Der Rosenkavalier—SUITE
                GR. 6, Vol. 1

Stravinsky:
The Firebird Suite—BERCEUSE
                GR. 1

The Firebird Suite—INFERNAL
DANCE OF KING KASTCHEI
                GR. 5, Vol. 2

Taylor: Through the Looking Glass—
GARDEN OF LIVE FLOWERS
                GR. 3, Vol. 2

Tchaikovsky:
The Sleeping Beauty—PUSS-IN-
BOOTS AND THE WHITE CAT
                GR. 3, Vol. 1
The Sleeping Beauty—WALTZ
                GR. 4, Vol. 1
Swan Lake—DANCE OF THE
LITTLE SWANS   **GR. 1**
Symphony No. 4—FOURTH
MOVEMENT   **GR. 6, Vol. 2**

Thomson:
Acadian Songs and Dances—THE
ALLIGATOR AND THE 'COON
                GR. 3, Vol. 2
Acadian Songs and Dances—
WALKING SONG   **GR. 1**

Vaughan Williams:
FANTASIA ON "GREEN-
SLEEVES"   **GR. 6, Vol. 2**
The Wasps —MARCH PAST OF
THE KITCHEN UTENSILS
                GR. 3, Vol. 1

Villa-Lobos: Bachianas Brasileiras No.
2—THE LITTLE TRAIN OF THE
CAIPIRA   **GR. 3, Vol. 1**

Wagner: Lohengrin—PRELUDE TO
ACT III   **GR. 6, Vol. 1**

Walton: Facade Suite—VALSE
                GR. 6, Vol. 2

Bowmar Orchestral Library   *Series 1, 2, and 3*

SERIES 1
ANIMALS AND CIRCUS (BOL # 51)
CARNIVAL OF THE ANIMALS,
Saint-Saens. (Introduction, Royal
March of the Lion, Hens and Cocks,
Fleet Footed Animals, Turtles, The
Elephant, Kangaroos, Aquarium,
Long Eared Personages, Cuckoo in
the Deep Woods, Aviary, Pianists,
Fossils, The Swan, Finale)
CIRCUS POLKA, Stravinsky
UNDER THE BIG TOP, Donaldson.
(Marching Band, Acrobats, Jug-
gler, Merry-Go-Round, Elephants,
Clowns, Camels, Tightrope Walker,
Pony Trot, Marching Band)

NATURE AND MAKE-BELIEVE (BOL # 52)
MARCH OF THE DWARFS, Grieg
ONCE UPON A TIME SUITE,
Donaldson. (Chicken Little, Three
Billy Goats Gruff, Little Train, Hare
and the Tortoise)
THE LARK SONG (Scenes of Youth),
Tchaikovsky
LITTLE BIRD, Grieg
DANCE OF THE MOSQUITO,
Liadov
FLIGHT OF THE BUMBLEBEE,
Rimsky-Korsakoff
SEASON FANTASIES, Donaldson.
(Magic Piper, The Poet and his Lyre,
The Anxious Leaf, The Snowmaiden)
TO THE RISING SUN (Fjord and
Mountain, Norwegian Suite 2),
Torjussen
CLAIR DE LUNE, Debussy

PICTURES AND PATTERNS (BOL # 53)
PIZZICATO (Fantastic Toyshop),
Rossini-Respighi
MARCH-TRUMPET AND DRUM
(Jeux d'Enfants), IMPROMPTU-
THE TOP (Jeux d'Enfants), Bizet
POLKA (Mlle. Angot Suite), GAV-
OTTE (Mlle. Angot Suite). Lecocq
INTERMEZZO (The Comedians),
Kabalevsky
GERMAN   WALTZ-PAGANINI
(Carnaval), Schumann-Glazounov
BALLET PETIT, Donaldson
MINUET, Mozart
A GROUND, Handel
CHOPIN (Carnaval),   Schumann-
Glazounov
VILLAGE DANCE, Liadov
EN BATEAU (In a Boat), Debussy
HARBOR VIGNETTES, Donaldson.
(Fog and Storm, Song of the Bell
Buoy, Sailing)

MARCHES (BOL # 54)
*ENTRANCE OF THE LITTLE
FAUNS*, Pierne
MARCH, Prokofieff
POMP AND CIRCUMSTANCE # 1,
Elgar

HUNGARIAN MARCH (Rakoczy),
Berlioz
COL. BOGEY MARCH, Alford
*MARCH OF THE LITTLE LEAD
SOLDIERS*, Pierne
MARCH (Love for Three Oranges),
Prokofieff
CORTEGE OF THE SARDAR (Cau-
casion Sketches), Ippolitov-Ivanov
MARCHE MILITAIRE, Schubert
STARS AND STRIPES FOREVER,
Sousa
*THE MARCH OF THE SIAMESE
CHILDREN* (The King and I),
Rodgers

DANCES, PART I (BOL # 55)
DANCE OF THE CAMORRISTI,
Wolf-Ferrari
DANCA BRASILEIRA, Guarnieri
GAVOTTE, Kabalevsky
SLAVONIC DANCE # 1, Dvorak
HOE-DOWN (Rodeo), Copland
FACADE SUITE, Walton (Polka,
Country Dance, Popular Song)
HUNGARIAN DANCE # 5, Brahms
SKATER'S WALTZ, Waldteufel
MAZURKA   (Masquerade   Suite),
Khatchaturian
GALOP (Masquerade Suite), Khatcha-
turian

DANCES, PART II (BOL # 56)
FOLK DANCES FROM SOMERSET
(English Folk Song Suite), Vaughan-
Williams
JAMAICAN RUMBA, Benjamin
BADINERIE, Corelli
DANCE OF THE COMEDIANS,
Smetana
CAN CAN (Mlle. Angot Suite), Lecocq
GRAND WALTZ (Mlle. Angot Suite),
Lecocq
TRITSCH - TRATSCH POLKA,
Strauss
TARANTELLA (Fantastic Toyshop)
WALTZ (Fantastic Toyshop),
Rossini-Respighi
ESPANA WALTZES, Waldteufel
ARKANSAS TRAVELER, Guion

RUSSIAN DANCE (Gayne Suite # 2),
Khatchaturian

359

WILD HORSEMEN, Schumann
HAPPY FARMER, Schumann
LITTLE WINDMILLS, Couperin
ARIETTA, Leo
MUSIC BOX, Liadov
FUNERAL MARCH OF THE MAR-
    IONETTES, Gounod
DANCE OF THE MERRY DWARFS
    (Happy Hypocrite), Elwell
LITTLE TRAIN OF CAIPIRA, Villa-
    Lobos

MUSIC, USA (BOL # 65)
SHAKER TUNE (Appalachian Spring),
    Copland
CATTLE & BLUES (Plow that Broke
    the Plains), Thomson
FUGUE AND CHORALE ON YAN-
    KEE DOODLE (Tuesday in Novem-
    ber), Thomson
PUMPKIN EATERS LITTLE
    FUGUE, McBride
AMERICAN SALUTE, Gould
POP GOES THE WEASEL, Cailliet
LAST MOVEMENT, SYMPHONY
    # 2, Ives

ORIENTAL SCENES (BOL # 66)
WOODCUTTER'S SONG, Koyama
THE EMPEROR'S NIGHTINGALE,
    Donaldson
SAKURA (Folk tune), played by koto
    and bamboo flute

FANTASY IN MUSIC (BOL # 67)
THREE BEARS, Coates
CINDERELLA, Prokofieff (Sewing
    Scene, Cinderella's Gavotte, Mid-
    night Waltz, Fairy Godmother)
MOON LEGEND, Donaldson
SLEEPING   BEAUTY   WALTZ,
    Tchaikovsky

CLASSROOM CONCERT (BOL # 68)
ALBUM FOR THE YOUNG, Tchai-
    kovsky. (Morning Prayer, Winter
    Morning, Hobby Horse, Mamma,
    March of the Tin Soldiers, Sick Doll,
    Doll's Burial, New Doll, Waltz,

Mazurka, Russian Song, Peasant
Plays the Accordion, Folk Song,
Polka, Italian Song, Old French
Song, German Song, Neapolitan
Dance Song, Song of the Lark,
Hand-organ Man, Nurse's Tale, The
Witch, Sweet Dreams, In Church)
OVER THE HILLS, Grainger
MEMORIES   OF   CHILDHOOD,
    Pinto. (Run, Run, Ring Around the
    Rosie, March, SleepingTime, Hobby
    Horse)
LET US RUN ACROSS THE HILL
    Villa-Lobos
MY DAUGHTER LIDI, TEASING,
    GRASSHOPPER'S   WEDDING,
    Bartok
DEVIL'S DANCE, Stravinsky
LITTLE GIRL IMPLORING HER
    MOTHER, Rebikov

SERIES 3
MUSIC OF THE DANCE: STRAVINSKY
    (BOL # 69)
FIREBIRD SUITE (L'Oiseau de Feu).
    (Koschai's Enchanted Garden, Dance
    of the Firebird, Dance of the Prin-
    cesses, Infernal Dance of Koschai,
    Magic   Sleep   of   the   Princess
    Tzarevna, Finale: Escape of Koschai's
    Captives)
SACRIFICIAL DANCE from "The
    Rite of Spring" (Le Sacre du Prin-
    temps)
VILLAGE FESTIVAL from "The
    Fairy's Kiss" (Le Baiser de la Fée)
PALACE OF THE CHINESE EM-
    PEROR from "The Nightingale"
    (Le Rossignol)
TANGO, WALTZ AND RAGTIME
    from "The Soldier's Tale" (L'Histoire
    du Soldat)

MUSIC OF THE SEA AND SKY (BOL # 70)
CLOUDS (Nuages), Debussy
FESTIVALS (Fêtes), Debussy
MERCURY from The Planets, Holst
SEA PIECE WITH BIRDS, Thomson

OVERTURE TO "THE FLYING DUTCHMAN" (Der Fliegende Holländer), Wagner
DIALOGUE OF THE WIND AND SEA from The Sea (La Mer), Debussy

SYMPHONIC MOVEMENTS, NO. 1 (BOL # 71)
FIRST MOVEMENT, SYMPHONY No. 40, Mozart
SECOND MOVEMENT, SYMPHONY No. 8, Beethoven
THIRD MOVEMENT, SYMPHONY No. 4, Tchaikovsky
SECOND MOVEMENT, SYMPHONY No. 4, Schumann
THIRD MOVEMENT, SYMPHONY No. 3, Brahms
FOURTH MOVEMENT, SYMPHONY No. 3, Saint-Saens

SYMPHONIC MOVEMENTS, NO. 2 (BOL # 72)
FIRST MOVEMENT, SYMPHONY No. 9, ("From the New World"), Dvorak
FIRST MOVEMENT, SYMPHONY No. 5, Beethoven
FIRST MOVEMENT, (Boisterous Bourrée), A SIMPLE SYMPHONY, Britten
SECOND MOVEMENT, SYMPHONY No. 2, Hanson
FIRST MOVEMENT, SYMPHONY No. 2, Sibelius

SYMPHONIC STYLES (BOL # 73)
SYMPHONY No. 99 ("Imperial"), Haydn (Adagio: Vivace Assai, Adagio, Minuetto, Vivace)
CLASSICAL SYMPHONY, Prokofieff (Allegro, Larghetto, Gavotte: Non troppo allegro, Molto vivace)

TWENTIETH CENTURY AMERICA (BOL # 74)
EL SALON MEXICO, Copland
DANZON from "Fancy Free," Bernstein
EXCERPTS, SYMPHONIC DANCES from "West Side Story," Bernstein
AN AMERICAN IN PARIS, Gershwin

U.S. HISTORY IN MUSIC (BOL # 75)
A LINCOLN PORTRAIT, Copland
CHESTER from NEW ENGLAND TRIPTYCH, Schumann
PUTNAM'S CAMP from "Three Places in New England," Ives
INTERLUDE from *FOLK SONG SYMPHONY,* Harris
MIDNIGHT RIDE OF PAUL REVERE from Selections from McGuffey's Readers, Phillips

OVERTURES (BOL # 76)
OVERTURE TO "THE BAT" (Die Fledermaus), Strauss
ACADEMIC FESTIVAL OVERTURE, Brahms.
OVERTURE TO "THE MARRIAGE OF FIGARO," Mozart
ROMAN CARNIVAL OVERTURE, Berlioz
OVERTURE TO "WILLIAM TELL," Rossini (Dawn, Storm, Calm, Finale)

SCHEHERAZADE BY RIMSKY-KORSAKOV (BOL # 77)
The Sea and Sinbad's Ship, Tale of the Prince Kalendar, The Young Prince and the Princess, The Festival at Bagdad

MUSICAL KALEIDOSCOPE (BOL # 78)
ON THE STEPPES OF CENTRAL ASIA, Borodin
IN THE VILLAGE FROM CAUCASIAN SKETCHES, Ippolitoff-Ivanoff
EXCERPTS, POLOVTSIAN DANCES FROM "PRINCE IGOR," Borodin
RUSSIAN SAILOR'S DANCE FROM "THE RED POPPY," Gliere
L'ARLESIENNE SUITE No. 1, Bizet Carillon, Minuet
L'ARLESIENNE SUITE No. 2, Bizet Farandole
PRELUDE TO ACT I, "CARMEN," Bizet
MARCH TO THE SCAFFOLD, from Symphonie Fantastique, Berlioz

361

MUSIC OF THE DRAMA: WAGNER (BOL # 79)
"*LOHENGRIN*" (Overture to Act 1, Prelude to Act 3)
"*THE TWILIGHT OF THE GODS*" (Die Götterdämmerung) (Siegfried's Rhine Journey)
"*THE MASTERSINGERS OF NUREMBURG*" (Die Meistersinger von Nürnberg) (Prelude, Dance of the Apprentices and Entrance of the Mastersingers)
"*TRISTAN AND ISOLDE*" (Love Death)

PETROUCHKA BY STRAVINSKY (BOL # 80)
COMPLETE BALLET SCORE WITH NARRATION

ROGUES IN MUSIC (BOL # 81)
TILL EULENSPIEGEL, Strauss
LIEUTENANT KIJE, Prokofieff Birth of Kije, Troika
HARY JANOS, Kodaly (Viennese Musical Clock, Battle and Defeat of Napoleon, Intermezzo, Entrance of the Emperor)

MUSICAL PICTURES: MOUSSORGSKY (BOL # 82)
PICTURES AT AN EXHIBITION (Promenade Theme, The Gnome, The Old Castle, Tuileries, Ox-Cart, Ballet of Chicks in their Shells, Goldenberg and Schmuyle, The Market Place at Limoges, Catacombs, The Hut of Baga Yaga, The Great Gate of Kiev)
NIGHT ON BALD MOUNTAIN

ENSEMBLES, LARGE AND SMALL (BOL # 83)
YOUNG PERSON'S GUIDE TO THE ORCHESTRA, Britten
CANZONA IN C MAJOR FOR BRASS ENSEMBLE AND ORGAN, Gabrieli

CHORALE: *AWAKE, THOU WINTRY EARTH*, Bach
FOURTH MOVEMENT, "TROUT" QUINTET, Schubert
THEME AND VARIATIONS FOR PERCUSSION QUARTET, Kraft
THEME AND VARIATIONS from *SERENADE FOR WIND INSTRUMENTS*, Mozart (K361)

CONCERTOS (BOL # 84)
FIRST MOVEMENT, PIANO CONCERTO, Grieg
FOURTH MOVEMENT, PIANO CONCERTO No. 2, Brahms
THIRD MOVEMENT, VIOLIN CONCERTO, Mendelssohn
SECOND MOVEMENT, GUITAR CONCERTO, Castelnuovo-Tedesco
THIRD MOVEMENT, CONCERTO IN C FOR TWO TRUMPETS, Vivaldi

MUSICAL IMPRESSIONS: RESPIGHI (BOL # 85)
PINES OF ROME (Pines of the Villa Borghese, Pines Near a Catacomb, Pines of the Appian Way)
FOUNTAINS OF ROME (The Fountain of Valle Giulia at Dawn, The Triton Fountain at Morning, The Trevi Fountain at Midday, The Villa Medici Fountain at Sunset)
THE BIRDS (Prelude)

FASHIONS IN MUSIC (BOL # 86)
ROMEO AND JULIET (Fantasy-Overture), Tchaikovsky
LITTLE FUGUE IN G MINOR, Bach
SUITE No. 2 FROM "*DAPHNIS AND CHLOË*," Ravel
ROMANZE from *A LITTLE NIGHT MUSIC* (Eine Kleine Nachtmusik), Mozart
PERIPETIA from *FIVE PIECES FOR ORCHESTRA*, Schoenberg

362

Keyboard Publications (Keyboard Jr.)

The following boxed units contain:

1. Material for each child to read
2. Teacher's guide
3. Recording with selected listening experiences
4. Enlarged theme charts
5. Pictures for bulletin board

I. Elements of music
   Patterns in Rhythm   Symbols of Sound
   Melody in Music

II. Instruments
   Drumbeats around the   The Story of the Piano
      World

III. Composers
   Sousa, the March King   Wolfgang Amadeus
   George Frederick Handel   Mozart
   Franz Joseph Haydn   Franz Schubert

IV. Musical Stories
   Mother Goose Suite   Stories Told in Music (*The
   The Magic Flute   Sorcerer's Apprentice* and
   Lohengrin   *Danse Macabre*)
   Till Eulenspiegel's Merry   Myths and Legends in
      Pranks   Music

V. Music of Many Lands
   Music of the American   Music of Hawaii
      Indian   Japanese Music
   Sounds of Mexico   Music of Spain
   South American Music   The World Dances

In addition to the above list of materials, prepared visual masters are also available with the following lessons:

The Music of Hungary
The Music of Poland
The Music of Russia
Scheherezade
String Instruments of the Orchestra

Brass Instruments of the Orchestra
The Holiday Spirit (December)
Woodwind Instruments of the Orchestra

Teaching records, teachers' guides, and children's materials accompany the following enlarged lessons:

America's History through Its Music
Masterpieces of Melody
Nature and Science in Music
Rhythm—the Heartbeat of Music

A fine publication is *New Pathways to Music* by Nick Rossi. It is a complete history of music in sight and sound, covering all periods from the early Christian era through the twentieth century. In addition to the narrated musical recordings, there are two filmstrips for each period—one covering arts and humanities, the other covering the musical aspects—composers, instruments, forms and styles. Teachers' guides and illustrated pamphlets for the students are also included:

Series I   Baroque
Series II   The Classic Period
Series III   The Romantic Period
Series IV   Impressionism
Series V–VIII will include: *The Renaissance; Late Romantic Era; Nationalism; Contemporary.*

Although *New Pathways to Music* was designed for the secondary level, it is excellent as an enrichment for the listening program in the sixth grade as well. Classroom teachers may find it very useful as a personal "refresher" in the history of music.

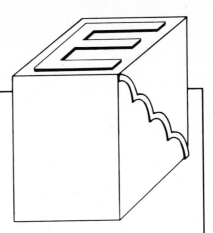

APPENDIX:

ADDRESSES
OF PUBLISHERS

Aberbach Group of Music Publishing Cos., 241 West 72d Street, New
   York
Allyn and Bacon, Inc., 150 Tremont St., Boston, Mass.
American Book Company, 55 Fifth Avenue, New York
Appleton-Century-Crofts, Inc., 440 Park Avenue South, New York
Associated Music Publishers, 609 Fifth Avenue, New York
Barnes & Noble, Inc., 105 Fifth Avenue, New York
Irving Berlin Music Corporation, 1290 Avenue of the Americas, New
   York
Big Three Music Corporation, 1350 Avenue of the Americas, New York
Boosey and Hawkes, 30 West 57th Street, New York
Bourne Company, 136 West 52d Street, New York

Bregman, Vocco and Conn, Inc., 1619 Broadway, New York
Wm. C. Brown Publishing Co., 135 South Locust Street, Dubuque, Iowa
Children's Record Guild, The Greystone Corporation, 100 Sixth Avenue, New York
Cooperative Recreation Service, Delaware, Ohio
Fearon Publishers, San Francisco, Calif.
Folkways Records and Service Corporation, 701 Seventh Avenue, New York
Follett Publishing Company, 1010 West Washington Boulevard, Chicago, Ill.
Sam Fox Music Publishing Co., 1841 Broadway, New York
Ginn and Company, Statler Building, Boston, Mass.
Girl Scouts of USA, 830 Third Avenue, New York
Harper & Row, Publishers, Incorporated, 49 East 33d Street, New York
Holt, Rinehart and Winston, Inc., 383 Madison Avenue, New York
Jan-Lee Music Co., 260 El Camino Drive, Beverly Hills, Calif.
Neil A. Kjos Music Co., 525 Busse, Park Ridge, Ill.
McGraw Hill Book Company, 330 West 42d Street, New York
Edward B. Marks Music Corporation, 136 West 52d Street, New York
Mills Music, Inc., 1790 Broadway, New York
MENC (Music Educator's National Conference), 1201 Sixteenth Street, N.W., Washington, D.C.
NEA (National Education Association) 1201 Sixteenth Street, N.W., Washington, D.C.
J. W. Pepper & Sons, 231 North Third Street, Philadelphia, Pa.
Prentice-Hall, Inc., Englewood Cliffs, N.J.
Richmond Organization, 10 Columbus Circle, New York
Saint Nicholas Music Co., 1619 Broadway, New York
G. Schirmer, Inc., 609 Fifth Avenue, New York
Schmitt, Hall and McCreary, 527 Park Avenue, Minneapolis, Minn.
Shapiro, Bernstein & Co., 666 Fifth Avenue, New York
Shawnee Press, Delaware Water Gap, Pa.
Silver Burdett Company, Morristown, N.J.
William Smith Publishing Co., 254 West 31st Street, New York
Summy-Birchard Company, Evanston, Ill.
Carl Van Roy, 51–17 Rockaway Beach Boulevard, Far Rockaway, N.Y.
Jerry Vogel Music Publishers, 121 West 45th Street, New York
Wadsworth Publishing Co., Belmont, Calif.
Warner Brothers–Seven Arts, 488 Madison Avenue, New York
Young Peoples Record Club, The Greystone Corporation, 100 Sixth Avenue, New York

Record Libraries Made Especially for Use in Elementary Schools

Some companies issue record libraries made especially for school use. Those listed are in this category.

1. *Adventures in Music*, RCA Victor
   RCA Victor Educational Sales, 155 East 42d Street, New York, N.Y. 10010
   Ten albums—one each for grades one and two; two each for grades three, four, five, and six. Accompanying pamphlets in each album are designed to aid teachers in exploring numerous teaching possibilities for each selection and to provide suggestions for related activities. (This series is a later publication than the *Basic Record Library for Elementary Schools*.)
2. *Basic Record Library for Elementary Schools* (selected portion only), RCA Victor. Six albums entitled *The Listening Program*, vols. 1–6; six albums entitled *The Rhythm Program*, vols. 1–6. Short selections from a wide variety of musical literature. The *Listening* and *Rhythm* albums may be used interchangeably. Each album has an accompanying pamphlet with teaching suggestions and information relative to each selection.
3. *Bowmar Orchestral Library*.
   Bowmar Records, Inc., 622 Rodier Drive, Glendale, Calif. 91201.
   Thirty-six albums: *Music USA*, *Animals and Circus*, etc. Teaching suggestions appear on the album jackets. Theme charts and overhead transparencies are available for each album.
4. *Keyboard Publications*, 1346 Chapel Street, New Haven, Conn.
   Boxed units with records, theme charts, reading material for the children, a teacher's guide, and pictures for bulletin boards. Overhead transparencies are available for some units. A new unit is available bi-monthly. These can be purchased through yearly subscription or individual order.
5. *Musical Sound Books*, by the Sound Book Press Society, Inc., Scarsdale, N.Y., Prepared by Lillian Baldwin. *Tiny Masterpieces for Very Young Listeners; Listener's Library; Young Listener's Library*.

In Appendix D (pp. 354–364), the libraries of RCA Victor *Adventures in Music* series, The Bowmar Orchestral Library, and Keyboard Publications are given just as they appear in their respective catalogs so that a teacher may determine whether he requires an entire library or simply a portion of it to meet his needs and/or the needs of the school. Many schools have a central record library that serves the entire school; however, some teachers prefer to keep certain records in their rooms at all times, necessitating their individual purchase. (Catalogs containing further information on publications are available from all companies upon request.)

SONG INDEX

369

SUBJECT INDEX

Transparency Masters

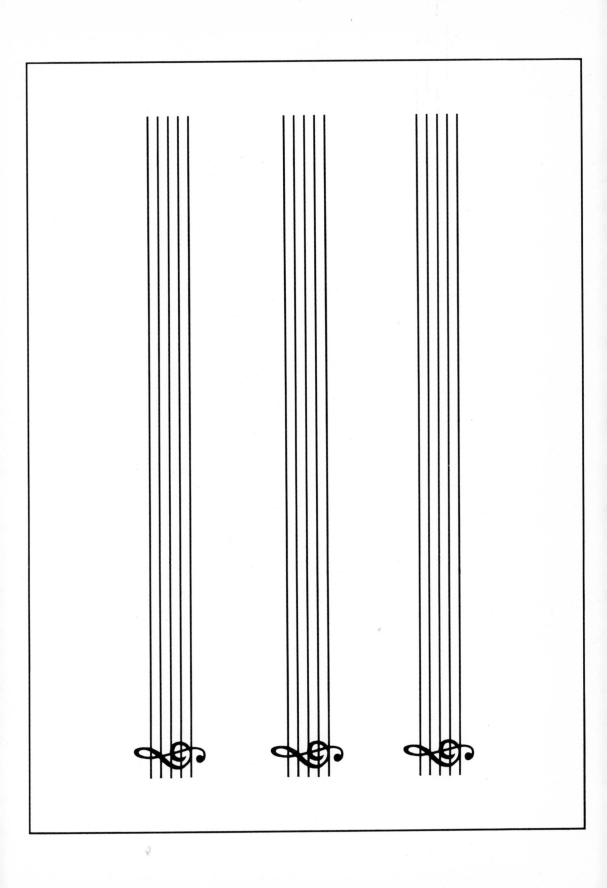

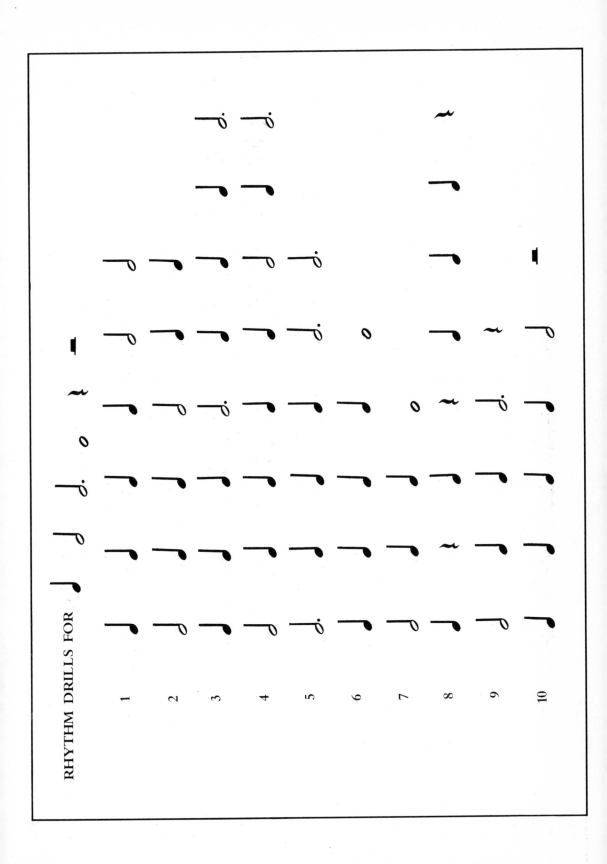

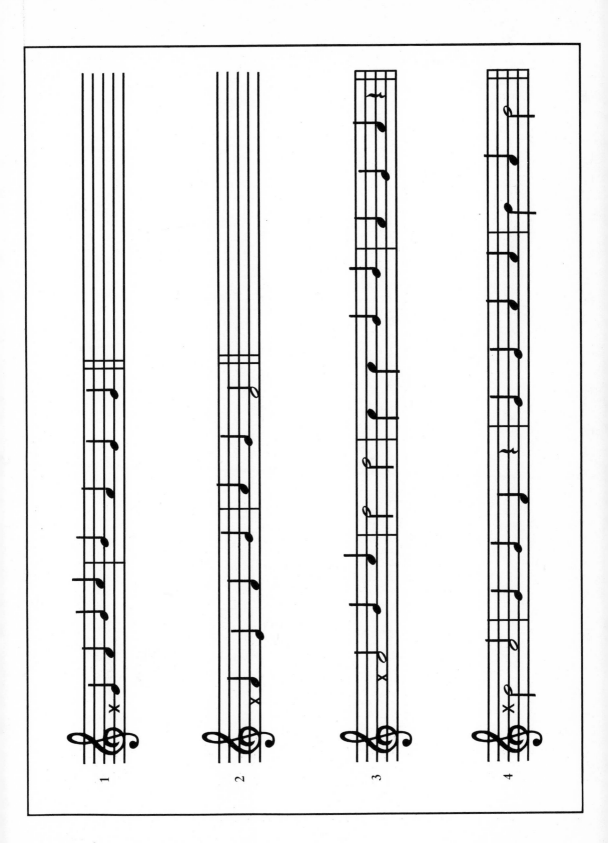

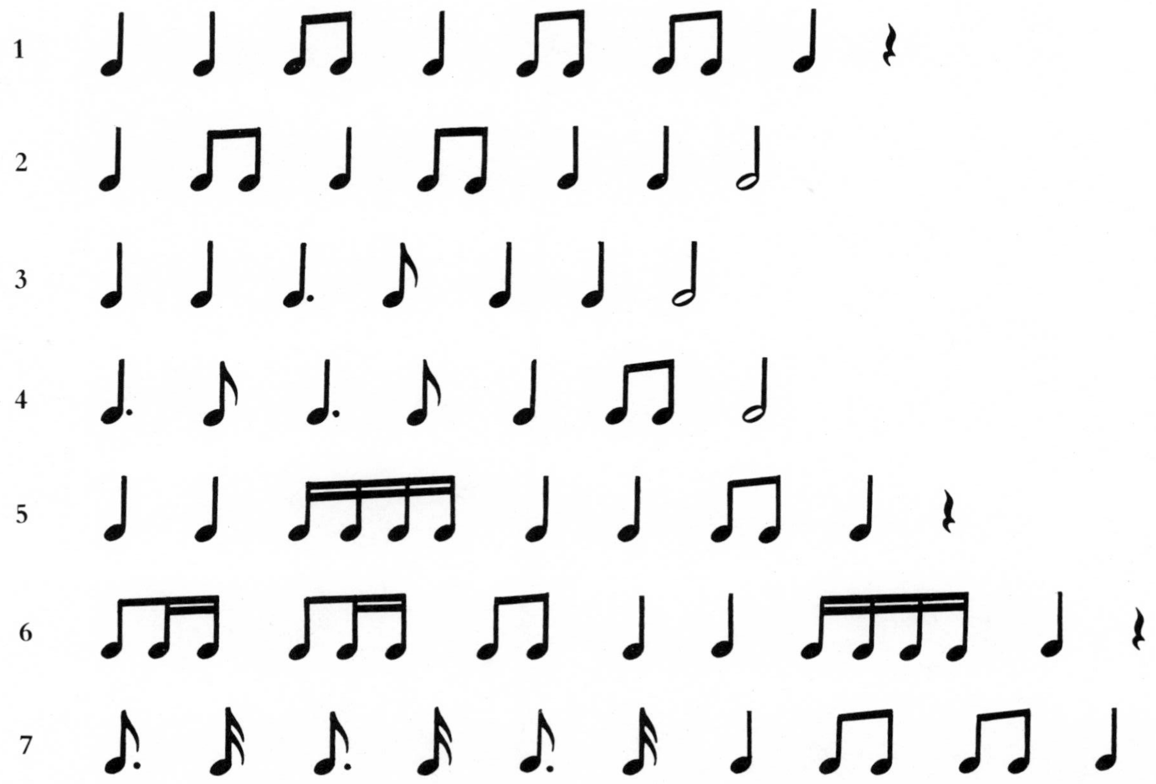
1
2
3
4
5
6
7

SIMPLE MELODIES USING EIGHTH NOTES

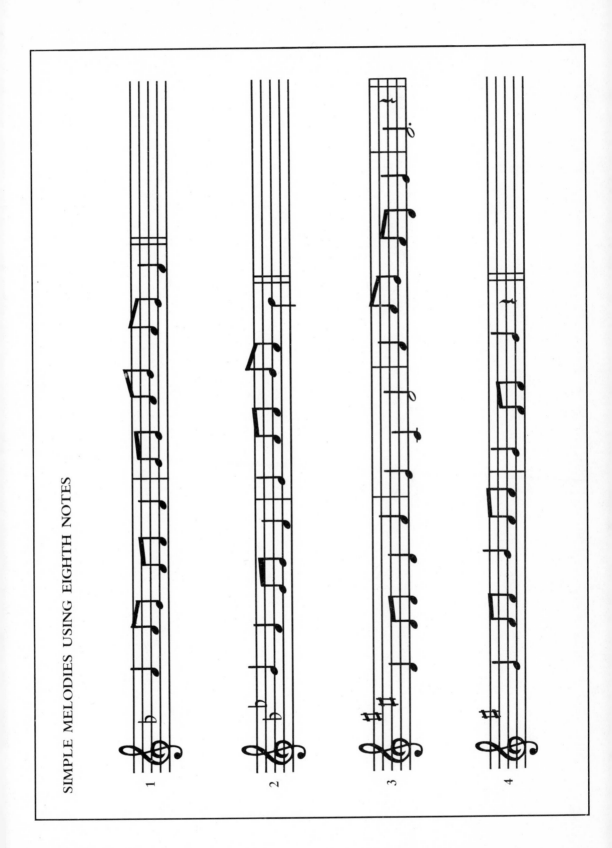

	I	IV	I	V7	I
GROUP 1 →	SOL	LA	SOL	SOL	SOL
GROUP 2 →	MI	FA	MI	FA	MI
GROUP 3 →	DO	DO	DO	TI	DO
	I	IV	I	V7	I

RHYTHM INSTRUMENT ORCHESTRATION
MINUET FROM EINE KLEINE NACHTMUSIK MOZART

R = RAP TAMBOURINE
S = SHAKE TAMBOURINE
C = CYMBALS

STICKS AND TAMBOURINE (8 MEASURES)

R R S S R R R S S R R R S R R R

WOOD BLOCK
(4 MEASURES)

C C C   FINE

STICKS
(4 MEASURES)

BELLS AND TRIANGLES (8 MEASURES)

DRUM
(4 MEASURES)

C   C C C C

BELLS AND TRIANGLES (8 MEASURES)

D. C. AL FINE

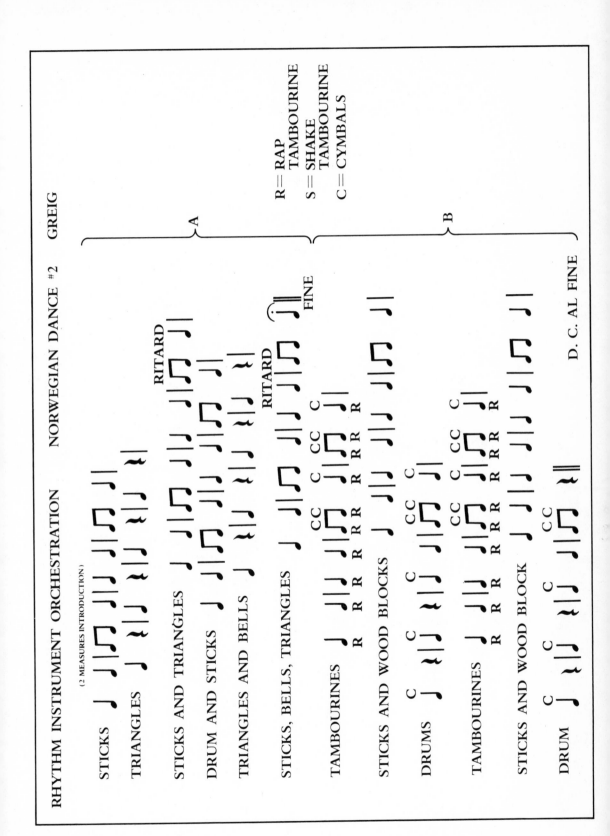

RHYTHM INSTRUMENT ORCHESTRATION   NORWEGIAN DANCE #2   GREIG

R= RAP TAMBOURINE
S = SHAKE TAMBOURINE
C = CYMBALS

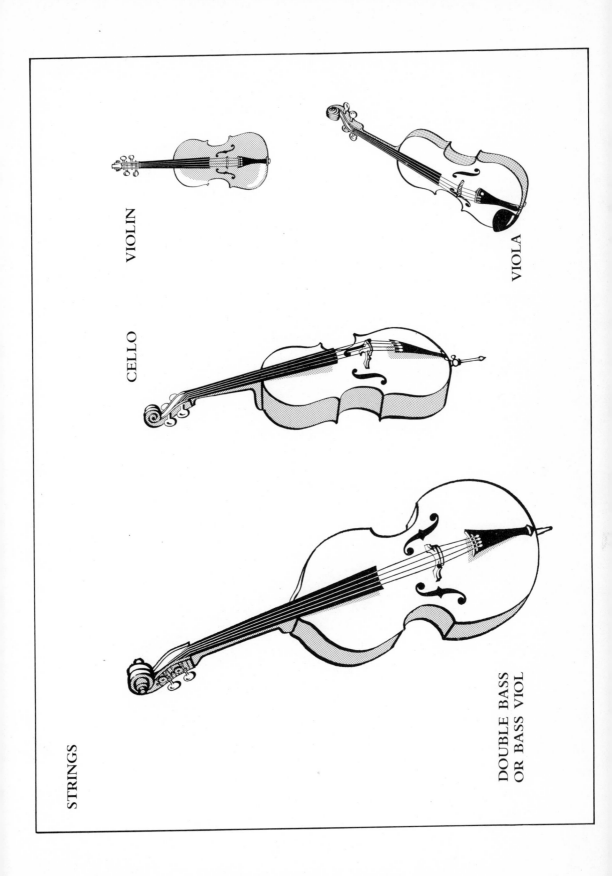

STRINGS

VIOLIN

VIOLA

CELLO

DOUBLE BASS
OR BASS VIOL

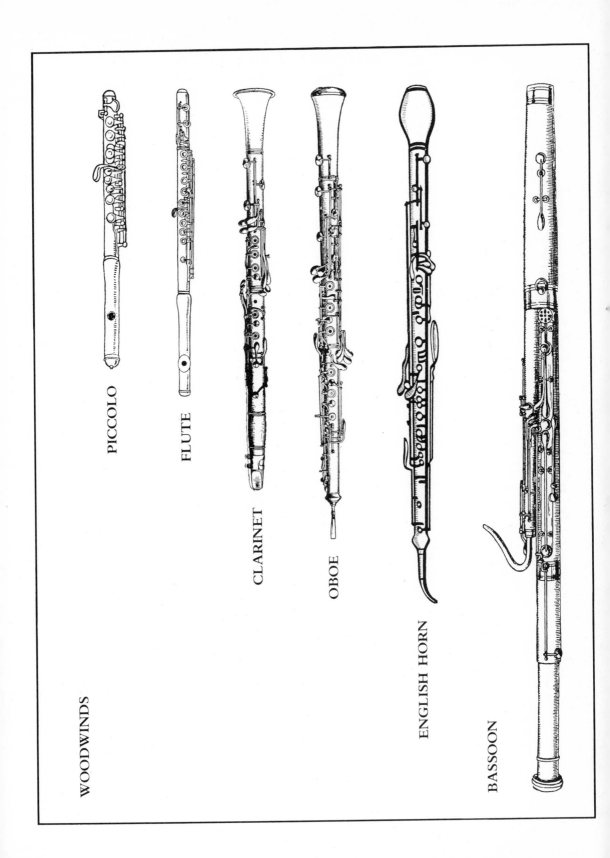

WOODWINDS

PICCOLO

FLUTE

CLARINET

OBOE

ENGLISH HORN

BASSOON

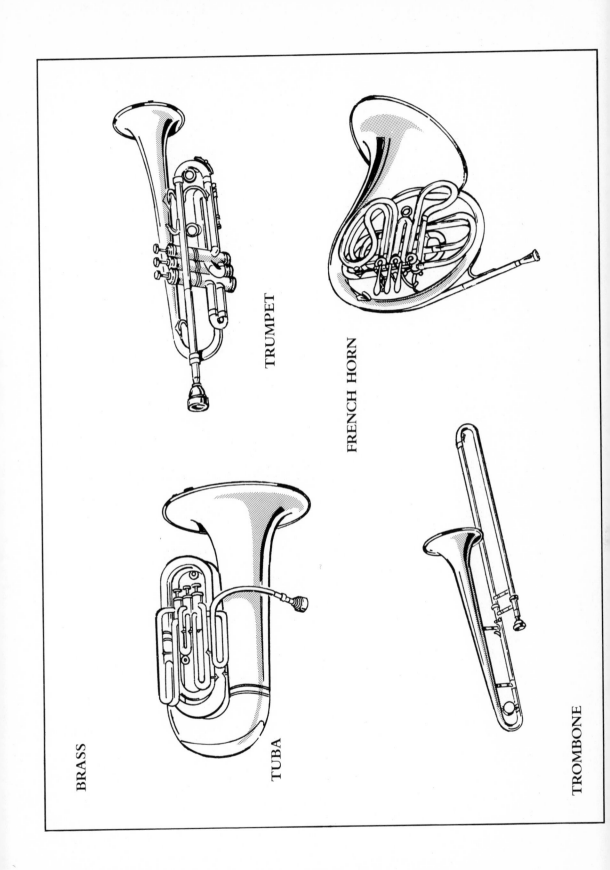

BRASS

TRUMPET

FRENCH HORN

TUBA

TROMBONE

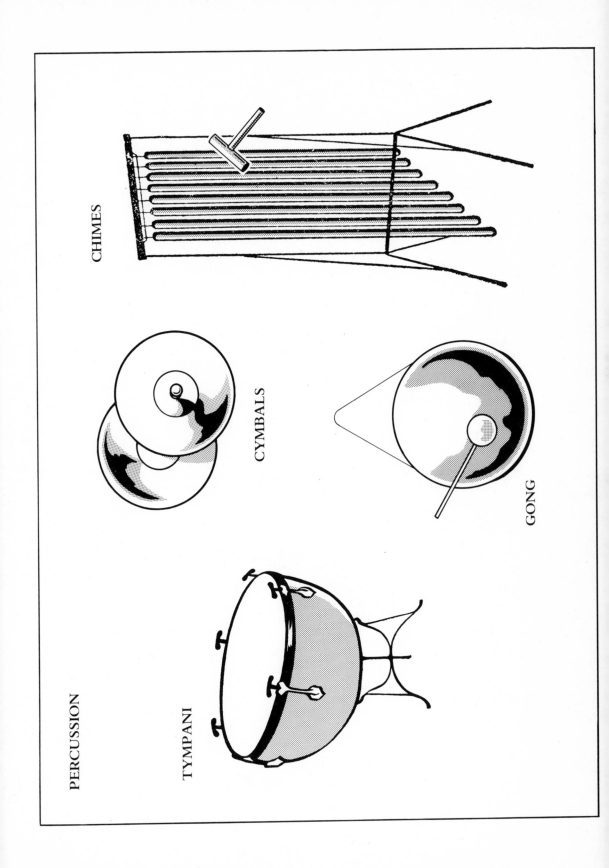

PERCUSSION

CHIMES

CYMBALS

GONG

TYMPANI

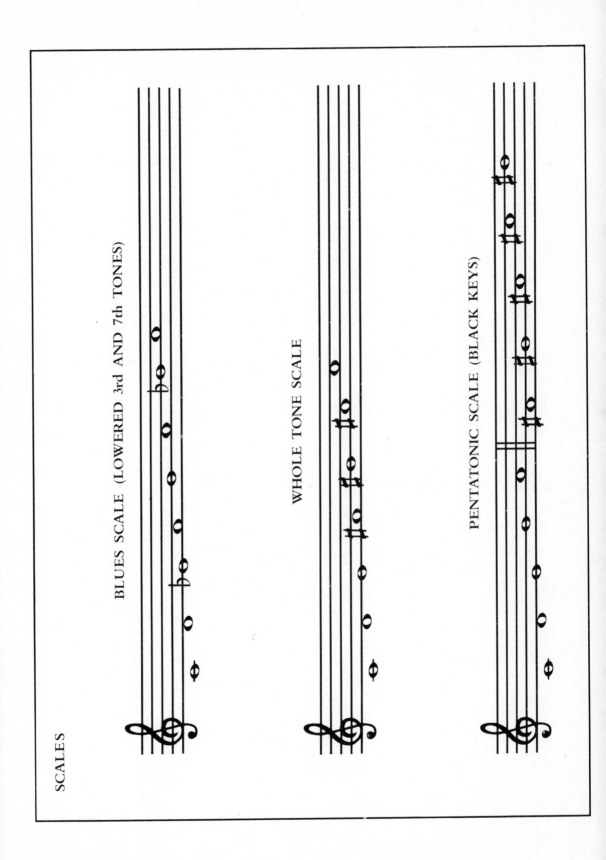

SCALES

BLUES SCALE (LOWERED 3rd AND 7th TONES)

WHOLE TONE SCALE

PENTATONIC SCALE (BLACK KEYS)

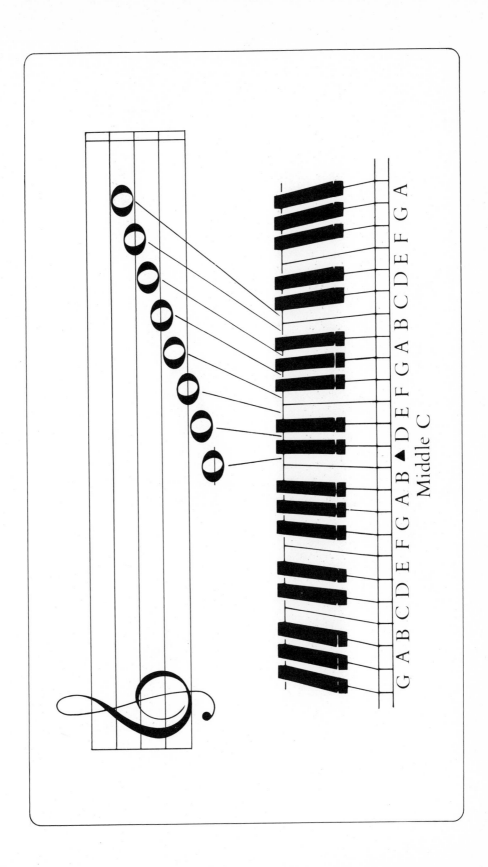